'This is a thoughtful and careful rethink of how we conceive EU law to have global governance effects. It is both insightful and novel and offers a truly alternative theorisation on the global reach of EU law.'

Professor Laurent Pech, University of Middlesex, UK

'This book is a timely analysis of the impact and effects of EU rules outside EU territory. It helps us understand why the EU seems to be shifting its attention from its own Member States to the rest of the world and how it does so. It also clarifies why third states accept EU-made rules. The book is an absolute must-have for everyone studying the international and transnational normative and regulatory impact of the EU.'

Professor Ramses A. Wessel, University of Twente, The Netherlands

The Global Reach of EU Law

The EU strives to be a leading rule-making organisation with global reach in both economic and non-economic fields. But how should we understand the science behind this? This book focuses upon unpacking the uncertainty, the form, and the directions of the global reach of EU law as a distinctive form of postnational rule-making. The work examines two central themes: the conceptual development of the global reach and effects of EU law, and the methodology of EU rule-making processes. It considers what specific impact and effects the EU's rules are having, and its approach to global reach. The book studies the EU's Area of Freedom, Security, and Justice (AFSJ) as a case of a non-economic field offering examples of ways and means in which the global reach of EU law can manifest itself in an evolving and sensitive field. Using this case study, the book develops a sharper focus upon the 'internal' and 'external' elements of EU law which make up our understanding of the global reach of EU law, and develops further why global reach is important as a scientific phenomenon.

The book will be a valuable resource for researchers and students in the areas of EU law, global governance, and the study of law beyond the nation state.

Elaine Fahey, Senior Lecturer and Associate Dean (International), The City Law School, City University London, UK.

Studies in Modern Law and Policy
Series Editor: Ralf Rogowski
Professor of Law, University of Warwick

Also in the series

Networking the Rule of Law
How Change Agents Reshape Judicial Governance in the EU
Cristina Dallara and Daniela Piana
ISBN: 978-1-4094-3305-7

Social Systems Theory and Judicial Review
Taking Jurisprudence Seriously
Katayoun Baghai
ISBN: 978-1-4094-5402-1

The EU Economic and Social Model in the Global Crisis
Interdisciplinary Perspectives
Edited by Dagmar Schiek
ISBN: 978-1-4094-5731-2

Constitutional Evolution in Central and Eastern Europe
Expansion and Integration in the EU
Edited by Kyriaki Topidi and Alexander H.E. Morawa
ISBN: 978-1-4094-0327-2

Central and Eastern Europe After Transition
Towards a New Socio-legal Semantics
Edited by Alberto Febbrajo and Wojciech Sadurski
ISBN: 978-1-4094-0390-6

Democracy, Law and Governance
Jacques Lenoble and Marc Maesschalck
ISBN: 978-1-4094-0395-1

The Global Reach of EU Law

Elaine Fahey

Routledge
Taylor & Francis Group
LONDON AND NEW YORK

First published 2017
by Routledge
2 Park Square, Milton Park, Abingdon, Oxon, OX14 4RN

and by Routledge
711 Third Avenue, New York, NY 10017

First issued in paperback 2018

Routledge is an imprint of the Taylor & Francis Group, an informa business

British Library Cataloguing in Publication Data
A catalogue record for this book is available from the British Library

Library of Congress Cataloging-in-Publication Data
Fahey, Elaine, author.
Title: The global reach of EU law / Elaine Fahey.
Other titles: Global reach of European Union law
Description: Abingdon, Oxon ; New York, NY : Routledge, 2017. |
Series: Studies in modern law and policy | Includes index.
Identifiers: LCCN 2016010428 | ISBN 9781138696563 (hbk)
Subjects: LCSH: Law–European Union countries–International unification. | International and municipal law–European Union countries. | Law and globalization–European Union countries.
Classification: LCC KJE969 .F34 2017 | DDC 341.242/2–dc23
LC record available at http://lccn.loc.gov/2016010428

ISBN 13: 978-1-138-60666-1 (pbk)
ISBN 13: 978-1-138-69656-3 (hbk)

Typeset in Galliard by
Cenveo Publisher Services

Contents

1 Introduction

On the spread of EU law

The global reach and effects of EU law,[1] or simply put for now, the 'spread' of EU law, is increasingly the subject of legal scholarship, which considers a broad range of its manifestations to other legal orders or systems, organisations or third countries, as an empirical phenomenon. For example, the so-called 'Brussels effect' is the subject of recent scholarship, assessing the perceived 'spillover' effect of EU regulatory standards on US rules in the realm of *inter alia* genetically modified foods, data privacy standards and chemical safety rules.[2] Equally, recent accounts consider the extent to which EU legal rules are actually transplanted in the US – for example, the transposition of EU environmental standards in California, Boston and Maine.[3] Included in these theorisations is the view that the size and scale of the EU, as a market and as a polity, has generated what is understood here as 'rule-transfer'. It has entailed that the EU has adopted rules and standards that other polities and markets have in turn adopted, compelled to do so or acting out of sheer necessity. This process of the 'outwards' adoption of EU rules elsewhere, particularly in the US, is conceptualised in various legal accounts. This concerns the actual practice-based transfer of rules, less so the process and the significance of the EU's promotion of norms. Such accounts offer normative explanations that are often dominated by market-based rationalisations, such as economic power, less so convergence or convenience.[4] However, as will be argued here, economic arguments may be insufficiently nuanced to similar practices of rule-making beyond economic areas. Legal and other scholarship examining the external adoption of EU rules

1 For clarity, EU law is referred to here as incorporating EU rule-making.

2 See Anu Bradford, 'The Brussels Effect' (2012), 107 Northwestern University, *LR* 1.

3 Joanne Scott, 'From Brussels with Love: The Transatlantic Travels of European Law and the Chemistry of Regulatory Attraction' (2009), 57 *AJCL* 897.

4 Zaidi Laïdi, 'European Preferences and Their Reception', in Zaidi Laïdi (ed.), *EU Foreign Policy in a Globalized World. Normative Power and Social Preferences* (Routledge, 2008), 1; R. Dan Kelemen, 'Globalizing European Union Environmental Policy' (2010), 17 *JEPP* 335; Gregory Shaffer and Daniel Bodansky, 'Transnationalism, Unilateralism and International Law' (2012), 1 *TEL* 31.

usually relies upon economic-based rationales to understand the process and outcome of such 'rule-transfer'. Similarly, convenience, mimicry, expertise, innovation and other technocratic rationales offer normative explanations for such transfers.[5] Very high EU legal standards as much as very low national standards may be equally open to 'mimicry', even where the social benefits come at a great economic cost.[6] Within the context of the US, the openness of federalism is depicted as an explanation for this rule-transfer, whereby the legal order at state level is inherently open to receiving best practices from external sources, constitutionally speaking.[7] This is argued here to be an excessively 'structural' account of such rule-transfer and not necessarily a very holistic account of the global reach and effects of EU law. At the other end of the spectrum, it has been recently argued that transfers of policies from the EU to the US – e.g. in socioeconomic areas, is inherently democracy-enhancing in so far as it purports to set high standards, which this account considers in detail.[8] Nonetheless, the normative story of the global reach and effects of EU law is innately bound up with the process surrounding it and it is one which this book seeks to develop further.

This book broadly explores what the 'global reach and effects' of EU law entails, theoretically, empirically and practically. It seeks deliberately to look beyond 'headline' approaches to the global reach of EU law in understanding EU rule-making, while also closely examining what is meant by the EU's self-expressed 'global approach' to EU rule-making or external dimensions to internal rule-making.[9] It focuses upon drawing together two specific strands so as to offer an integrated account of rule-making processes: (1) how the EU promotes external norms and (2) its relationship to internal rule-making. This focus draws from the evolution in legal scholarship of predominantly empirical work, whereby EU law scholars have charted the adoption in the US of vast ranges of EU rules in very recent times, as well as the broader idea of the global impact or

5 See Shaffer and Bodansky, ibid.; Kelemen, ibid.; R. Dan Kelemen and David Vogel, 'Trading Places: The Role of the United States and the European Union in International Environmental Politics' (2010), 43 *CPS* 427.

6 Consider regulatory competition across the EU and beyond it to introduce smoking bans in bars, the law on the sale, or alternatively use of, plastic bags in retail. See 'Smoking Curbs: The Global Picture' (3 February 2011): www.bbc.com/news/world-11845158, accessed 23 December 2015.

7 For example, Judith Resnik, Joshua Civin and Joseph Frueh, 'Ratifying Kyoto at the Local Level: Sovereigntism, Federalism, and Translocal Organizations of Government Actors (TOGAs)' (2008), 50 Arizona *LR* 709; Judith Resnik, 'Foreign as Domestic Affairs: Rethinking Horizontal Federalism and Foreign Affairs Preemption in Light of Translocal Internationalism' (2007), 57 *Emory LJ* 31.

8 For example, Katarina Linos, *The Democratic Foundations of Policy Diffusion: How Health, Family, and Employment Laws Spread Across Countries* (Oxford University Press, 2013).

9 See Chapter 2.

10 See Bradford, n. 2; Joanne Scott, 'Extraterritoriality and Territorial Extension in EU Law' (2014), 62 *AJCL 87; Joanne Scott, 'The New EU Extra-territoriality'* (2014), 51 *CMLR* 1343.

spread of EU law.[10] However, for all of their merits, there may be said to be many shortcomings of existing studies outlined above. The distinctions drawn there raise fundamental methodological issues which are explored here further – for example, what analytical method is best used, what is being transferred, why and how? And is it legitimate or transparent what EU law achieves? And what is explicitly aimed at in rule-making?

One specific theoretical methodology used to sketch the broader themes of this account and explore specific case studies is the phenomenon of 'EU rule-transfer', expanded upon here next. More practically, the book traces norm promotion in rule-making and purports to carefully identify and separate the external from the internal in distinct case studies. It is argued that defined methodologies are only embryonic in EU law scholarship. For example, there is currently a movement in scholarship to reconstruct methodology and take into account the multi-disciplinarity of the subject, its highly diverse range of actors, instruments and processes.[11] It advocates approaches which accommodate *inter alia* the plurality of sources of EU law and which explicitly enunciate its method. An attempt to trace transparently a source-based construction of EU rule-making is argued here to accommodate contemporary concerns rather than conform to the practices of other disciplines and subject-confines, usually structured interviews or practice-based accounts.

On EU rule-making

EU rule-making has long existed as a 'black box' within European Union (EU) law scholarship, whereby a limited amount of traceable output thereof has become the subject of vast sectors of scholarship. The 'black box' itself has become more transparent, traceable and accessible over time.[12] Yet still to speak about EU rule-making poses elementary questions as to its meaning that may appear striking. There is no common, standard description of EU 'rule-making' that is shared across disciplines in a holistic sense. Instead, temporal stages of *inter alia* lobbying, negotiation, consultation and input, decision-making, implementation, enforcement and judicial decision-making in EU law have been analytically

11 See Rob van Gestel and Hans-W. Micklitz, 'Why Methods Matter in European Legal Scholarship' (2014), 20 *ELJ*, 292, 313–316 ('An Agenda for a European Debate'); Tamara Hervey, Robert Cryer, Bal Sokhi-Bulley, Alexandra Bohm, *Research Methodologies in EU and International Law* (Hart Publishing, 2011); Rob van Gestel, Hans-W. Micklitz and Miguel Poiares Maduro, 'Methodology in the New Legal World,' EUI Law Working Paper 2012/13; Ulla Neergaard, Ruth Nielsen and Lynn Roseberry (eds), *European Legal Method* (DJOF, 2011); cf. 'The New History of EU Law' project, University of Copenhagen: http://europeanlaw.saxo.ku.dk/, accessed 23 December 2015.

12 On recent efforts to deploy this terminology and thereby reconstruct the history of EU law, see Antoine Vauchez and Bruno De Witte, *Lawyering Europe. European Law as a Transnational Social Field* (Hart, 2013).

developed piecemeal by legal scholars, often later than other disciplines on the same fields.[13] The absence of such an understanding of EU rule-making is argued here to emasculate transparency. Accordingly, this account considers EU rule-making in a holistic sense, both as a process and as a normative idea, and specifically focuses upon understanding its methodology from a legal perspective. It uses the term 'rule-making' so as to encompass active and dynamic practices arising in postnational rule-making that may not fit conventional or traditional models of law-making or specific understandings of 'law'.[14] This terminology draws a wider lens so as to capture its impact as postnational rule-making, focusing upon its method, its instruments and aims in a global context. This particular approach of focusing upon methodology also involves tracing its active or 'bottom-up' construction in various case studies.

No rule-making project, whether a new legal order or constitution or otherwise has ever truly begun as a *tabula rasa*. They have influences, sources and borrowings that are commonplace, which range from the formal and explicit to the informal, osmotic or organic.[15] EU rule-making has never been reluctant to draw inspiration, to emulate or to replicate best international standards, practices or rules of its Member States.[16] As the EU as an organisation evolves, its strategic

13 The subject of many recent monographs: for example, on enforcement: Marise Cremona (ed.), *Compliance and the Enforcement of EU Law* (Oxford University Press, 2012); on the negotiation and conclusion of international agreements: Henri de Waele and Jan Jap Kuipers (eds), *The European Union's Emerging International Identity: Views from the Global Arena* (BRILL, 2013); Piet Eeckhout, *EU External Relations Law* (2nd edn, Oxford University Press, 2011); Mario Mendez, *The Legal Effects of EU Agreements* (Oxford University Press, 2013); on rule-making: Joana Mendes, *Participation in Rule-Making: A Rights-Based Approach* (Oxford University Press, 2011).

14 See Joost Pauwelyn, Ramses Wessel and Jan Wouters (eds) *Informal International Lawmaking* (Oxford University Press, 2012); on postnational rule-making, see Karl H. Ladeur, 'The Theory of Autopoiesis as an Approach to a Better Understanding of Postmodern Law – From the Hierarchy of Norms to the Heterarchy of Changing Patterns of Legal Inter-relationships' *Law*, No. 99/3, *EUI Working Papers*; Erik Eriksen, Christian Joerges, Florian Rödl (eds) *Law, Democracy and Solidarity in a Post-national Union: The Unsettled Political Order of Europe* (Routledge, 2008); Erik Eriksen, Christian Joerges and Florian Rödl (eds) 'Law and Democracy in the Post-National Union', *Arena Report* 1/2006; Damian Chalmers, 'Post-nationalism and the quest for constitutional substitutes' (2000), 27 *JLS* 178; Neil Walker, 'Postnational Constitutionalism and Postnational Public Law: A Tale of Two Neologisms' (2012), 3 *T LT* 61; Gregory Shaffer, 'A Transnational Take on Krisch's Pluralist Structure of Postnational Law' (2012), 23 *EJIL* 565; Nico Krisch, *Beyond Constitutionalism: The Pluralist Structure of Postnational Law* (Oxford University Press, 2011).

15 This has long been the study of the subject of comparative law: see Pierre Le Grand and Roderick Munday, *Comparative Legal Studies: Traditions and Transitions* (Cambridge University Press, 2003); H. Patrick Glenn, *Legal Traditions of the World: Sustainable Diversity in Law* (4th edn, Oxford University Press, 2010).

16 See the early effort of the Court of Justice in the landmark *Handelsgesellchaft* decision on fundamental rights to incorporate as many national standards so as to construct a de jure European property right: Case 11/70, *Internationale Handelsgesellschaft mbH v Einfuhr- und Vorratsstelle für Getreide und Futtermittel*, EU:C:1970:114.

internalisation of external norms has also evolved. Similarly, the global impact of its rules and choices have too. There are distinct normative challenges posed by an inherent openness to absorbing, emulating or integrating all international standards, member state existent standards and values. Furthermore, the scale of the EU as an economic bloc and its evolving reputation as a global governance actor render the adoption of its rules mandatory, essential or simply useful for many outside of its territory, creating issues of social acceptance and legitimacy. To study how the EU engages in rule-making and its effects thus involves studying an ecosystem of processes. What this book focuses upon, then, is the unpacking of the 'ecosystem' of EU rule-making processes. Its study is argued to demand a particularly integrated view of the 'internal' and 'external' of the EU law, one which is advocated here to be conducted through developing a methodology of EU rule-making.

This book thus takes as its central theme two specific issues: (1) understanding conceptually the global reach and effects of EU law, including its democratising and legitimising effects and challenges, which are argued to be inadequately exposed and (2), understanding the methodology of EU rule-making processes in this context through the lens of 'EU rule-transfer' and select security-based case studies. As a result, this book considers what specific impact and effects the EU's rules are having. What is the EU trying to do when it uses external norms? What third parties are accepting the EU's rules and why? What rules, standards or values is the EU accepting? And what relationship do its practices have to international political processes that it participates in?

Using EU rule-transfer to frame the global reach of EU law

This book provides a legal theorisation of the global reach and effects of EU law conducted through rule-transfer. As a multi-directional phenomenon, with internal and external, and inwards and outwards dimensions, it is argued here to have both positive and negative effects for democracy, offering insights into the flourishing as much as the failings of EU integration processes. Outwards EU rule-transfer is demonstrated through a series of case studies to manifest itself in largely economic-orientated domains and is widely accounted as being 'democracy enhancing' for its recipients or is perceived as beneficial, market enhancing, market creating or sustaining.[17] Existing accounts are argued not to be sufficiently nuanced to the relationship between direct and indirect outwards

17 See Josephine Van Zeben, *The Allocation of Competence in the European Trading Emissions Scheme* (Cambridge University Press, 2014; outwards participation in the global legal order); Chad Damro, 'Market Power Europe' (2012), 19 *JEPP* 682 (outwards transfers of rules); see from a fundamental rights perspective, Federico Fabbrini, *Fundamental Rights in Europe* (Oxford University Press, 2014), juxtaposing transnational law and fundamental rights and outwards focused participation in transnational law.

rule-transfer. The legitimacy of these processes is argued to be sometimes questionable and highly variable and dependent upon social acceptance thereof. By contrast, inwards rule-transfer irrespective of whether the EU is the initial source of rules or simply where external sources and norms are transferred largely tends to create contexts whereby democracy is perceived to be thwarted or adversely impacted through such transfers. This is shown to occur more frequently in non-economically oriented areas. External norms are often used by the EU to legitimise these same processes, particularly in these non-economic fields.[18] In this regard, this book considers the question of the social legitimacy of the operation of inwards and outwards EU rule-transfer – i.e. its external acceptance by third countries, parties and organisations. In sociological terms, even if it is an objective fact, legitimacy is socially constructed.[19] Legitimacy is a multifaceted entity which comprises both social credibility and social acceptance. It may be pragmatic or normatively or cognitively based and is not necessarily a study of legal formalism or legal validity. Legitimacy can differ across time and space, and between actors, systems and contexts, and is characterised by malleability. It may change but it may also be resilient.[20] Legal scholarship often focuses upon normative or cognitive bases of legitimacy rather than on whether 'X' is regarded as legitimate.[21] It is argued here that to focus upon questions of social legitimacy assists in opening up EU rule-making practices. Theorisations excessively dependent upon sociological and/or behavioural analysis take undue advantage of the malleability of vocabulary at the expense of analytical sharpness. Nonetheless, many practices of postnational rule-making are argued here to be heavily dependent upon their acceptance and it is this lens which is deployed here.[22] The intersection and relationship between the internal and external in EU law is argued to be of much significance in understanding these questions and is the subject of many case studies here, Chapters 4 and 5 (AFSJ rule-making and AFSJ data transfer – inwards) and Chapter 6 (cybercrime and cybersecurity – outwards).

The book argues that the shortcomings of inwards transfers tend to be difficult to 'compensate' for 'downstream' in EU rule-making processes, which will be demonstrated amply by certain case studies – for example, on EU data transfer (in Chapter 5). These shortcomings tend to be difficult to correct and can evoke a misplaced faith in the *ex ante* 'corrective' power of EU civil society or *ex post*

18 As will be argued in Chapter 4.

19 W. Richard Scott, *Institutions and Organizations* (SAGE, 2001).

20 James Gibson and Gregory Caldeira, 'The Legitimacy of the Court of Justice in the European Union: Models of Institutional Support' (1995), 89 *APSR* 356.

21 Julia Black, 'Constructing and Contesting Legitimacy and Accountability in Polycentric Regulatory Regimes' (2008), 2 *Regulation and Governance* 137.

22 Ellen Cohn and Susan White, *Legal Socialization: A Study of Norms and Rules* (Springer-Verlag, 1990); Ellen Cohn *et al.*, 'An integrated model of legal and moral reasoning and rule-violating behaviour: The role of legal attitudes' (1990), 34 *Law and Human Behaviour*, 295.

facto judicial review.[23] EU rule-making processes generally involve demanding standards and strive for the highest possible goals in law, policy and implementation. They generate what is known as the 'perfectionism' conundrum of EU law.[24] Even where EU rule-making is explicitly minimalist, it remains dominated by concerns for 'perfect' effectiveness in its enforcement and measurements, manifesting itself in the use of, for example, scoreboards.[25] Paradoxically, perfectionism in EU rule-making exists *ex ante*, from the outset, rather than *ex post*. It thus contrasts with the significance of judicial activism or judicial discretion in EU law, contributing to 'expansionism' as a broader normative theme of EU law scholarship.[26] The external expansion of the EU of, for example, its territory, directly or indirectly through rule-making as a result of its economic prowess and/or its use of competences, clashes with EU 'perfectionism'.[27] A focus then on methodology is argued to accommodate a bifurcated analysis of rule-making, which looks both internally and externally at its manifestations. It thus offers a more substantive and holistic theorisation of EU rule-making. As a result, this book focuses upon the relationship between what will be developed here as outwards and inwards 'rule-transfer' from a legal perspective, through internal and external interlinked case studies. Furthermore, it examines questions of legitimacy and democracy in rule-transfer and their interrelationship. Specifically, this book also considers the rule-making that the EU concludes with its external partners where these instruments are later adopted internally, as much as the transfer or movement of norms by the EU. As such, the focus of the text is upon the EU but is not limited to a study of its enlargement practices, accession, conditionality or development as rule-transfer would conventionally dictate.

23 Beate Kohler-Koch and Christine Quittkat, *De-Mystification of Participatory Democracy EU-Governance and Civil Society* (Oxford University Press, 2013). Contrast Yannis Papadopoulos, *Democracy in Crisis? Politics, Governance and Policy* (Palgrave Macmillan, 2013), 79.

24 Jacco Bamhoff, 'Perfectionism in European Law' (2011–2012), 14 CYELS 75; Damian Chalmers, 'Gauging the cumbersomeness of EU law' (2009), 62(1) *CLP* 405. See, by contrast, the discussion in the context of European Private law by Martijn Hesselink, 'Private Law Principles, Pluralism and Perfectionism,' *Centre for the Study of European Contract Law Working Paper Series*, No. 2013–02; Ulf Bernitz, Xavier Groussot and Felix Schulyok (eds), *General Principles of EU Law and European Private Law* (Kluwer, 2013), 21; Hugh Collins, *The European Civil Code The Way Forward* (Cambridge University Press, 2008), 165. On the architecture of the rule-making processes and European private law, see Hugh Collins 'Regulatory Competition in International Trade: Transnational Regulation through Standard Form Contracts' (talk delivered at the University of Amsterdam, 2013), available as a video on www.arils.uva.nl, last accessed 23 December 2015.

25 That is, to measure enforcement. This is now also part of the AFSJ since 2013: EU Justice Scoreboard http://ec.europa.eu/justice/effective-justice/scoreboard/index_en.htm, last accessed 23 December 2015.

26 See Maurice Adams, Henri de Waele, Johan Meeusen and Gert Straetmans (eds), *Judging Europe's Judges: The Legitimacy of the Case Law of the European Court of Justice* (Hart, 2013); Gerard Conway, *The Limits of Legal Reasoning and the European Court of Justice* (Cambridge University Press, 2012); Niamh Nic Shuibhne, *The Coherence of EU Free Movement Law: Constitutional Responsibility and the Court of Justice* (Oxford University Press, 2013).

27 See n. 24.

Defining and developing EU rule-transfer

This account purports to develop, through case studies, a specific legal understanding of the term 'rule-transfer'. Of course, this begs the question as to what rule-transfer is and why would a legal account use it? 'Rule-transfer' may be described as a term of art of political science and international relations scholarship which is concerned with how the EU evolves as an organisation through rule-making processes. Rule-transfer is formally understood as a means or process by which EU legal rules are adopted in third country legal orders. Rule-transfer is conventionally deployed in at least three ways in non-legal scholarship on governance and in particular on accession to the EU and EU development policies, so as to depict, first, the mandatory transposition of EU rules in third countries, second, the non-mandatory transposition of EU rules in third countries and third, the extension of EU governance.[28] It is a term deployed predominantly in non-legal scholarship on governance and policy development, which focuses upon the reasons for the adoption of rules by the EU or promotion of the adoption of rules.[29] However, it has a distinctive legal component, given that it has as its subject and/or object legal rules. And while such taxonomy of this literature can be formulated, it is important to state that there is a wide deployment of the term without definition in governance scholarship, which instead focuses upon its character as a form of external governance.[30] Rule-transfer is *stricto senso* derived from strands of Europeanisation and governance scholarship, within the boundaries of political science and international relations. It encompasses both internal and external questions of aspirant member states, the adoption of EU rules and of candidate and EU conduct. Usually, it concerns the process and methods of conditionality in accession to the European Union (EU), through the adoption by candidate countries of the *acquis communitaire.* Yet it has an almost seamless application from the European Neighbourhood Policy,[31] accession and enlargement, to the adoption of EU rules in China.[32] More generally and of significance to the present account, it is understood as the

28 Sandra Lavenex, 'The power of functionalist extension: how EU rules travel' (2014), 21(6) *JEPP* 885.

29 See, for example, its use without any formal definition of its legal content by Frank Schimmelfennig and Ulrich Sedelmeier, 'Governance by conditionality: EU rule transfer to the candidate countries of Central and European Europe' (2004), 11 JEPP 669; Sandra Lavenex and Frank Schimmelfennig (eds), *EU External Governance: Projecting EU Rules Beyond Membership* (Routledge, 2010). See, for example, the account of Mathieu Rousselin, 'But why would they do that? European External Governance and the Domestic Preferences of Rule Importers' (2012), 8, *Journal of Contemporary European Research*, 470, examining the reasons for the process of rule transfer; Mathieu Rousselin, 'Constraint and Consent in the Transfer of European Rules: The Case of China' (2014), 19 *EFAR* 121.

30 E.g. Lavenex and Schimmelfennig (n. 29).

31 Lavenex (n. 28).

32 See Mathieu Rousselin, 'The EU as a Multilateral Rule Exporter: The Global Transfer of European Rules via International Organizations', KFG Working Paper Series, No. 48, November 2012; *Kolleg-Forschergruppe* (KFG) 'The Transformative Power of Europe', *Freie Universität*, Berlin.

external projection of EU rules, standards or policies.[33] Governance scholarship deploys the specific term 'governance seekers' so as to depict the 'users' of rule-transfer.[34] In doing so, the lexicon of such scholarship is permeated by an implicit valorisation of the users of EU rules. It seeks to depict in very clear-cut terms the nature and actors of the processes, but less so the means used. Moreover, relatedly, to depict the role of the US as portrayed in Bradford's 'Brussels Effect' as a 'governance seeker' vis à vis the EU[35] might be said to pose assumptions as to power dynamics that are not objectively testable. Also normatively, as much as linguistically, it presents a challenge within a crowded rubric. How can one assess its legitimacy and effectiveness within this dynamic of designated takers and seekers if it presupposes the legitimacy of the nature of the rules?

The combined perspective of law and governance presents diverse visions of the phenomenon studied here. Recent legal scholarship draws a sharp distinction between the EU's outwards transfer of legal rules and governance practices externally.[36] In doing so, they argue that the transfer of rules constitutes an exportation of rules alone and is separate or apart from governance. However, this book argues that contemporary rule-making suggests otherwise and that law and governance may have a complex combined function, warranting a closer focus upon method. For example, practices in evolving fields, traditionally sacrosanct for the nation state such as security, do not necessarily support this reasoning. For example, when the EU imports EU–US 'security' rules into its own legal order, one witnesses a transfer of law and governance.[37] There may be thus a fusion of rules and governance practices together in certain subject areas, such as security, where the transfer of rules themselves may be insufficient without incorporating governance mechanisms together.

Developing the legal components of rule-transfer

The analysis in non-legal scholarship of the process of the adoption of EU rules in EU candidate accession states increasingly appears highly formalistic in

33 See one of the few (holistic) legal accounts of these processes, focusing upon Central and Eastern European Enlargement: Wojciech Sadurski, *Constitutionalism and Enlargement in Europe* (Oxford University Press, 2012).

34 Rousselin (n. 29).

35 Ibid.

36 See Grainne De Búrca, 'EU External Relations: The Governance Mode of Foreign Policy' in Bart Van Vooren, Steven Blockmans and Jan Wouters (eds), *The EU's Role in Global Governance: The Legal Dimension* (Oxford University Press, 2013), 39.

37 See Elaine Fahey, 'Law and Governance as Checks and Balances in Transatlantic Security: Rights, Redress and Remedies in EU-US Passenger Name Records and the Terrorist Finance Tracking Program' (2013), 32 *YEL* 1. Security is employed here as shorthand expression for rules related to the Area of Freedom, Security and Justice and it is this dimension of the AFSJ which is focused upon rather than rights, remedies or redress concerns usually associated with analyses of AFSJ rule-making.

contrast with emerging empirical work of legal scholars.[38] Existing scholarship on rule-transfer is also argued here to offer a limited perspective on integration between legal orders or even may be said to be currently blinkered to its legal content. It underestimates and even excludes the promotion of and success of the transfer of EU law. Irrespective of its definition, its legal component may be said to be 'dominant', given that it depicts EU legal rules being accepted and adopted outside the EU, often for accession to the EU. However, the relevance or centrality of legal rules and legal theorisations of rule-making processes do not form part of existing scholarship.[39]

While rule-transfer may be predominantly about legal rules, it remains a topic 'apart' from legal scholarship. Nevertheless, it is argued here that rule-transfer invariably has both a legal component and a legal objective and, as will be explored, mostly has components with both internal and external facets. It is argued to accommodate the need for methodology in studying EU rule-making from a legal perspective. It also accommodates well the behavioural direction of EU law analysis, commenting upon EU action as social practices, socialising behaviour in the global legal order, causation dynamics as well as their legitimacy.

EU rule-transfer conventionally concerns the external functioning of EU law – e.g. within accession states – and internal ideals ('the EU') through and by law. Rule-transfer thus usually concerns democratic processes whereby the rule of law is developed. It carries a particular assumption as to the democratic benefits of the operation of EU law upon its subjects. As a result, one may say that its normative edge tends often to appear blunt or perhaps a bit hollow because EU rule-transfer is the means and the end thereof. Rather, the legitimacy and the effectiveness of these processes is subsumed within an analysis from the outset. Nevertheless, it offers a particular empirical or practical insight into the EU's role in the world and its global impact through law. The study of rule-transfer is argued to offer a practical insight into the EU's role in the world and its global impact. Such a study is, of course, more usually 'internally' focused rather than externally so – i.e. upon the EU and its subjects rather than the world. As a result, this book draws from EU rule-transfer in substance, scope, method and outlook by an explicit development of its theorisation beyond its conventional contours. The book deploys the term to depict internal and external focused methods of rule-making. It deploys the term to depict the movement of rules and to include the external acceptance or adoption of EU law.

38 For example, Bradford (n. 2).

39 Recent rule-transfer scholarship emphasises increasingly a narrative of the functionalist extension of governance which travels outside the EU. This narrative of functionalist extension of governance divides up subject domains sharply. For example, Lavenex maintains that EU external relations display a 'dual character' such that a fundamental distinction exists between Type 1 and Type II (ESDP/foreign policies versus territorially defined strategies – for example, ENP, EEA: Lavenex (n. 28). See De Búrca (n. 36); Schimmelfennig and Sedelmeier (n. 29).

Distinguishing Europeanisation, policy diffusion, transposition and rule-exportation

For the purposes of this account, rule-transfer must be distinguished and separated from various other methods of depicting processes of the 'movement' of EU rules – e.g. Europeanisation, policy diffusion, transposition and rule-exportation. First, Europeanisation is understood as reshaping politics in the domestic arena in ways that reflect policies, practices or references advanced through the EU systems of governance.[40] Just like rule-transfer, Europeanisation is a dynamic process but is factually limited to the period before and after the admission of a new member state to the EU. It thus has no necessarily obvious or clear-cut application to third countries who mirror, mimic or otherwise 'take' EU rules, a process which is considered in this book. Moreover, Europeanisation is usually associated with institutionalisation and specifically horizontal institutionalisation,[41] through a widening of the group of actors whose actions and relationships are normatively structured. It must be acknowledged as having a highly specific technical and even technocratic meaning, one which has not been availed of much in legal scholarship.[42]

There is a body of international relations and political science scholarship describing the diffusion of values from the EU to the US legal order across legal fields.[43] Can we distinguish between forms of rule-transfer and mere policy diffusions?[44] Such questions demonstrate the importance of examining the normative rationale for rule-transfer and how it informs its definition, its direction, its content but also its subjects and objects, which are considered here throughout. However, this formulation focuses more upon the reasons for this diffusion rather than the process itself. While this scholarship draws more broadly across subjects, it focuses upon neither the methodology nor the normative content of rule-transfer.[45] Political science/ IR scholars sharply divide the effects of specific subject domains, in particular, the internal market and external relations.[46]

40 Ian Bache and Andrew Jordan, *The Europeanization of British Politics* (Palgrave Macmillan 2008), 5; Fabrizio Caffagi *et al.*, 'Europeanization of Private Law in Central and Eastern Europe Countries (CEECs): Preliminary Findings and Research Agenda', EUI LAW Working Paper 2010/15.

41 Schimmelfennig and Sedelmeier (n. 29).

42 Caffagi *et al.*, ibid.

43 Linos (n. 8); Gregory Shaffer, 'Globalization and Social Protection: The Impact of Foreign and International Rules in the Ratcheting Up of U.S. Privacy Standards' (2001), 25 Yale *JIL* 1; Bradford (n. 2); Scott (n. 3); David Vogel, *The Politics of Precaution: Regulating Health, Safety, and Environmental Risks in Europe and the United States* (Princeton University Press, 2012).

44 Linos (n. 8); Claudio Radaelli, 'Diffusion without Convergence: How Political Context Shapes the Adoption of Regulatory Impact Assessment' (2005), 12(5) *JEPP* 26.

45 David Bach and Abe Newman, 'Self-Regulatory Trajectories in the Shadow of Public Power: Resolving Digital Dilemmas in Europe and the United States' (2004), 17 *Governance* 387.

46 Lavenex (n. 28).

However, legal accounts depicting variants of rule-transfer are based upon either projects of the external impact of internal market laws or the fluid intersection of the internal and external in EU. Such accounts have not captured the EU's most evolving and dynamic field, its Area of Freedom, Security and Justice (AFSJ) in their work. Even when they do, they adopt very narrow depictions of its components, despite its possible significance for this work. It is argued here that existing legal accounts conceptualise in limited fields the actual practice-based transfer of rules, less so the broader question of the process of the EU's promotion of norms. They also largely overlook developments in the AFSJ, despite evidence of their growing significance. It is further argued here that theorisations of EU rule-transfer as the functionalist extension of governance may have serious limitations, focusing unduly on the nature of the fields and less so on their external or global effects and possibly being less suited to depicting developments under analysis by legal scholars.

Literature on 'rule-exportation' tends to have a heavy instrument-specific focus and is dominated by concerns for autonomy.[47] Also legal transplants do not focus upon the particularities of the supranational context, or even broader international adoptions. Comparative law assumes that there are 'parent' legal orders and thus is a rough tool to capture the nuances of EU law as postnational rule-making. As Teubner states, there is a 'false dichotomy' arising from the binary image of recipients either repulsing or accepting legal transfers.[48] As such, his 'legal irritant' is indicative of legal transfers that do not automatically displace pre-existing legal meanings and practices but instead trigger a new set of unpredictable choices. Nevertheless, there are many conceptual shortcomings and limitations of the term 'legal irritant'.[49] Some have sought to suggest that legal transplants and legal irritants are one of the same family.[50] Others caution about paying too much attention to descriptive metaphors in formulating theories.[51] Nor could it be adequately captured as a mere legal transplant, as studied by comparative law, capturing only haphazardly and micro-analytically specific instruments, rules or practices, less the overall process or overarching conduct of the EU and its relevance to global actions.

47 For example, European Private Law: Yane Svetiev and Hans Micklitz, 'Consumer Law Travels' (2013), 36(3) *JCP* 209; Yane Svetiev and Hans Micklitz, 'From Rule Export to Institution Building: Consumer Law at the EU's Doorsteps' (2013), 36 (3) *JCP* 1.

48 Gunther Teubner, 'Legal Irritants: Good Faith in British Law or How Unifying Law Ends Up in New Divergences' (1998), 61 *MLR* 11, 12.

49 John Gillespie, 'Towards a discursive analysis of legal transfers into developing East Asia' (2008), 40(3) *NYUJILP* 657, 665.

50 David Nelken, 'Beyond the Metaphor of Legal Transplants? Consequences of Autopoietic Theory for the study of Cross-Cultural Legal Adaptation' in Jiri Priban and David Nelken (eds), *Law's New Boundaries: The Consequences of Legal Autopoiesis* (Aldershot, 2001); David Nelken, 'Rethinking Legal Transfers' in Pierre Legrand and Roderick Munday (eds), *Comparative Legal Studies: Traditions and Transitions* (Cambridge University Press, 2002).

51 Gillespie (n. 49).

Language is inherently flexible and so the term of art of 'legal transposition' has been devised to overcome limitations as to the 'legal transplant' terminology. However, it is argued here to have many limitations, especially in the EU context, for understanding the methodology of rule-making practices.[52] The transposition of legal rules is a concept which is an elementary, even rudimentary, part of EU rule-making. It forms an essential Member State's obligations of its membership of the EU. As a result, the EU has been a fertile ground for those studying comparative implementation processes. Transposition in this sense depicts an implementation process as much as a legal phenomenon of EU law – i.e. the mandatory obligation of loyal cooperation.[53] We may say that it depicts a highly formal, conventional and rather structured process. It is shielded as an internal process within or about the territory of the EU. Transposition is not usually deployed to depict more nuanced movements of rules from the EU beyond its borders. For example, transposition does not describe the acceptance by third countries of EU rules, nor is it understood to. Similarly, a process whereby the EU enacts rules with third countries which are then 'evolved' into internal EU rules is neither usually nor accurately captured by the formal legal term of transposition. There are many forms of adoption of EU rules beyond the territory of the EU that compel us to understand power dynamics and rule-making processes that may occur with or without intent for their movement. For this reason, the structure and formalism of the implementation process is argued to be a limited framework to consider rule-making.

The case study of the EU's Area of Freedom, Security and Justice

This leads to the more practical question of who are the subjects and objects of the process depicted here, EU rule-transfer, and whether or how they may be separated. The focus of this work is on the specificity and taxonomy of practices, rules and instruments in the broader context of EU rule-making. Rule-transfer conventionally understood largely concerns instances of vertical authority, legal obligations and mandated transpositions from the EU to candidate countries. The practices of rule-transfer as understood here may concern transfers of instruments in the absence of any legal authority, between legal orders. This book is thus concerned with both external and internal transfer – i.e. both outwards and inwards transfer. In this regard, rule-transfer is considered here as a means to study EU action, directly and indirectly, actively and passively, because it considers both acceptance and acquiescence by both the subjects and objects of rule-transfer.

There is a 'directional' specificity to all accounts that frames their subject and object in a specific way, which is dependent upon the subject matter. For example,

52 See Esin Orucu, '*Law as Transposition' (2002), 51 ICLQ* 205, 208.

European private lawyers have charted EU rule-export outside the EU, in a specific field where national authority and parental norms have a distinct role to play.[54] Rule-exportation in this context then is fundamentally a unidirectional idea, predicated upon institution building. The 'unidirectional' nature of many case studies on the success of the outwards-only transfer of EU rules to third countries and organisations may in reality be only part of the story. It is argued to fall short of depicting the operation of the global reach and effects of EU law as a holistic process. Rather, how the EU strategically seeks external norms, exports and imports norms, which impacts upon the study of its subjects and objects, is explored here.

This account focuses upon one subject domain as the object of study where the 'internal' and 'external' dimensions to EU law, policy and governance are particularly pronounced and evolving – in the EU's AFSJ, a newly regularised part of EU law.[55] The relationship between the 'internal' and 'external' within EU law is argued to play a central role in the operation of the global reach and effects of EU law. It is a complex dichotomy and is under-explored in legal scholarship, arguably having fallen out of fashion in other disciplines for its sheer complexity or constant evolving state.[56] The AFSJ is argued to be instructive as to the operation of the global reach and effects of EU law through the study of rule-transfer. It is arguably the most sensitive and dynamic field of the EU, with a wide range of policies, governance and instruments, that has evolved heavily influenced by external norms. However, it is only newly regularised as a field and certain rule-making practices are under development. As will be explored in Chapter 5, EU 'internal' security readily embraces 'external' security. EU security rules under development are argued to demonstrate the migratory effects of external rules by way of some form of 'rule-transfer' – i.e. the movement of rules between legal orders. Yet how we understand these specific rule-making processes, their evolution, their methodology or their taxonomy is an unfixed science. To subsume such processes within a characterisation of functional 'movement' alone (e.g. as rule-migration or exportation) risks bypassing 'the

53 See Marise Cremona (ed.), *The Compliance and Enforcement of EU Law* (Oxford University Press, 2012), xl.

54 Micklitz and Svetiev (n. 47).

55 On the regularisation of it as a domain of law as to enforcement, compliance, procedures, see Chapter 4.

56 See Helena Carrapiço and Florian Trauner, 'The External Dimension of EU Justice and Home Affairs after the Lisbon Treaty: Analysing the Dynamics of Expansion and Diversification' (2012) 17 *EFAR* 1, Table 1; Sandra Lavenex and Nicole Wichmann, 'The External Governance of EU Internal Security' (2009), 31(1) *JEI* 83; Florian Trauner, 'The internal-external security nexus: more coherence under Lisbon?' (EUISS Occasional Paper No. 89, March 2011). See Elaine Fahey, 'The EU's Cybercrime and Cyber-Security Rule-Making: Mapping the Internal and External Dimensions of EU Security' (2014), 1 *EJRR* 46. It is a complex subject area perceived to exist somewhere between a policy area and subject field, one which has been mainstreamed in the latest treaty reforms: see Carrapiço and Trauner, ibid.

bigger picture'. As a result, the EU's AFSJ represents a useful case study on account of its evolving and dynamic content.

Legal scholarship tends to adopt a narrow understanding of EU security. It is largely limited as to former second pillar defence activities, or now Common Security and Defence Policy, responsibility to protect and dispute settlement, or focuses upon the work of fledgling EU security agencies.[57] Some recent non-legal scholarship has sought to develop a broader understanding of security beyond traditional definitions, to incorporate climate change, migration, piracy and counter-terrorism, as well as development aid.[58] Such a view is argued here to be consistent with contemporary EU rule-making and accordingly is adopted. Through case studies this account systematically identifies external norm primacy in AFSJ rule-making. In doing so, it seeks to contribute to the debate on shifting practice in the understanding of security. The book also uses three specific case studies (EU cybercrime and cybersecurity, AFSJ data transfer and directives in the post-Lisbon AFSJ) with pronounced internal and external contours that represent evolving areas which are the subject of limited legal scholarship to date. As the subject and object of study, AFSJ has an advantage of being a dynamic area which is amenable to process-oriented study. There, the relationship between the 'internal' and 'external' is explicit, transparent and evolving. Through security-oriented case studies focusing upon method, directionality, international political processes, the book formulates the global reach and effects of EU law as a phenomenon and process in a less economically oriented field. This approach has a broader appeal. Much scholarship of transnational law in particular is dedicated to dissecting its process-oriented structures or architecture whereas the approach here is instead bottom-up.[59] The case studies employ a textual 'tracing' methodology which explicitly develops their internal and external dimension, developed in detail internally. As a result, this book develops a methodology which is transparent and explicit to capture the processes depicted.

Aims of the text

Understanding the EU as a postnational actor

This leads to the broader question as to what is meant to pinpoint the global reach and effects of EU law or to delineate patterns and tendencies as a phenomenon. The role of the EU as an esoteric organisation and as a unique legal actor

57 For example, Martin Trybus and Nigel White (eds), *European Security Law* (Oxford University Press, 2007); Panos Koutrakos, 'The European Union in the Global Security Architecture' in Van Vooren, Blockmans and Wouters (eds) (n. 36).

58 See *Christian Kaunert and Kamil Zwolski, The EU as a Global Security Actor – A Comprehensive Analysis Beyond CFSP and JHA* (Palgrave Macmillan, 2013).

59 Contrast Peer Zumbansen, 'Administrative Law's Global Dream: Navigating Regulatory Spaces Between "National" and "International"' (2013), 11(2) *I.CON* 506.

entails that the spread of its rules is multifaceted, as are understandings thereof. Understanding how the EU intends, aims and formulates the effects of its rules globally is both a descriptive and normative project which has considerable ramifications for the constitutional fabric of the EU as a project. This aspect of the study of the global reach and effects of EU law is conducted here in two ways. The first is more discrete and considers the place of the EU as an actor within postnational rule-making. The conceptualisation of 'actors' engaging in rule-making is central to theorising power, autonomy, influence and even legitimacy in rule-making. However, there is no consensus in scholarship on what it means to be an actor, despite its centrality to discussions on rule-making, power and influence.[60] To view an institution as an actor in their own right is technically an inaccurate one.[61] Legal scholarship employs formal, limiting criteria to assess what we may frame here loosely as 'actorship' qualities, such as legal personality, legal authority to act and institutional autonomy.[62] Yet such formalism may pose many limitations. Even if it is able to collect a Nobel Peace Prize, have its own diplomatic service or have nearly every EU executive actor and agency endowed with a global mandate,[63] the EU does not function as a unitary actor in the world. It does not participate as a state in the global legal order. Although it has 'single legal personality' – i.e. formal authority to act – the EU has a broad range of 'statuses' in international organisations.[64] Sometimes it acts alongside its member states, although sometimes it does not. It faces the reality that international agreements cannot be easily renegotiated. These challenges are not limited to the EU in the outside world. Internally, the EU comprises very powerful institutional components that sometimes appear more powerful than the sum of its parts. They are broadly understood as actors engaged in rule-making after the state.

60 See Elaine Fahey, *The Actors of Postnational Rule-Making: Contemporary Challenges of European and Public International Law* (Routledge, 2015), Introduction; Christopher Hill, 'The Capability-Expectations Gap, or Conceptualizing Europe's International Role' (1993), 31(3) *JCMS* 305; Joe Jupille and James Caparaso, 'States, Agency and Rules: The European Union in Global Environmental Politics', in Carolyn Rhodes (ed.), *The European Union in the World Community* (Lynne Rienner, 1998), 213.

61 See Michael Barnett and Martha Finnemore, *Rules for the World International Organizations in Global Politics* (Cornell University Press, 2004).

62 See, for example, Dan Sarooshi, *International Organizations and Their Exercise of Sovereign Powers* (Oxford University Press, *2005)*; Richard Collins and Nigel White (eds), *International Organizations and the Idea of Autonomy: Institutional Independence in the International Legal Order* (Routledge, 2011); Jan Klabbers, 'Presumptive Personality: The European Union in International Law', in Marti Koskenniemi (ed.) *International Law Aspects of the European Union*, (Martijnus Nijhoff, 1998), 231; Andrea Bianchi (ed.), 'Relativizing the Subjects or Subjectivizing the Actors? That is the Question' in Andrea Bianchi (ed.), *Non-State-Actors and International Law* (Ashgate, 2009).

63 Deirdre Curtin, 'Challenging Executive Dominance in European Democracy' (2014), 77(1) *MLR* 1.

64 Piet Eeckhout, *EU External Relations Law* (2nd edn, Oxford University Press, 2011); Mathias Ruffert 'Personality under EU-Law: A Conceptual Answer towards the Pluralisation of the EU' (2014), 21 *ELJ* 346.

Yet doctrinal or formalist understandings of 'actors' engaged in rule-making are unable to capture new manifestations of 'executive' actors widely found in the EU or its powerful and independent judicial components or its transnational parliament.[65] There is a paradox as to the state of the EU: it is an empowered, sophisticated legal actor. Yet it faces as many external and internal hurdles in its development as what is argued here later to be its embryonic sovereignty evident in the global reach and effects of EU law. The contemporary formulation of the global reach and effects of EU law does not grapple with the inconsistencies, incoherence and challenges of EU action in the world, by articulating the complexities of 'actor'-related questions. Nevertheless, as the case studies pursued in Chapters 5 and 6 on data transfer and cybercrime and security will demonstrate, the tensions between the internal and external in EU law often flow from the autonomy exercised by its actor components. This results from the 'bicepheral' stance of the EU in theory and practice. It is argued here to be excusatory and indulgent of the overreach of EU powers, as exemplified in accounts of the global reach and effects of EU law. Behavioural understandings of EU action dominate EU law and governance scholarship – e.g. observing its practices, assessing its action and locating its place in a broader global context. In this regard, a closer focus upon how we understand and depict actors in rule-making develops resonance with this scholarship.

Understanding postnational sovereignty

The second aspect of the study is conducted through sovereignty, often considered as the core ideal of public law and elementary tenet of power, constitutionalism and authority.[66] Accounts which depict or describe postnational rule-making processes, constitutionalism or democracy do not tend to invoke sovereignty, either as a construct, or as a method or process. Instead, such accounts are more concerned with the place within breakdowns of orthodoxy conceived broadly, the shortcomings of postnational democracy and its institutional components and rule-making practices. Sovereignty receives little or no attention in the post-Lisbon context, even after considerable structural, constitutional and policy

65 On the executive: Deirdre Curtin, *Executive Power of the European Union: Law, Practices and the Living Constitution* (Oxford University Press, 2009). On courts: Karen Alter, *The New Terrain of International Law: Courts, Politics, Rights* (Princeton University Press, 2013); Elaine Fahey, 'The EU Emission Trading Scheme and the Court of Justice: the High Politics of the Indirect Promotion of Global Standards' (2012), *GLJ* 1247; R. Dan Kelemen, *The Transformation of Law and Regulation in the European Union* (Harvard University Press, 2012). On transnational parliaments: Davor Jancic, 'Interactions between the EU and US legal order' in Elaine Fahey and Deirdre Curtin (eds), *A Transatlantic Community of Law'* (Cambridge University Press, 2014); Neil Walker, 'Postnational Constitutionalism and Postnational Public Law: A Tale of Two Neologisms' (2012), 3 *TLT* 61.

66 Bert Van Roermund, '*Sovereignty: Unpopular and Popular*' in Neil Walker (ed.), *Sovereignty in Transition: Essays in European Law* (Hart, 2003), 33.

changes to the EU itself.[67] Sovereignty is arguably neither popular nor conventional, nor does it transpose itself into discourses of rule-making beyond the nation state. For some, to speak of sovereignty in the context of global governance leads to the bewildering identification processing of identifying a 'global sovereign'.[68] It has been argued here that those who argue that new and evolving international institutions do not necessitate a new conceptualisation of sovereignty are unduly myopic to the challenge of postnational rule-making. EU scholarship on sovereignty begins from the premise of its exceptionalism. However, much scholarship on sovereignty and the EU has been developed prior to more recent invocations in the EU treaties to evolve as a postnational democracy.

The case studies of AFSJ norm promotion, transatlantic data transfer and cybercrime and cybersecurity are argued to demonstrate significant internal and external incoherence between the aims and means of EU rule-making. They generate major challenges as to coherence, competence and boundaries. It is argued that there is a need to engage with the blurring of sovereignty, authority and territory within these developments. However, as a broader proposition, the space of EU rules is argued here to require more nuancing, method and case studies as to its components. The book argues overall that the merger of sovereignty, territoriality and jurisdiction in a global world is an emerging matter for EU law.

On methodology: tracing EU norm promotion

This account considers how the EU actually promotes norms in its rule-making – i.e. to consider its actual practices as to its values, instruments and rules deployed so as to cause or generate rule-transfer. As a result, a specific methodology used here to capture these phenomena is to focus upon the values, instruments and rules, broadly defined, which the EU actually adopts in its rule-making. The formulation of 'life cycles of norms' as developed by Finnemore and Skikkink ('norm emergence', 'norm cascade' and 'norm internalisation') have proven to have had a significant impact upon the study of international politics.[69] The increasing use of this rubric by legal scholars, exploring the similarity between

67 See further Chapter 7. Jean Cohen, *Globalization and Sovereignty Rethinking Legality, Legitimacy, and Constitutionalism* (Cambridge University Press, 2012); Beth Simmons, 'Review Essay: Is Sovereignty still Relevant' (2000), 94(1) *AJIL* 226; Hans Lindahl, 'Why Sovereignty?' in Richard Rawlings, Peter Leyland and Alison Young (eds), *Sovereignty and Law: Domestic, Regional & Global Perspectives* (Oxford University Press, 2013); Steven Krasner, *Sovereignty. Organized Hypocrisy* (Princeton University Press, 1999); Wouter Werner and Marc de Wilde, 'The Endurance of Sovereignty' (2001), 7 *European Journal of International Law* 283; Neil Walker, 'The Cosmopolitan Local: Neil Mac Cormick's Post Sovereign World' in Jon Fossum and Augustin Mendedez (eds), *The Post-Sovereign Constellation* (Springer, 2011).

68 See Chapter 7.

69 Martha Finnemore and Katherine Sikkink, 'International Norm Dynamics and Political Change' (1998), 52 *International Organisation* 887. See further references in Chapter 4.

norms and law in the domestic and international context, is drawn from and further developed here.[70] It is argued that at the heart of understanding EU rule-transfer lies the fact that international organisations such as the EU often act as norm agents or entrepreneurs but do not do so with a sufficiently transparent method.[71] Norms act as a focal point for decentralised networks of organisations and individuals and, as a result, international organisations may act as major promoters of norms in world politics.

Law performs an important communicative function in the EU legal order.[72] However, as Sunstein states, law is not an agent and cannot speak, lacking personality or personification, and law is a complex construct for the visualisation of rule-making. Rather, law can make statements and so the expressive function of law and its impact upon prevailing social norms is part of the structures of our society.[73] The EU usually communicates its norms externally, such as the rule of law or the promotion of fundamental rights, in clauses of the formal agreements with neighbouring countries, candidate countries and trade partners.[74] Alternatively, the EU issues local statements – for example, in Gaza recently the EU expressed its views on the death penalty in a public statement.[75] More usually, though, the enunciation of EU norms is usually communicated to the subjects and objects of the agreement with legal authority – i.e. by formal and consensual agreement with a third party. However, the EU has a patchy record with regard to the enforcements of these norms. For example, it rarely enforces its suspension rights for breach thereof in the context of trade.[76] Moreover, the EU maintains an ostensibly 'transparent' treaty register, where it formally

70 See further in Chapter 4.

71 Finnemore and Sikkink (n. 69).

72 Albeit without defining what law is: Cass Sunstein, 'On the Expressive Function of Law' (1995), 144 *University of Pennsylvania LR* 2021, 2024; Cass Sunstein, 'Social Norms and Social Roles' (1996), 96 *Columbia LR* 903. But see Matthew Adler, 'Expressive Theories of Law: A Skeptical Overview' (2000), 148 *University of Pennsylvania LR* 1363.

73 For example, it might be contested whether the EU's 'advocacy' before the US Supreme Court could be considered as law or whether legislation alone is captured by Sunstein, hence the adoption of rule-making here: Elaine Fahey, 'On the Use of Law in Transatlantic Relations: Legal Dialogues Between the EU and US' (2014), 20(3) *ELJ* 368.

74 For example, European Commission, Inventory of Agreements containing the Human Rights Clause, DG RELEX/B2 – Treaties Office, 7 July 2011; available at http://ec.europa.eu/world/agreements/viewCollection.do, accessed 23 December 2015.

75 For a list of locally issued EU views on the death penalty, see the website of the European External Action Service: http://eeas.europa.eu/human_rights/adp/index_en.htm, accessed 23 December 2015.

76 For example, unilateral EU suspension of treaties has occurred in relation to countries such as Zimbabwe, Liberia, Togo, Fiji, Guinea and Mauritania. The EU has also invoked trade sanctions for human rights violations without a human rights clause strictly providing for it in the case of Myanmar: Bruno De Witte, 'The EU and International Legal Order: The Case of Human Rights' in Malcolm Evans and Panos Koutrakos (eds), *Beyond the Established Legal Orders: Policy Interconnections Between the EU and the Rest of the World* (Hart, 2011), 481; Laurent Pech, 'The Rule of Law as a Guiding Principle of EU's External Action', CLEER Working Paper, 2012/3.

categorises the types of norms that it promotes in its external relations.[77] However, there are many shortcomings to these practices, substantive – e.g. what it communicates overall – and how it does this – e.g. transparently – considered next, that impact upon the manner in which we may understand the methodology of EU rule-transfer.

As a general proposition, there is a variety of subject matters through which to consider the concept of EU norm promotion through law, either internally or externally. The theme of exportation of EU values has a very broad interpretation and considerable span of subject areas, beyond security.[78] The EU frequently imports values and norms, and itself acts often as a model for values through its rule-making, on account of the success, novelty and effectiveness of its rules.[79] By contrast, internal rule-making processes may generate differing practices and processes as to norm promotion. The dominant focus of much scholarship upon the actors of norm promotion as norm agents has given centre-stage to newly empowered actors in evolving policy – for example, to the European Parliament in the Area of Freedom, Security and Justice (AFSJ).[80] Such a focus appears useful in specific policy fields but may be less useful in a broader theorisation of EU action and the boundaries thereof in rule-making. It may also fail to capture the nuances of postnational rule-making, especially with regard to the evolving external dimension to EU action.

This book argues that we must look beyond the prism of 'norm internalisation' in studying rule-making, commonly deployed in IR and social sciences literature, whereby the internal adoption of norms from external sources is a specific focus.[81] Similarly, judicially focused accounts of norm internalisation by legal scholars do not offer a holistic – i.e. a complete and unified – account of multi-directional rule-making processes. Instead, this book argues that a holistic account is achieved through a study of rule-making processes 'bottom-up'. Norm internalisation lacks a focus upon the methodology of rule-making processes and does not focus upon rule-based content usually. It may be argued to presuppose a process – for example, the internationalisation of European law, which may not sit well with nuances of contemporary EU rule-making. For example, IR scholarship has focused upon the EU's internationalisation of US norms in post 9/11 rule-making. However, it excludes rule-making practices

77 See http://ec.europa.eu/world/agreements/default.home.do.

78 See also Sonia Lucarelli and Ian Manners (eds), *Values and Principles in EU Foreign Policy* (Routledge, 2006).

79 Marise Cremona, 'Values in EU Foreign Policy' in Evans and Koutrakos (n. 76), 275, 285. The European Convention on Human Rights or the Geneva Convention on the status of refugees are examples of the former, the evolution of the legal order of ASEAN might represent the latter. See also Marise Cremona, 'The European as a Global Actor: Roles, Models and Identity' (2004), 41 *CMLR* 553.

80 Ariadna Ripoll Servent and Alex MacKenzie, 'The European Parliament as a "Norm Taker"? EU–US Relations after the SWIFT Agreement' (2012), 17 *EFAR* 71.

81 See Chapter 4.

such as the subsequent adoption by the EU rule-making adopted initially with the US bilaterally.[82] It is a narrative of post-9/11 security that perhaps is insufficiently nuanced to contemporary rule-making in security and is explored in Chapter 5.

A brief outline of the chapters of the book are sketched below.

Outline of the book chapters

Chapter 2 ('The boundaries of the global reach of EU law') examines the phenomenon and formulation of the global reach of EU law. The chapter considers the nature of competence as a construct in EU law and reflects upon the fluidity of the boundaries of the 'internal' and 'external' giving rise to the global reach of EU law and their nexus. The chapter then examines three distinct and discrete meanings of the global reach of EU law: the externalisation of the internal market, extra-territoriality of EU law and the global reach of the EU in international organisations. It assesses in each section their place in judicial review before the Court of Justice in certain recent proceedings. It argues that the global reach of EU law as it evolves may cause its formal and even social legitimacy much 'slippage', exacerbated by few meaningful checks from the Court of Justice.

Chapter 3 ('The EU as an actor in rule-making') explores how we conceptualise actors in rule-making. It argues that the EU as a legal and political actor in global governance seemingly defies categorisation. Leading theorisations of EU action in the world are argued not to account for contemporary practices in EU law. The chapter examines initially descriptive issues such as, first, paradoxes and limitations of the EU as a legal actor in the world, followed by, second, an analysis of the institutional components of organisations as actors. It considers thereafter practical limitations on how the EU acts in the world – i.e. what the EU 'does' to promote good global governance in the world and the relationship between EU law and Normative Power Europe (NPE). This chapter then assesses the paradoxes and limitations involved in considering the EU as a unified legal actor in the world. The evolution of living institutional components and their place within the theory and practice of actors in rule-making are outlined. The dominance of Normative Power Europe as a means of understanding the normative dimension to EU action in the world is then considered, while the final section assesses pressures upon the 'construct' of actors in rule-making beyond the nation state, from the perspective of organisations as structures, subject matter and operationally.

Chapter 4 ('External norm primacy and EU law: AFSJ directives in the post-Lisbon legislative cycle') begins the overarching methodological study of the book and begins with the consideration of the case study of the EU's place in

82 Javier Argomaniz, 'The Passenger Name Records Agreement and the European Union Internalisation of US Border Security norms' (2009), 31 *JEI* 119.

international organisations that it promotes in rule-making, focusing upon external norms in internal rule-making. The chapter traces the output of one instrument of EU rule-making in a select field – namely, its AFSJ. It considers how external norms – i.e. understood predominantly as instruments of international law, including but not limited to conventions, agreements, treaties, agreements qua norms – 'cascade' and 'internalise' into AFSJ rule-making in 17 proposed and adopted directives in the post-Treaty of Lisbon – i.e. in the 2009–2014 legislative cycle. It considers (1) norm promotion practices, (2) legislative self-characterisation and (3) the formulation of 'norm cascade' into EU law. The chapter examines the primacy of external norms as an overall process.

Chapter 5 ('Tracing transatlantic rule-transfer') explores rule-transfer by an examination of select areas of transatlantic relations – namely, EU–US Passenger Name Records (PNR) and EU–US Terrorist Finance Tracking Programme (TFTP) 'Swift' Agreement and their effects upon EU security rules. In the first section, it explores select areas of transatlantic imprints on EU security rules, examining the operation of rule-transfer and considers the question of importation and exportation of values via EU law, as well as the context of mutual recognition in transatlantic security agreements. The chapter then sets out an analysis of two transatlantic agreements and their impact upon and link to internal EU security rules. Finally, it considers the mooted 'global approach' of the EU to PNR. The chapter shows how the stringency of the measures arising as transatlantic legal imprints should be of some concern in the absence of a clear understanding of the adequacy of operation and safeguards of transatlantic rule-making. Moreover, the origins of the EU internal security rules remain of significance for understanding how the resulting rules themselves should be reviewed. The exercise of tracing transatlantic rule-transfer provides an insight with which to view the global reach and effects of EU law. It demonstrates the precariousness of the internal and external, which the EU readily exploits.

Chapter 6 ('The EU's cybercrime and cybersecurity rule-making') conducts a case study of the relationship between internal and external security policies of the EU in EU rule-making in the area of cybercrime and cybersecurity. It explores how the EU gives primacy to external norms – i.e. the Council of Europe Cybercrime Convention, in both its contemporary internal and external rule-making in the case study, appears to produce very different regulatory results despite the commonality of the norms used. The chapter starts by examining the evolution of the instruments of the EU's internal regulation of cybersecurity and cybercrime in the EU cyber strategy, its supporting directive along with the development of a cybercrime directive. It then examines the formulation of risk therein, and finally contrasts rule-making between the EU and US in cybercrime and cybersecurity and its relationship to internal EU rule-making. The traditionally asserted 'fluidity' of external and internal security is argued to be inaccurate when considered from this perspective.

Chapter 7 ('The EU's participation in the global legal order: manifestations of sovereignty') draws together the strands of the case studies and text, and considers the global reach and effects of EU law as manifestations of sovereignty. This chapter argues that postnational rule-making practices conducted by the EU may usefully be captured by sovereignty as an overarching framework. Much scholarship on sovereignty and the EU has been developed prior to more recent invocations in the EU treaties to evolve as a postnational democracy. Participation by the EU in the global legal order requires reflection on what the EU is and what it does. The chapter assesses the understandings and many paradoxes of sovereignty. It considers the exceptionalism of EU sovereignty, including EU sovereignty, as developed by Walker. Finally, it considers the EU's participation in the global legal orders and how it does this, in four subsections, as to (1) its goals, (2) its social practices, (3) the 'space' of and for EU rules, and (4) the construction of (trans)boundaries under EU law.

2 The boundaries of the global reach of EU law

Introduction

The phrase 'global reach' has long had connotations of 'world reach, success or influence', in a commercial context.[1] Understandings of the reach of law globally traditionally have had a high Anglo-American rather than European content and relate predominantly to the extra-territoriality of US law.[2] Nevertheless, from areas as diverse as the internal market,[3] EU refugee law,[4] data protection,[5] EU environmental law, EU banking and financial services and taxation law,[6] to EU competition law,[7] it is now perceived as a commonplace occurrence of EU law that it has global reach in whatever form. In legal accounts, the global reach of EU law is usually considered as a phenomenon relative to its subject areas, perhaps less so as to its causation or its constitutional significance.[8]

1 For example, www.collinsdictionary.com/dictionary/english/global-reach, accessed 23 December 2015.

2 A search on Westlaw international generates thousands of hits, predominantly from US journals. For example, from a vast selection, the literature arising from extra-territoriality: Noah Feldman, 'Cosmopolitan Law' (2007) 116 *Yale Law Journal* 1022; see the US Alien Tort Statute controversy in *Kiobel* v. *Royal Dutch Petroleum Co.*, 133 S.Ct 1659 (2013), 'Developments in the Law-Extra-territoriality' (2011), 124 *HLR* 1226; Hannah Buxbaum, 'Territory, Territoriality, and the Resolution of Jurisdictional Conflict' (2009) 57(2) *AJCL* 631.

3 Anu Bradford, 'The Brussels Effect' (2012), 107 *NULR* 1; Piet Eeckhout, *The European Internal Market and International Trade – A Legal Analysis* (Oxford University Press, 1994).

4 For example, Helen Lambert, Jane McAdam and Maryellen Fullerton (eds) *The Global Reach of European Refugee Law* (Cambridge University Press, 2013).

5 See the evolution of the territorial scope of the Data Protection Regulation: www.statewatch.org/eu-dp.htm, accessed 23 December 2015.

6 Suzanne Kingston, 'Territoriality in EU (Taxation) Law: A Sacred Principle, or Dépassé?' in Joachim Englisch (ed.) *International Tax Law and New Challenges from Constitutional and Legal Pluralism* (IBFD, 2015).

7 See Florian Wagner-von Papp, 'Competition Law, Extra-territoriality and Bilateral Agreements' in Ariel Ezrachi (ed.), *Research Handbook on International Competition Law* (Edward Elgar, 2012).

8 Non-legal accounts of the EU as a global regulator claim to be considerably more accurate where they are sectorally specific. See Alison Young, 'The European Union as a Global Regulator? Context and comparison' (2015), 22 (9) *JEPP*: www.tandfonline.com/toc/rjpp20/22/91233.

The global reach of EU law often appears as a dynamic idea which has many equally compelling manifestations. For example, some suggest that the global reach of EU law comprises the spread of its norms and values or contextual standards rather than law or that it is an effects-based formulation.[9] From a purely textual and practical perspective, however, it is far from unexpected that EU law would have global reach. The externalisation of the internal market is an evolving phenomenon in EU law. For example, EU policy documents and legislation regularly attempt to link the internal to the external in EU law and policy with much transparency, including more frequently mooting its extra-territoriality.[10] EU politics also emphasises the global ambitions of EU law, as warranting exploitation.[11] Yet what are the formal constitutional limits or boundaries to these ambitions? The global reach of EU law often appears triggered by forms of constitutional flexibility arising from the fluidity of the 'internal' and 'external' in EU law. They are argued here to raise questions as to what boundaries, if any, there are to the global reach of EU law.

Arguably, one of the most complex features of the global reach of EU law is to decipher its subjects and objects. While the enquiry as to the subjects and objects of public international law is one long scorned as fruitless,[12] the Court of Justice in its landmark decision in *Van Gend en Loos* determined that the subjects of EU law were fundamentally distinct from public international law as a new legal order and it remains a vibrant differentiating characteristic.[13] As the EU's internal and external competences have evolved, it increasingly captures a broader range of actors and interests as its subjects and objects. As a result, there is a growing amount of case law on the boundaries of the global reach of EU law, which is the subject of analysis here.

This chapter considers three specific examples of the shifting boundaries of the global reach of EU law that have arisen recently before the Court. These include, first, the externalisation of the internal market and second, the EU participation in international organisations. Second, these form distinctive forms of legislative and executive action that are revealing of the internal and external boundaries of EU law and the flexibility of the meaning of 'reach' beyond mere legislation.

9 See Lambert *et al.* (n. 4). See Joanne Scott, 'Extraterritoriality and Territorial Extension in EU Law' (2014), 62 *AJCL* 87; Joanne Scott, 'The New EU Extra-territoriality' (2014), 51 *CMLR* 1343: Bradford (n. 3)

10 See n. 5 or Directive 2008/101/EC of the European Parliament and of the Council of 19 November 2008 amending Directive 2003/87/EC so as to include aviation activities in the scheme for greenhouse gas emission allowance trading within the Community [2009], *OJ L* 8/3, recital 25.

11 For example, European Council Brussels, 27 June 2014, EUCO 79/14, seeking 'to fully exploit the potential of the single market in all its dimensions'.

12 See Rosalyn Higgins, ***Problems and Process: International Law and How We Use It*** (Oxford University Press, 1994).

13 Case 26/62 *Van Gend en Loos* EU:C:1963:1 [1963], I-ECR 1. See, generally, Bruno De Witte, 'EU law: Is it International law?' in Catherine Barnard and Steve Peers (eds), ***European Union Law*** (Oxford University Press, 2014) Chapter 7; Joseph H.H. Weiler, 'Van Gend en Loos: The Individual as Subject and Object and the Dilemma of European Legitimacy' (2014), 12 (1) *I.CON* 94.

Third, challenges to EU extra-territoriality have also arisen frequently in the post-Lisbon period, also possibly indicative of the shifting actual boundaries of EU law. In all strands of case law arising in these fields, the Court of Justice appears unwilling to engage with the evolving subjects and objects of EU law and has largely upheld all legislation and action challenged. It will be argued here that the aggrandisement of EU competence, scope and even territory through the flexible boundaries of the global reach of EU law may score lowly in terms of social legitimacy, both inside and outside the EU. This state of affairs appears unaided by the form of review conducted by the Court of Justice.

This chapter thus explores in the following section the place of competence as a construct in EU law and reflects upon the fluidity of the boundaries of the 'internal' and 'external' giving rise to the global reach of EU law and their nexus. It then examines the externalisation of the internal market, EU participation in international organisations and the extra-territoriality of EU law. It assesses in each section their place in judicial review before the Court of Justice in recent proceedings. The final section considers the shifting boundaries of the phenomenon of the global reach of EU law.

The construct of competence: on the boundaries between the internal and external in EU law

The global reach and effects of EU law provide evidence of the flexibility and innovation in law-making techniques as well as the fluidity of the boundaries of the 'internal' and 'external' of competence in EU law. Until the end of the 1990s there was 'astonishingly' little literature in legal competence.[14] It was a considerable time before competence issues were integrated into the treaties.[15] A 'court-centric' view of competence is common because the Court is usually depicted 'as the main institutional actor dealing with the issue', albeit one that is agreed not yet to have developed a doctrine on the definition of EU competence.[16] It has been recently argued that important discrepancies exist between the formal allocation of powers provided for in the treaties and actual legal practice.[17] Although true, arguably this 'opposition' between theory and practice may not be explicable of the global reach of EU law. This is because competence allocation under the treaties does not formally distinguish with any particularity between internal and external competences of the EU and does not establish any clear 'venue preference.'[18] It is thus a dynamic which warrants further consideration.

14 See Loïc Azoulai, 'Introduction' in Azoulai (ed.), *The Question of Competence in the European Union* (Oxford University Press, 2014), 1.

15 Ibid., 2.

16 Ibid., 14. See also Christian Timmermans, 'ECJ Doctrines on Competence' in Azoulai (ed.) (n. 14), Chapter 7.

17 Ibid., 1.

18 Bruno De Witte and Anne Thies, 'Why Choose Europe: The Place of the European Union in the Architecture of International Cooperation' in Bart Van Vooren, Steve Blockmans and Jan Wouters (eds), *The EU's role in Global Governance: The Legal Dimension* (Oxford University Press, 2010), 23, 34.

This account next outlines the core elements of the 'internal' and 'external' competence and their nexus in EU law. It considers the boundaries of the 'internal' and internal market, the 'external' boundaries of EU law and the internal–external regulatory dynamic in EU law.

The boundaries of the 'internal' and the internal market

As a matter of EU law, extraordinary flexibility surrounds the contemporary internal market. The case law of the CJEU is remark-worthy for its light-touch review of legal competence to act in this area.[19] In the history of EU law, only once has legal competence resulted in a directive being struck down on legal competence grounds pursuant to Article 114 TFEU, the legal basis for harmonisation. While the seminal decision of the Court of Justice in tobacco advertising striking down EU legislation for want of competence may have marked an extraordinary constitutional moment in EU law, virtually no EU legislation in a decade has been struck down on competence grounds thereafter.[20] As a decision, it remains accused of its irrelevance to contemporary law and practice.[21] The very definition of the contemporary internal market has long been approached for at least two decades as a study in 'competence creep' or even 'competence sweep'.[22] A competence catalogue introduced in the Treaty of Lisbon has had limited impact upon this state of affairs.[23] This status quo appears to have incentivised the legislature to adopt ambitious and flexible constructions of the internal market. As a result, the flexibility of the 'internal' is the predominant tool of the contemporary EU legislator. This leads first to a consideration of the boundaries of the external in EU law.

The boundaries of the 'external' in EU law and EU action

There is as yet no unified methodology to EU external relations law, which continues to be dominated by practice and a proliferation of actors. Practices of EU external relations law have not tended to lend themselves easily to classification or typologies. The external dimension to most internal policies has

19 See Loic Azoulai, 'The "Retained Powers" Formula in the Case Law of the European Court of Justice: EU Law as Total Law?' (2011), 4 *European Journal of Legal Studies* 193; Bruno De Witte, 'A Competence to Protect: The Pursuit of Non-market Aims through Market Legislation' in Phil Syrpis (ed.), *The Judiciary, the Legislature and EU Internal Market* (Cambridge University Press, 2011), Chapter 2, 25–27.

20 See C-376/98 *Germany* v. *Parliament and Council* EU:C:2000:544 [2000] ECR 1-8419. See Stephen Weatherill, 'The Limits of Legislative Harmonisation Ten Years after Tobacco Advertising: How the Court's Case Law Has Become a "Drafting Guide"' (2011), 12 *GLJ* 827.

21 Derrick Wyatt, 'Community Competence to Regulate the Internal Market' in Michael Dougan and Samantha Currie (eds), *50 Years of the European Treaties* (Hart Publishing, 2009), 93; see also Alexandre Saydé, *Abuse of EU Law and Regulation of the Internal Market* (Hart, 2014).

22 Stephen Weatherill, 'Competence and Legitimacy' in Catherine Barnard and Okeoghene Odudu (eds), *The Outer Limits of European Union Law* (Hart, 2009); Azoulai 'Introduction', (n. 14).

23 See Weatherill (n. 22), 17.

developed on the basis of the implied powers doctrine and residual power clause. Later amendments have provided a scattered range of explicit external powers, from environmental policy, education, vocational training, culture, public health, trans-European networks, research and technological development, and space to social policy and energy. Nonetheless, the treaties have enabled the EU to undertake a wide variety of external action, often 'impressively so'.[24] The Treaty of Lisbon is widely agreed to have codified the core jurisprudence of the Court of Justice somewhat awkwardly.[25] Post-Lisbon, sharp distinctions between the Court and various Advocates General on the scope of exclusive competence do little to bolster the credibility of the EU's competence catalogue.[26]

It is also difficult to name a field of law and policy that would fall outside a potential Union competence and all areas of shared competence provided for by Article 3(2) TFEU, except for cases of parallel competence, have the potential of becoming exclusive. Yet from a practical perspective, the distinction between exclusive, shared, shared but parallel, supportive and national competence appears as a sliding scale rather than as fixed categories because practice is not always based on purely legal categorisations.

The EU often finds pragmatic ways to allow its member states to act alongside it even where there is partial exclusivity, which further blurs our comprehension of boundaries or 'fault-lines'.[27] Pre-Lisbon, this pragmatism induced extensive litigation from member states contesting its authority.[28] Mixed agreements have been viewed as a pragmatic means to cope with the issue of competence in external action. Post-Lisbon, however, one may eventually witness a fall in their use in the interests of securing simpler and more coherent EU action, as will be discussed further.[29] Sometimes the EU acts alone with the blessing of the member states for reasons of political credibility and pragmatism rather than with strict legal propriety.[30] However, such credibility or pragmatism is increasingly at the expense of member state sovereignty and autonomy, that which remains at

24 Piet Eeckhout, *EU External Relations Law* (2nd edn, Oxford University Press, 2011), 212.

25 Marise Cremona, 'Defining Competence in EU External Relations: Lessons from the Treaty Reform Process' in Alan Dashwood and Marc Maresceau (eds), *Law and Practice of EU External Relations: Salient Features of a Changing Landscape* (Cambridge University Press, 2008), 34. Piet Eeckhout, 'Exclusive External Competences: Constructing the EU as an International Actor' in *The Court of Justice and the Construction of Europe: Analyses and Perspectives on Sixty Years of Case-Law* (Springer, 2012), 613.

26 As to the Common Commercial Policy: Case C-414/11 *Daiichi Sankyo* EU:C:2013:520, Opinion of A.G. Cruz Villalon, 31 January 2013; Case C-137/12 *Commission* v. *Council* EU:C:2013:675; Opinion of A.G. Kokott, 27 June 2013.

27 See Marise Cremona, 'EU External Relations: Unity and Conferral of Powers' in Azoulai (n. 14), 65.

28 For example, the 'Open Skies' case law; see Christophe Hillion, 'A Look Back at the Open Skies Judgments' in Mielle Bulterman (ed.), *Views of European Law from the Mountain: Liber Amicorum Piet Jan Slot* (Kluwer, 2009), 257.

29 For example, *Commission* v. *Council* (n. 26); Christophe Hillion and Panos Koutrakos (eds), *Mixed Agreements Revisited – The European Union and its Member States in the World* (Hart, 2010).

30 For example, this often occurs between the EU and US for more effective negotiations as in the EU–US Agreements on Extradition and Mutual Legal Assistance.

the international level and cannot be assumed to be a trouble-free equilibrium.[31] In this regard, some of the most significant contemporary EU global action operates in the pragmatic grey zone between the idea of 'outside in' and 'inside out'. This leads to the issue of to how to frame the internal–external nexus as a regulatory dynamic in EU law.

The EU internal–external regulatory dynamic

Apart from Article 21(3) TEU requiring consistency between internal and external practices, and passing references to consistency in policies, actions and activities (e.g. Article 7 TFEU or 13 (1) TEU), there is little by way of formal structured conceptualisation of the interrelationship between internal and external competence in the treaties. EU external action may 'lead' or even eclipse internal policy development 'outwards in', which is not necessarily obvious as a matter of EU law.[32] For example, certain international agreements entered into by the EU have acted as the spur for internal EU legislation. The EU–US Passenger Name Records Agreements and EU–US Transatlantic Financial Tracking Programme (TFTP) ('Swift') Agreement have triggered the development of comparable internal EU legislative proposals.[33] Controversies surrounding these internal proposals demonstrate how such external action may be very 'far' from internal ideals.

The specific dynamic emerging is also difficult to judge conclusively such is its constant recalibration. For example, powers in Article 207 TFEU grant the EU much autonomy to pursue a distinctive external EU strategy as to the Common Commercial Policy. Nevertheless, the EU has sought to externalise the internal market instead of or in addition to using such powers post-Lisbon.[34] While previously it might have been thought that mixed agreements could facilitate EU action and flexible constructions of competence, recent post-Lisbon case law suggests an end to the externalisation of the internal market in favour of exclusive external competence.[35]

31 See the emphasis of the Bundesverfassungsgericht in its Treaty of Lisbon judgment: Judgment of 30 June 2009 – 2 BvE 2/08 ECLI:DE:BVerfG:2009:es20090630.2bve000208 para 375.

32 Cremona (n. 27), 74 onwards.

33 Agreement between the United States of America and the European Union on the use and transfer of Passenger Name Record Data to the United States Department of Homeland Security of 17 November 2011; [2012] *OJ L* 215/5. See Proposal For a Directive on the use of Passenger Name Record data for the prevention, detection investigation and prosecution of terrorist offences and serious crime, COM(2011) 32. The EU–US PNR agreement originally relied upon *inter alia* Article 114 TFEU which was struck down by the Court as beyond the scope thereof: Joined Cases C-317/04 *European Parliament* v. *Council and Commission* EU:C:2006:346 and C-318/04, EU:C:2005:190 [2006] ECR I-04721. See Elaine Fahey, 'Law and Governance as checks and balances in Transatlantic Security' (2013), 32 *YEL* 1.

34 Marise Cremona, 'Expanding the Internal Market: An External Regulatory Policy for the EU?' in Blockmans, Van Vooren and Wouters (n. 18), Chapter 10.

35 For example, *Commission* v. *Council* (n. 26).

However embryonic, the internal–external regulatory dynamic is also significant given its impact upon the EU's ability to contribute to global governance.[36] The failed Anti-Counterfeiting Trade Agreement (ACTA) is a useful example of the intricacies of the relationship between internal and external competence. There, the EU insisted upon not transposing ACTA, the plurilateral treaty, which aimed to improve the domestic enforcement of intellectual property (IP) rights, because of its alleged consistency with EU law.[37] ACTA was ultimately rejected by the European Parliament for reasons of inadequate information pursuant to its new information powers in Article 218(10) TFEU, as to the regulatory dynamic between the treaty and the acquis. It dealt a significant blow to the ability of the EU to act externally. In this regard, the rise in status of the European Parliament in international relations post-Lisbon could also alter the internal–external regulatory dynamic and put its transparency and also its legitimacy into sharper perspective in the future.

Framing the legitimacy challenges

The internal–external regulatory dynamic has recently caused some concern at national level and the review of EU competences conducted recently in the UK and the Netherlands is instructive. The Dutch report alone considered the challenges of EU law operating as global governance and its relationship to subsidiarity.[38] It is a political debate that may arise with more frequency in the future as to the opposition between the internal and external in EU law. This is especially so where the member states increasingly lose international presence after the Treaty of Lisbon changes to external competence embed further.

The tendency of the EU legislator and executive to exploit the flexibility of its tools may be argued to bear harsh consequences for its *social* legitimacy in the long run.[39] As EU law continues to generate more global reach, it may result in

36 Cremona (n. 34), 177.

37 See Christina Eckes, Elaine Fahey and Machiko Kanetake, 'International, European and US Perspectives on the Negotiation and Adoption of the Anti-Counterfeiting Trade Agreement (ACTA)' (2012), 20 *Currents* 20.

38 Review of the Balance of Competences between the United Kingdom and the European Union presented to Parliament by the Secretary of State for Foreign and Commonwealth Affairs by Command of Her Majesty, July 2012, 13; '*Inventarisatie EU-regelgeving op subsidiariteit en proportionaliteit – Nederlandse lijst van actiepunten, bijlage bij Kamerbrief inzake uitkomsten subsidiariteitsexercitie' MINBUZA*-2013.184321, 21 June 2013.

39 The three 'dominant' taxonomies of legitimacy – legal, moral and social – are not necessarily regarded as self-contained social legitimacy, which is understood as its projection on to an action, rule, actor or system by an actor's belief that the action, rule, actor or system is morally or legally legitimate. It does not make a normative commitment to any relationship of power and is an empty concept without an account of the moral or legal framework to which the believer subscribes social legitimacy: Joseph Weiler, 'Europe in Crisis – On "Political Messianism", "Legitimacy" and the "Rule of Law"' (2012), *SJLS* 248; Fritz Scharpf, *Reflections on Multilevel Legitimacy* (2003); *Max Planck Institute for the Study of Societies Working Paper* 07/03; Chris Thomas, 'The Uses and Abuses of Legitimacy in International Law' (2014), 34(4) *OJLS* 729.

much slippage to its formal and social legitimacy. The longer term dependency of the EU upon external social acceptance should not be understated. Moreover, from an inwards–out perspective, the interaction between internal and external competence may warrant significant revision at some point should the weight of the EU's external competences upon national sovereignty bear even more heavily. From an outwards–in perspective, far more attention may need to be given to the impact of the global reach of EU law on a systematic basis.

The study of legitimacy in EU law is mostly conducted 'court-centrically'.[40] Ostensibly, this amounts to a limited enquiry when it comes to reflecting upon the global reach of EU law on account of its expanding subjects and objects. The relative significance of the Court in developing the external and internal objectives of EU law is argued to differ greatly where the former have a lesser telos than the latter.[41] Perhaps the rising incidence of the global reach of EU law highlights the significance of this nexus between the internal and external. As it stands, the Court appears predominantly as a frequently invoked check upon the global reach of EU law and thus warrants closer attention.

Accordingly, the focus here next turns to specific forms of judicial review as checks on EU action with global reach. Three means by which EU law currently achieves global reach are considered, along with instances of their judicial review – namely, externalisation of the internal market, the participation of the EU in international organisations and extra-territoriality and EU law.

With regard to 'the externalisation of the internal market', the case studies of the Trade in Seals Regulation, the 'CRD' legislation and EU–Swiss Relations are considered first, followed by their analysis (analysing litigation of the externalisation of the internal market).

Reviewing the boundaries of EU global reach

Externalisation of the internal market

The notion of an internal market is a largely unspecified idea in international economic law and political science.[42] Perhaps profiting from this uncertainty, the objects of the EU's internal market have evolved considerably in the treaties in recent times. The externalisation of the EU's internal market is a recent development following on from two decades of the completion of the Single Market.

40 For example, Maurice Adams, Henri de Waele, Johan Meeusen and Gert Straetmans (eds), *Judging Europe's Judges: The Legitimacy of the Case Law of the European Court of Justice* (Hart, 2013), 261; James Gibson and Gregory Caldeira, 'The Legitimacy of the Court of Justice in the European Union: Models of Institutional Support' (1995), 89(2) *APSR* 356.

41 Marise Cremona, 'A Reticent Court? Policy, Objectives and the Court of Justice' in Marise Cremona and Anne Thies (eds), *The European Court of Justice and External Relations Law* (Hart, 2015), 15.

42 See Sieglinde Gstöhl, 'Political Dimensions of an Externalisation of the EU's Internal Market', *EU Diplomacy Papers* 3/2007, 4; Piet Eeckhout, 'The External Dimension of the EC Internal Market A Portrait' (1991), 15 World Competition 5; Eeckhout (n. 3).

Official EU policy provides that the external dimension to the internal market is an explicit and unambiguous element thereof. In this regard, the leading policy documents of the EU, past and present, from the Lisbon Strategy, the Europe 2020 Strategy to Global Europe have all harboured both internal and external objectives with much transparency.[43] Nonetheless, some harbour ambiguity about the meaning of this nexus – for example, stating that '[v]irtually all Internal Market policies carry to some degree an "international dimension."'[44] This ambiguity also raises questions as to its coherence.[45] There is no formal description of the mechanics for the externalisation of the internal market in the treaties. Article 21(3) TEU makes an explicit link between internal and external policies in the pursuit of the EU's global rule-making goals. However, the same formula is not reciprocated in comparable internal market provisions – e.g. Article 26 TFEU or even Article 114 TFEU also setting out regulatory objectives. In this regard, whether the 'inside–out' and 'outside–in' dynamic of EU law is transparent is far from clear. Although diminishing, post-Lisbon free trade agreements tend to be mixed agreements, which are supposedly less likely to externalise the internal market.[46] It has thus been argued that the Common Commercial Policy (CCP) has sometimes been disregarded post-Lisbon and superseded by efforts to externalise the internal market.[47] This context puts into perspective the diversity and flux of the concept of externalisation.

There are many diverse examples of the externalisation of the internal market in recent EU law post-Lisbon and three examples of its spectrum are considered here – namely: the trade in seal products regulation, third country banks in the 'CRD' legislative package, and free movement of persons in EU–Swiss relations.

Trade in seal products regulation

An instructive example to begin with is Regulation 1007/2009 on the trade in seals which was enacted prior to the Treaty of Lisbon pursuant to ex Article 95 EC (now Article 114 TFEU), applying to seal products imported from third countries.[48] The regulation contained an exception only for seal products from indigenous communities, which principally benefited Greenland but not the other remaining seal trade jurisdictions, Canada and Norway ('IC exception'). However, as a regulatory instrument, it was concerned primarily less with products and

43 For example, European Commission, 'Europe 2020: A European Strategy for Smart, Sustainable and Inclusive Growth', COM(2010) 2020 final, 8; European Commission, 'Lisbon Strategy Evaluation Document' SEC(2010) 114 final, 7.

44 See http://ec.europa.eu/internal_market/ext-dimension/index_en.htm, accessed 23 December 2015.

45 Ibid.

46 See Sieglinde Gstöhl and Domink Hanf, 'The EU's Post-Lisbon Free Trade Agreements: Commercial Interests in a Changing Constitutional Context' (2014), 20 *ELJ* 733.

47 See further Cremona (n. 34).

48 Regulation (EC) No. 1007/2009 of the European Parliament and of the Council of 16 September 2009 on trade in seal products ('Seal Regulation').

more with animal welfare – and perhaps even more accurately, third country animal welfare.[49] For instance, the regulation provided that for its rules to be fully effective it *had* to apply to both products originating in the community and those from third countries, and went on to expressly protect the interests of Inuit communities.[50]

After the enactment of the regulation, Canada and Norway challenged the regulation at the World Trade Organisation, alleging that it discriminated against their industries. The EU confirmed in its argument to the Appellate Body (AB) that the regulation was designed to address EU public morals regarding seal welfare and that the regulation could be acknowledged to have depressed the EU seal market, which would inevitably reduce the potential for global demand, citing public international law on the rights of indigenous peoples.[51] A WTO AB decision handed down in 2014 found that the EU's regulation violated the General Agreement on Tariffs and Trade (GATT) (1994), but upheld the regulation on animal welfare grounds in a landmark decision on the protection of public morals.[52] A 'tougher' seals regulation looks set to be adopted shortly so as to bring the regulation into line with the WTO findings.[53]

In 2015, after all these developments, the Court of Justice gave judgment on an appeal against a decision of the General Court which had dismissed an action for annulment of the regulation taken by a broad range of plaintiffs from within the EU and beyond it.[54] The Court, in a terse decision which repeatedly stressed the procedural confines of the case on appeal, upheld the finding of the General Court as to the use of ex Article 95 EC. It held that the legislature was not required to specify which national law diverged so as to justify recourse to ex Article 95 EC and that the General Court had validly taken into account supplementary information of the Commission in the litigation.[55] The decision must be said to be so procedurally framed and confined in its analysis as to hardly amount to a substantive decision of the regulation. Notably, it contained no reference to the WTO AB decision nor the proposed amendment to the regulation. Either way, it appears to set a very low standard for a review of the legal base in this context.

While the regulation is now credited with saving the lives of 2 million seals globally and thus constitutes an effective externalisation of the internal market, it is perhaps also a useful reminder of the legitimacy issues surrounding EU law in the wider world. Some have argued that it is entirely lawful, common and even essential for the EU legislator to legislate for non-internal market interests,

49 Recital 8.

50 Recitals 13 and 14.

51 'EC – Measures Prohibiting the Importation and Marketing of Seal Products' (DS400 and 401) WTO Appellate Body Decision 14/3051 (22 May, 2014), pp. 44–50.

52 Gregory Shaffer and David Pabian, 'The WTO EC-Seal Products Decision: Animal Welfare, Indigenous Communities and Trade' (2015), 109 *AJIL* 154.

53 See Council doc. 6015/15.

54 Case C-398/13 P *Inuit Tapiritt Kanatami and others* EU:C:2015:535 [2015], I-ECR 000; Case C-583/11 P *Inuit Tapiritt Kanatami* EU:C:2013:625 [2014], I-ECR 000.

55 Paras 21–41.

drawing upon the fundamentals of the internal market constitution and the legislator's limited toolbox in support.[56] This defence of the *internalisation* of non-internal market values is arguably distinct from the *externalisation* of the internal market, because it is weaker in its link to the values of the internal market constitution. Although animal welfare is now post-Lisbon articulated as a value in Article 13 TFEU, one may ask how 'deterritorialised' a value should be. Seal welfare must be understood as a direct and 'inwards–out' externalisation of the internal market through EU law. The regulation thus brought the innovative and flexible character of EU rule-making to the global stage, but it has not necessarily received a welcome reception.[57]

'CRD' legislative package

Another example of the externalisation of the internal market is how third countries and third-party actors may legitimately need the benefit of internal market rules in order to trade with or even set up in the EU.[58] This is to be found in the controversial new banking legislative package passed in the wake of the financial crisis known as 'CRD IV' based on Article 53 TFEU with provisions for relations with third country banks.[59] It contains a title on relations with third countries, including provisions relating to the establishment of third country banks, which are stated to be 'essential' for the achievement and 'smooth operation' of the internal market.[60] Of note is that Article 92 provided that 'the application of [the directive] shall be ensured by competent authorities for institutions at group, parent company and subsidiary levels, including those established in offshore financial centres'.[61] A recent challenge by the UK as to *inter alia* how the internal market was being externalised in these forms of provisions was withdrawn after an adverse advocate general's opinion.[62]

56 See De Witte (n. 19), 25–27.

57 The decision, rather than the EU, has been criticised *inter alia* for opening up floodgates of other similar moral claims: see Robert Howse, Joana Langille and Katie Sykes, 'Pluralism in Practice: Moral Legislation and the Law of the WTO After *Seal Products*' 506/ 2015. New York University Public Law and Legal Theory Working Papers.

58 See Piet Eeckhout, *EU External Relations Law* (2nd edn, Oxford University Press, 2011), 144 onwards.

59 See Article 47: Directive 2013/36/EU of the European Parliament and of the Council of 26 June 2013 on access to the activity of credit institutions and the prudential supervision of credit institutions and investment firms, amending Directive 2002/87/EC and repealing Directives 2006/48/ EC and 2006/49/EC [2013] *OJ L* 176/338. See also Cremona, 'Expanding the Internal Market' (n. 34), 162, 164, at n. 17.

60 Recitals 5 and 6.

61 See also Article 109(2) CRD: 'Competent authorities … had to ensure that parent undertakings and subsidiaries subject to this Directive implement such arrangements, processes and mechanisms in their subsidiaries not subject to this Directive.'

62 See C-507/13 *UK* v. *Council* EU:C:2014:2481 [2015], I-ECR 000, Opinion of the AG, 24 November 2014. See 'Banks seek to clarify new bonus rules with Brussels', *Financial Times* (25 August 2015).

It is arguable that the dividing line between the externalisation of the internal market in the CRD and extra-territorial questions appears particularly murky. Such an externalisation of the internal market through its extension as broadly as possible adopts an 'inwards–out' perspective on the internal market, rather than an 'outwards–in' perspective, which would act as an enabling provision for third parties. The unanswered question remains as to what prospective plaintiffs, if any, remain.

Free movement of persons in EU–Swiss relations

Another more frequent form of externalisation of the internal market is to grant externally the advantages and freedoms of the internal market to third country partners. For example, the benefits of the internal market externally form an integral part of third country and European Economic Area (EEA) and Swiss relations with the EU. The Court of Justice has held that the Swiss Confederation is to be equated with a member state of the EU for the purposes of free movement of persons and represents the high water mark of these relations.[63] Recent EU–Swiss agreements on aspects of the free movement of persons are based on Article 218(9) TFEU in conjunction with Articles 46, 53 and 62 TFEU.[64] They follow on from a series of sectoral agreements signed in 1999 after the confederation's rejection of the EEA agreement in 1992. However, this genre represents a more integrated understanding of the territory of the EU as opposed to dealing with mere third parties or actors, whereby such entities such as the EEA or Switzerland actively obtain the benefits of the internal market through their relationships with the EU. There is thus specific greater authority within this genre to draw upon the internal market in the light of the express goals of EU–Switzerland relations, as a structured and territorialised externalisation of the internal market.

Litigating the externalisation of the internal market: **Commission *v.* Council** *(conditional access services)*

There are few means to actually test the externalisation of the internal market in EU law other than by litigation. Moreover, the absence of active protagonists with a vested interest and ability to litigate may also generate gaps as to checks and balances. Third parties affected by EU law may not always pursue their claims with ease within the EU legal order.[65] Nevertheless, litigation may

63 See Case C-247/09, *Alketa Xhymshiti* v. *Bundesagentur für Arbeit* EU:C:2010:698 [2010], I-11845.

64 See Council decision on the position to be taken by the European Union within the EU–Swiss Joint Committee established by Article 14 of the agreement between the European Community and its member states, of the one part, and the Swiss Confederation, of the other, on the free movement of persons, with regard to the replacement of Annex III (mutual recognition of professional qualifications) thereto, 2011/467/EU [2011] *OJ L* 195/7; COM /2015/076 final. See to similar effect Council Decision (EU) 2015/771 of 7 May 2015, with the same legal bases.

65 See the case law in n. 54.

sometimes legitimise the prior exclusion of interests in law-making by affording those affected not previously participating in the law-making process to participate in the courtroom.[66] It thus represents another important dimension to understanding the externalisation of the internal market and is considered here as a result. Judicial review of the externalisation of the internal market in recent case law has arisen in respect of the nexus between the Common Commercial Policy and the externalisation of the internal market. The decision in *Commission* v. *Council* is argued here to demonstrate an instance of 'strong' judicial review of the externalisation of the internal market in so far as it subjected EU action purporting to export the acquis to stringent judicial review.[67]

Commission v. *Council* concerned the European Convention on the legal protection of services on or consisting of conditional access adopted by the Council of Europe in 2001 with the participation of the then European Community.[68] The Convention was concerned principally with piracy of television, radio or Internet content, illicit activities and unlawful access at pan-European level.[69] In 2011, the Council adopted Decision 2011/853 as a means to extend the provisions of Directive 98/84/EC on the legal protection of services based on or consisting of conditional access and establish a law on services based on conditional access available throughout the continent of Europe, with Article 207 TFEU, the legal basis for the common commercial policy, and 114 TFEU, governing internal market harmonisation, as legal bases for the conclusion by the EU of an international agreement.[70] The Commission along with the European Parliament complained that the decision was adopted on the wrong legal base recently before the Court in *Commission* v. *Council.*

Advocate General Kokott in her opinion held that Article 114 TFEU had been inappropriately used because the Convention did not establish uniform rules but rather engaged in external harmonisation[71] through an attempt to export the union's acquis beyond its borders. The Court of Justice largely agreed with the advocate general and held that the *primary* objective of the Convention was to extend legal protection of services beyond the territory of the EU, while the functioning of the internal market had been a purely *incidental* one.[72] The Court in annulling the Council Decision held that Article 207(4) TFEU together with Article 218(5) TFEU formed the correct basis

66 See Rachel Cichowski, *The European Court and Civil Society: Litigation, Mobilization and Governance* (Cambridge University Press, 2007).

67 Case C-137/12, *Commission* v. *Council*, EU:C:2013:675.

68 Council decision 2011/853/EU of 29 November 2011 on the signing on behalf of the Union of the European Convention on the legal protection of services based on conditional access, [2011] *OJ L* 336/ 1. Seven Member States were members at the time of the litigation.

69 CETS No. 178, 2001.

70 The Court also considered whether the Union's competence to conclude the agreement was exclusive within the meaning of Article 2(1) TFEU or Article 3 TFEU.

71 Para. 46.

72 Para. 71.

for the decision and not Article 114 TFEU because the Convention fell within the exclusive competence of the EU pursuant to Article 3(1)(e) TFEU.

Commission v. *Council* ostensibly affirms that the internal market may not act as a 'crutch' to support international trade qua external action. The de jure illegality of exporting the EU's acquis in this fashion appears as the chief ratio of the decision. Nevertheless, the outcome of the decision is also a de facto loss for Member State sovereignty and their international presence.[73] The Court in its decision adopts a highly formalistic approach to the internal market, which also simultaneously incises the member states from external action. It sits ill with other more procedural case law – for example, handing down a light-touch review of the seals regulation. We are thus left with a rather cloudy understanding of what other forms of externalisation could be problematic.

The account next considers a judicial review of EU participation in international organisations as a form of global reach through EU external action.

The participation of the EU in international organisations

Overview

The ability of the EU to engage in the global legal order and act in international organisations is argued here to be a literal and active component of the global reach of EU law. This ability pertains to the very boundaries of external action and EU participation in international organisations, as *actual* global reach.[74] It is worth recalling that the EU has had a very limited impact in the global legal order with respect to its membership of international organisations in the post-Lisbon period.[75] The EU has not managed to gain full membership status in international organisations despite its acquisition of legal personality and worldly ambitions. In general, the external environment is perceived to be less than hospitable to the EU's ambitions in international relations.[76] The status of the EU in the global legal order does not appear to be improving outside of the UN, where its esoteric status also falls short of optimal full membership.[77] It has a varied range of statuses in UN bodies, which appear 'privileged' compared to its

73 See Joris Larik, 'No mixed feelings: The post-Lisbon Common Commercial Policy in *Daiichi Sankyo* and *Commission* v. *Council* (Conditional Access Convention) (2015), 52 *CMLR* 779, 798.

74 External action is understood here as defined in the treaties.

75 See Henri de Waele and Jan Jap Kuijper (eds), *The Emergence of the European Union's International Identity – Views from the Global Arena* (Brill, 2013).

76 Jan Wouters, Anna-Louise Chané and Jed Odermatt, 'The European Union: A Shadowy Global Actor? The UN System as an Example' in Elaine Fahey (ed.) *The Actors of Postnational Rulemaking: Conceptual Challenges of European and Public International law*' (Routledge, 2015).

77 UN General Assembly Resolution 65/276 on 3 May 2011.

place in other international organisations.[78] The EU has obtained observer status in most UN fora, been given enhanced participation rights in some and only granted status as a member organisation in a few exceptional cases.[79] The barriers that the EU faces in developing its status in international organisation have many internal and external dimensions, both within the EU itself and the targeted organisation.[80] It also faces many effective bars, such as the rules of an international organisation.[81]

There are no treaty provisions regulating possible EU membership of an international organisation.[82] Nor are there treaty provisions governing the enhanced statuses of the EU in international organisations. Perhaps, as a result then, there has been very little case law on the interaction of the member states and the EU in international organisations where the EU is not a member. What has been considered but not necessarily litigated with greater frequency is the formulation of a union position in international organisations, where that body will lay down acts with legal effects upon the EU acquis.[83] Until recently, Article 218(9) TFEU was understood to apply to the procedures surrounding the negotiating of international agreement *and* the suspension of the aforesaid.[84] Beyond this, the duty of cooperation generally governs unilateral action of the member states. However, member states are argued to be increasingly under a duty to remain silent, irrespective of the nature of competence and scenario at stake.[85] A transparent and holistic understanding of the evolving status of the EU and its participation in international organisations is arguably far from the status quo.

This section considers next the interaction between the *Germany* v. *Council* EU and Member States in international organisations, litigating global reach and external action as global reach.

78 See Frank Hoffmeister, 'Outsider or Frontrunner? Recent Developments under International and European Law on the Status of the European Union in International Organizations and Treaty Bodies' (2007), 44 *CMLR* 41.

79 See Wouters, Chané and Odermatt (n. 76), 163–66.

80 Ibid.

81 See Mauro Gatti and Pietro Manzini 'External Representation of the European Union in the Conclusion of International Agreements' (2012) 49 *CMLR* 170.

82 Eeckhout (n. 24), 222.

83 See P.J. Kuijper, 'Caselaw of the Court of Justice of the EU and the Allocation of External Relations Powers' in Cremona and Thies (n. 41) Chapter 6, 108.

84 Article 218(9) TFEU provides that: 'The Council … shall adopt a decision suspending application of an agreement and establishing the positions to be adopted on the Union's behalf in a body set up by an agreement, when that body is called upon to adopt acts having legal effects, with the exception of acts supplementing or amending the institutional framework of the agreement.' See Kuijper, ibid.; Inge Govaere, 'Novel Issues Pertaining to EU Member States' Membership of Other International Organisations: The OIV Case' in Inge Govaere, Erwan Lannon, Peter van Elsuwege and Stanislas Adam (eds), *The European Union in the World: Essays in Honour of Marc Maresceau* (Martinus Nijhoff Publishers, 2013), 225.

85 See Joris Larik and Andrés Delgado Casteleiro, 'The Duty to Remain Silent: Limitless Loyalty in EU External Relations' (2011), 36 *ELR* 524.

The interaction between the EU and member states in international organisations

Existing salient case law on international organisations that the EU is not part of, while numerically small, is perhaps all the more esoteric because it concerns the International Maritime Organisation (IMO), a specialist UN agency in maritime affairs which does not allow an international organisation to join and of which all EU Member States are members.[86] This case law mostly has as its common denominator a ratio as to the duty of sincere cooperation on member states with respect to the acquis. The application of this duty in this context has allowed the Community (as it then was) to rely upon its non-membership and negate the legal effects of external norms.

In its well-known decision in *Intertanko*, the Court considered the effects of the Convention on marine pollution, Marpol 73/78, an IMO Convention which all states had concluded but not the Community.[87] The Court held that the Convention was not binding on the Community because it had not assumed under the EC treaty the powers previously exercised by the member states and so a challenged directive could not be read in the light of the Convention.[88] However, it held that it still had to interpret the directive taking into account the Convention in view of the customary international law principle of good faith and the principle of sincere cooperation. Subsequently, in the landmark transboundary pollution dispute in *Commune de Mesquer* v. *Total*,[89] the Court considered the relationship between a directive and the effects of IMO conventions which limited liability (i.e. the International Convention on Civil Liability for Oil Pollution and the International Convention on Establishment of International Fund for Compensation for Oil Pollution Damage), which the Community was not a party to but which the member states were. The Court did not accept that the Conventions were binding on the Community as it had not acceded to them.[90] More recently, albeit prior to the Treaty of Lisbon, in *Commission* v. *Greece*, the Court considered whether Greece was entitled to submit a proposal to the IMO on its own behalf and not that of the Community in an area covered by Community law.[91] The Court held that the Community's competence was exclusive in this field and that the Greek proposal could lead to the adoption by the IMO of new rules which would affect Community law and be in breach of Article 4(3) TFEU and the common transport policy, even if not binding. The Court thus held that lack of membership did not prevent the Community's competence from being exercised. Nevertheless, the duty of cooperation was perceived to be the governing principle by which member states in international organisations of which the EU is not a member were governed.

86 See www.imo.org/en/Pages/Default.aspx accessed 23 December 2015.

87 Case C-308/06 *Intertanko* EU:C:2008:312 57.

88 See para. 47.

89 Case C-188/07 *Commune de Mesquer* v. *Total France* EU:C:2008:359 [2008], ECR I-4501.

90 See para. 85.

91 Case C-45/07, *Commission* v. *Greece*, EU:C:2009:81 [2009], ECR I-701.

However, recent case law has stretched the limits of this specific provision in Article 218(9) TFEU.[92] Thus, the decision of the Grand Chamber in *Germany* v. *Council* (OIV) grants considerable powers to the EU to 'develop' itself in international organisations and act so as to protect its acquis where the EU has no formal status and not all Member States are members – yet where EU law still prevails.[93] It is argued to constitute a distinctive example of the global reach of the EU taking effect through EU law.

Litigating global reach: **Germany *v.* Council** *(OIV)*

Germany v. *Council* concerned resolutions that had been adopted on behalf of the EU in the International Association for Vine and Wine (OIV), an intergovernmental organisation with competences in the areas of vines, wines and related products, and the provisions of Article 218(9) TFEU as to the adoption of a position for the Union.[94] The EU was not yet a member, nor were all of the Member States and the EU had not acquired any special status in the OIV – for example, observer status. The Council had not yet given the Commission authorisation to negotiate accession to the OIV.

Secondary law had previously introduced references to OIV resolutions and it raised the question of their 'internal' effects as 'external norms'. Moreover, previous resolutions adopted by the OIV were not classified as relevant to the EU's acquis. For over a year after the entry into force of the Treaty of Lisbon, Commission proposals for a Union position in the OIV were rejected by the Member States. The Member States in 2011 adopted resolutions by consensus, which were deemed to affect the EU's acquis, and under pressure of infringement proceedings, a proposal was adopted with four member states voting against it and one abstaining. A Council decision was then adopted by a qualified majority on the basis of Article 43 TFEU as to the common agricultural policy, in conjunction with Article 218(9) TFEU, for the resolutions to be passed and certain Member States voted against it, including Germany.

Germany sought the annulment of the decision on the basis that the latter was not the appropriate legal basis and argued that it could not be used where the EU was not a member to the organisation. It also argued that the article presupposed a binding act, with legal effects, which was not the case for an OIV resolution. The case thus concerned the generic reference in Article 218(9) TFEU to 'an agreement', *without* distinguishing between cases where the EU was and was not a member and the legal effects then of a Union position. Arguably, a literal interpretation might have put the question beyond dispute in favour of the member

92 See also Opinion 1/13 (Child Abduction) EU:C:2014:2303.

93 C-399/12, *Germany* v. *Council* EU:C:2014:2258.

94 www.oivint/oiv/info/enmembresobservateurs?lang=en accessed 23 December 2015. By 2014, there were 21 EU Member States and 46 Member States, marginally more than at the time of the litigation.

states. It is worth remarking that at the time of the pending decision, the Council once again failed to agree on a position.[95]

Advocate General Cruz Villalón held that Article 218 TFEU concerned a *lex specialis* whereby the EU *had* to be a party to the agreement setting up the body in order to act. He held that arguments seeking to apply its provisions to the fact 'by analogy' could not be made so as to stretch the application of Article 218 TFEU where barriers in international law would be removed which would circumvent the EP's competences and upset the new institutional balance struck in the treaties in the area of EU external action.[96] By contrast, the Grand Chamber of the Court of Justice found that the wording of Article 218(9) TFEU was not limited to the negotiation and conclusion of agreements.[97] The resolution decisively influenced EU law because it related to the common organisation of wine markets, which fell under the Common Agricultural Policy. As a result, the EU was entitled to establish a position in light of their direct impact on the EU's acquis.

External action as global reach

The only case cited in the entire decision of the Grand Chamber decision is *Commission* v. *Greece*. However, as the duty of sincere cooperation does not feature in its reasoning, it renders it less convincing to support this construction of the application of Article 218 TFEU. The technical and even procedural nature of the decision should not emasculate its result which puts significant obligations upon Member States, not limited to or even based on the duty of cooperation.[98] This is especially so given the smaller number of states that are members of the OIV (currently 21) compared to *all* in the IMO. The decision could thus severely hamper member state autonomy on the international stage and amounts to a very questionable extension of global reach through the procedural terms of Article 218 TFEU, as a thin veneer of legality.[99]

Germany v. *Council* (OIV) is an important example of 'weak' judicial review of external action giving rise to EU global reach because the decision appears to give the EU considerable powers in a broad array of international organisations where the EU is not yet a member, without exploring as much. The light-touch review of external action therein also sits ill with the stricter review of EU expansionism in *Commission* v. *Council* (Legal Services Convention), although it similarly 'sidelines' member state presence at international level. The decision appears to force a Union position through a few member states, a form of 'global reach' that appears both undesirable and highly questionable. It goes surprisingly far as 'reach' in an organisation where the EU lacks observer status.[100]

95 Council doc. 9350/13.
96 See para. 113 in particular.
97 Para. 54.
98 See Govaere, who describes this omission as 'illogical': (n. 84), 238.
99 Ibid., 225–43.
100 All of which are scientific or expert organisations.

Its aftermath is worthy of reflection. Recent Council decisions on positions to be established by the EU in the OIV provide for a highly reductionist role for the EU member states there. For example, it provides that the member states shall act jointly in the interests of the Union and provides for the postponement of voting in particular circumstances.[101] This essentially holds international organisations 'hostage' to the EU voting position.[102] Although an isolated decision, the effects of the Court's decision clearly enable significant global reach to take effect through judicial review.

This particular example of global reach perhaps reflects the realities of the EU's struggle to evolve itself. However, it also serves as a further example of the fluidity of the construct of competence. Weak review thereof appears to do little for the social legitimacy of the EU as an evolving entity in the global legal order.

Judicial review of claims of EU extraterritoriality

Overview

Despite the perceived merger of questions of territory, sovereignty and jurisdiction beyond the State, the place of 'territoriality' appears to form a significant part of the global reach of EU law.[103] However, territory is a highly nationalistic idea that appears to sit ill with the development of the EU as a postnational democracy. The consistency of EU law with international law principles is also far from straightforward. It is universally accepted that States must show some restraint in the exercise of their powers and choose criteria or connecting factors establishing a link to their territory or to their nationals.[104] While it is still disputed whether a reasonableness requirement can be regarded as international customary law, it reflects a tendency in contemporary international adjudication.[105] The extent to which this may be said to form part of EU law is less clear-cut. The Court of Justice has held that the EU must respect customary international law in the exercise of its powers and, more recently, perhaps also in

101 For example, Proposal for a Council Decision establishing the position to be adopted on behalf of the EU with regard to certain resolutions to be voted in the framework of the International Organisation for Vine and Wine (OIV) COM(2014) 528 final, Article 1: 'position of the Union ... shall be expressed by the Member States which are members of the OIV, acting jointly in the interests of the Union'.

102 See Govaere, n. 84. The OIV places much importance upon international standards and their adoption – for example, Codex Alimentarius, and thus affects the dynamics of the EU's input and output into international rule-making.

103 See, for example, Gunther Handl, Joachim Zekoll and Peer Zumbansen (eds), *Beyond Territoriality: Transnational Legal Authority in an Age of Globalization* (Martinus Nijhoff, 2012).

104 See Cedric Ryngaert, *Jurisdiction in International Law* (Oxford University Press, 2008), and in particular at 9.

105 For example, see third restatement of foreign relations law of the US, 1986, ss. 402, 403.

the adoption of its legislation.[106] A consistent viewpoint on the place of territory, sovereignty and jurisdiction is not necessarily shared by the Court of Justice, EU institutions or the Member States alike. For example, post-Lisbon, the EU, its Member States and national authorities have opposed the extraterritorial application of US law in different intensities, in contexts as diverse as human rights law, tort law and competition law.[107] This state of affairs is of note given an asserted rise in EU extraterritoriality in a variety of forms in EU law and policy, although not always per se territorial or even legal in nature.[108] It supports the view that there is considerable use and even exploitation of the boundaries of the 'internal' and 'external' by the EU legislature.

Judicial review of these developments before the Court of Justice has been increasing and, for the most part, as will be argued here, appears 'light-touch'. The Court has shown little appetite to engage with those contesting extraterritoriality. Neither has it shown a desire to develop the conceptualisation of the subjects and objects of EU law, nor the competence dimension to EU extraterritoriality.

Four specific recent cases are briefly outlined here to consider the broadening of regulatory capture, examining extraterritoriality of EU animal welfare law, extraterritoriality of financial and banking legislation, extraterritoriality of EU competition law and extraterritoriality of the EU environmental law. The selection is not exhaustive and other examples are also found – for example, in the area of data protection.

The extraterritoriality of EU animal welfare law: Zuchtvieh-Export GmbH *v.* Stadt Kempten

The protection of the welfare of animals as 'sentient beings' is provided for in Article 13 TFEU, as warranting integration into internal policies. With regard to its external dimension, while the EU Strategy for the Protection of Welfare of Animals 2012–2015 with trading partners made a commitment to the inclusion of animal welfare in bilateral trade agreements and to be active in international organisations,[109] the international dimension to EU animal welfare has seen little recent development. The Council of Europe Convention for the Protection of Animals during International Transport was signed by the European Community in 2003. It followed from disagreement among the member states on the

106 C-286/90 *Anklagemyndigheden* v. *Peter Michael Poulsen and Diva Navigation Corp*, EU:C:1992:453; C-366/10 *Air Transport Association of America* v. *Secretary of State for Energy and Climate Change* EU:C:2011:864. See now Article 3(5) TEU.

107 For example, in *Kiobel* v. *Royal Dutch Petroleum Co.*, 133 SCt 1659 (2013) – for example, Germany and European Commission; in *Re Visa and Mastercard*, US District Court of Eastern District of New York (27 August 2010) noted in Viven Rose (ed.) *Bellamy and Child European Community Law of Competition* (2nd suppl., Oxford University Press, 2010), at 1.101.

108 See the work of Scott, emphasising their governance rather than legal character (n. 9).

109 'The European Union Strategy for the Protection and Welfare of Animals' 2012–2015, COM (2012) 6 final; http://ec.europa.eu/food/animals/welfare/international/index_en.htm, accessed 23 December 2015.

introduction of EU legislation and later formed the basis for an EU regulation on animal transport enacted thereafter, Regulation 1/2005, concerning the protection of animals during transport.[110] The introduction of the principle of 'individual responsibility' in the regulation was perceived as a ground-breaking attempt to devolve responsibility to enforcement authorities. However, animal welfare groups have decried the non-enforcement of the regulation.[111] The territorial reach of the regulation came up for analysis for the Court of Justice recently in *Zuchtvieh-Export GmbH* v. *Stadt Kempten*.[112]

There, a German authority had refused clearance for a consignment of cattle to travel approximately 7,000km from Germany to Uzbekistan via Poland, Belarus, Russia and Kazakhstan. The national court had questioned the applicability of the regulation to a journey taking place in third countries, the planning checks that the competent authority in the departure state had to provide and how they were to demonstrate compliance.[113] At the hearing, the Commission attempted to limit the application of the regulation to checks only with *its* fundamental requirements.[114]

Advocate General Bot held that the territorial scope of the regulation was 'unambiguous' and applied only 'within the Community'.[115] He further held that the legislature could have provided otherwise had it wished for compliance with its rules after the exit point. By contrast, the Court, taking a considerably broader view, held that the regulation referred explicitly not only to long journeys between Member States but also to third countries. It held that no distinction was provided for with regard to transport within the EU and transport with a destination in a third country, so the journey log had to include long journeys, including those with a destination in a third country. Nevertheless, the Court held that a margin of discretion was conferred upon the competent member state authority to accept realistic planning for transport, which would safeguard the animal welfare equivalent to the EU rules.[116]

The Court thus appeared to eschew the direct consequences of its reasoning by devolving decision-making on mutual recognition to the member state authority but notably diverging from the limitations that the Advocate General had sought to place upon the regulation. The place of third countries as the

110 Council Regulation (EC) No. 1/2005 of 22 December 2004 on the protection of animals during transport and related operations and amending Directives 64/432/EEC and 93/119/EC and Regulation (EC) No. 1255/97 [2005], OJ L 3, 1.

111 See Compassion in World Farming analysis of the Food and Veterinary Organisation reports for the European Commission: www.ciwf.org.uk/media/3817823/analysis-of-fvo-reports-on-enforcement-of-transport-regulation.pdf, accessed 23 December 2015.

112 Case C-424/13, *Zuchtvieh-Export GmbH* v. *Stadt Kempten* EU:C:2015:259; Opinion of AG Bot, 11 September 2014.

113 Article 1 of the regulation expressly provided that it applied to the transport of live animals entering or leaving the customs territory of the then European Community.

114 Described by the Advocate General as a 'middle way' solution: para. 84, Opinion.

115 For example, paras 47, 57.

116 Paras 52, 54.

subjects and objects of EU rules was not problematic for the Court. Indeed, the place of third countries as an explicit and legitimate regulatory subject appears central to its reasoning.

Extraterritoriality of financial and banking legislation: **UK *v.* Council *(FTT)***

While the mere promotion of national economic policy is not a sufficient territorial link by the standards of public international law,[117] extraterritoriality has formed a significant part of EU banking and financial legislation introduced in the wake of the financial crisis. For example, the EU's Market Abuse Regulation concerning insider dealing, the unlawful disclosure of inside information and market manipulation all have an extraterritorial scope.[118] The EU's Regulation on Derivatives (EMIR) is to similar effect.[119] Another proposed EU directive with extraterritorial implications, the EU's Financial Transaction Tax (FTT), began as a directive that the EU had mooted bringing to G20 level, reminiscent of the once-mooted global 'Tobin tax'.[120] The tax became mired in disagreement at Council level and thus led to a Council decision in 2011, taken under enhanced cooperation.[121] The geographical reach of this proposal was initially condemned as excessive because of, *inter alia*, its broad definition of establishment.[122]

A revised proposal in 2013 provided that it would apply to 'all' financial transactions on the condition that one party to the transaction was established in the territory of a participating member state and that a financial institution in the territory of a participating member state was a party to the transaction.[123] However, it was still argued that the FTT did not comprehensively assess the consequences for non-participating states.[124] Moreover, unlike other similarly enacted legislation,

117 See Andrea Bianchi 'Unity v. Fragmentation: Jurisdictional Rules in Customary International Law (Discussant)' in Karl Meessen (ed.), *Extraterritorial Jurisdiction in Theory and Practice* (Kluwer, 1996), 74, 87–88.

118 It applied in Article 2 to 'instruments traded on a multilateral trading facility or organised trading facility in the EU', as well as 'instruments the price or value of which are dependent on the price or value of EU traded instruments'.

119 EU Derivatives Regulation (EMIR) 648/2012 on OTC derivatives, central counterparties and trade repositories. It subjected counterparties concluding derivatives contracts to *inter alia* clearing and risk mitigation obligations even if established outside the EU, with a direct substantial and foreseeable effect within the EU. See also Kingston (n. 6).

120 See Van Vooren, 'The Proposed Financial Transaction Tax Directive: The quest to Create Momentum at the G 20 Level through Internal Legislation' in Van Vooren, Blockmans and Wouters (n. 18).

121 Proposal for a Council Directive on a common system of a financial transaction tax and amending Directive 2008/7/EC COM(2011) 594 final; proposal for a Council Directive implementing enhanced cooperation in the area of financial transaction tax, COM(2013) 71 final.

122 See Joachim Englisch, John Vella and Anzhela Yevgenyeva, 'The Financial Transaction Tax Proposal under the Enhanced Cooperation procedure: legal and practical considerations' (2013), *British Tax Review*, 223, 229.

123 Article 3. The concept of financial transactions was also broadly defined in Article 2(2).

124 See Englisch *et al.* (n. 122), 231.

the FTT directive did not have a governance framework and thus appeared unduly highly revenue oriented and eventually led to litigation.[125]

In *UK* v. *Council*, the UK sought to annul the FTT and claimed that the decision permitted the introduction of an FTT applicable to institutions, persons or transactions situated or taking place in the territory of non-participating states, and thus adversely affected their competences and rights.[126] It also claimed that the legislation produced transterritorial effects through the 'counterparty' and 'issuance' principle. The CJEU (Third Chamber) in an extraordinarily brief decision of two paragraphs gave short shrift to the arguments.[127] It held that the principles of taxation challenged were not in any way constituent elements of the impugned Council decision. The Court also held that the counterparty principle corresponded to an element of the 2011 proposal mentioned in recital 6 of that decision and the issuance principle first appeared in the 2013 proposal. It thus held that the decision had no provision related to the issue of expenditure linked to the implementation of enhanced cooperation.

The dismissive nature of the Court's decision sits uncomfortably with the political and legal history of the tax as a global tax. On account of its procedural nature, the decision was even reported 'as leaving the door open to a future legal challenge', perhaps allowing uncertainty to fester around the tax and its future plaintiffs.[128] The limited reasoning of the Court was perhaps unsurprising, given that the UK was seeking to defend its prerogatives as part of a broader litigation strategy. Nevertheless, its claims here were met with considerable indifference.

Extraterritoriality of EU competition law: **Innolux Corporation *v.* Commission**

With commercial activities having a global impact, the investigation of alleged antitrust violations is no longer the exclusive preserve of a single regulator.[129] Yet although Articles 101 and 102 TFEU are silent on whether they apply extraterritorially, their extraterritorial application has been extensive. Most agree that bilateral agreements and soft law have dramatically reduced its incidence in EU competition law.[130] Nevertheless, the Court of Justice has developed doctrines that are perceived to be far-reaching.[131] The extraterritorial application of EU competition law by the Commission is currently pending in several high-profile

125 For example, EMIR: see Scott, 'The New EU Extra-territoriality' (n. 9), 1371–1373.
126 C-209/13 *UK* v. *Council* EU:C:2014:283.
127 That is, paras 36 and 37.
128 'Court dashes drive to resist tax on City', *Financial Times*, 30 April 2014.
129 Damian Geradin, Marc Reysen and David Henry, 'Extraterritoriality, Comity and cooperation in EU Competition Law' in A. Guzman (ed.), *Cooperation, Comity and Competition Policy* (Oxford University Press, 2010), 44.
130 See Wagner-von Papp (n. 7).
131 See Kingston (n. 6).

cases and investigations.[132] The Court's doctrines of implementation and qualified effects are so far-reaching that no actual effects need to be shown to have territorial jurisdiction.[133]

In the recent decision of *Innolux Corp* v. *Commission*, the Advocate General and Court fundamentally differed on the extraterritorial application of EU competition law and its impact upon third parties.[134] There, the Commission had imposed a fine on six Korean and Taiwanese producers of liquid crystal displays (LCD panels) for their participation in a cartel from 2001 to 2006 for direct sales in the EEA of cartelised panels incorporated into finished products and through transformed products of cartelised panels incorporated into finished products sold on to another undertaking in the EEA. The General Court had set the fine imposed on the appellant at €288 million, after having reduced the original amount fined of approximately €648 million. The grounds of appeal thus principally related to whether the facts fell within the scope of *inter alia* Article 101 TFEU by the mere fact that the LCD panels were incorporated as components in factories sold in the EEA and the fining calculation. The facts were complicated by the fact that it concerned similar proceedings on similar facts arising around the same time period as in the US in *Motorola Mobility* v. *AU Optronics*, where the Belgian Competition Authority made submissions against the extraterritoriality of US antitrust law. Moreover, at the same time as the European Commission had acted, the Chinese competition law authority (National Development and Reform Commission) was also prompted to impose similar fines extraterritorially for the first time also as to the same product.[135]

Advocate General Wathelet held that the Commission had gone too far in fining a cartel relating to products manufactured and sold outside the EEA because the products were transformed or incorporated into other products which arrived in the EEA.[136] He held that it was prima facie difficult to link the sales in Asian with the EEA rules, and that the reasoning of the Commission was woefully inadequate with regard to the question of effects.[137] Instead, the Commission had to interpret their own guidelines restrictively, in light of Article 6 ECHR. By contrast, the Court of Justice (Third Chamber) held that the sales 'inevitably' had to be taken into account because they were inevitably affected by the infringement that the Commission had had territorial jurisdiction to pursue.[138] They had colluded on prices to be charged to customers in the EEA and were taking part in collusion which had the object and effect of restricting competition within the internal market. The appeal predominantly concerned

132 For example, Case C-413/14 *Intel* v. *Commission*; *Japan Airlines International* v. *Commission;* Case T-36/11 and *Samsung SDI* v. *Commission* Case T-84/13 (pending). See Marek Martyniszyn, 'On Extra-territoriality and the Gazprom case' (2015), 36(7) *ECLR* 291.

133 See joined cases C-89/85, C-104/85, C-114/85, C-116/85, C-117/85 and C-125/85 to C-129/85 *Ahlström Osakeyhtiö and others* v. *Commission* (*Woodpulp*) EU:C:1994:12; Case T-102/96 *Gencor Ltd v Commission of the European Communities*, EU:T:1999:65.

134 Case C-231/14 P, *Innolux Corp* v. *Commission*, EU:C:2015:451.

the calculation of the amount of the fine to be imposed for that infringement and there was no legal principle – e.g. *ne bis in idem* – which the Commission had to have regard to with respect to non-member states.

The decision of the Court of four short paragraphs amounts to a highly benign review of the impugned extraterritorial conduct or links with the internal market, conduct which the Advocate General had found otherwise, explicitly referencing human rights standards in support of his analysis. The decision makes no mention whatsoever of the developments on the same facts in the US in litigation there and hands a wide scope to the Commission to collect swingeing fines for products that may be pursued readily now, given the nature of such component parts. TV and computer parts have historically delivered the highest cartels fines in EU law. Accordingly, the decision may be said to embody the truly global reach of EU competition law, pursued at all costs.

Extraterritoriality of EU environmental law: Air Transport Association of America *v.* Secretary of State

EU and public international law have begun to incorporate a more extensive range of positive duties to protect, participate and consult in the area of transboundary environmental law.[139] Historically, the EEC had attempted to develop the global reach of EU environmental law some time ago. Its efforts to do so in the field of marine conservation were upheld by the Court shortly thereafter.[140] A more recent example of EU regulation of transboundary matters arose as to the EU Emissions Trading Scheme (ETS), which was the first international scheme for the trading of greenhouse gas emission allowances. It arose out of a failure of the International Civil Aviation Organisation (ICAO) to evolve a global scheme.[141] When, as a result, in 2008 an EU directive included aviation under the scheme and also explicitly referenced territoriality,[142] it ignited a global controversy that would eventually come before the Court of Justice.[143]

135 No. 14-8003 US Court of Appeals, 7th Circuit; www.bbc.com/news/technology-20910299, accessed 23 December 2015.

136 At para. 44.

137 At para. 53.

138 Para. 70.

139 See C-188/90, *Commune de Mesquer* v. *Total France SA and Total International Ltd* EU:C:2008:359, [2008], ECR I-4501.

140 See n. 77; Council Regulation No. 1626/94, laying down certain technical measures for the conservation of fishery resources in the Mediterranean [1994], *OJ L* 171/1.

141 COM(2010) 265 final, 26 May 2010; COM(2010) 86 final.

142 EC Directive 2008/101 of 19 November 2008, amending Directive 2003/87/EC [2009], *OJ L* 8/3, in recital 25.

143 Prior to the decision, the US House of Representatives voted to prohibit US aircraft operators from participating in the EU ETS: European Union Emissions Trading Scheme Prohibition Act of 2011, HR 2594.

Air Transport Association of America v. *Secretary of State* arose from a challenge by a range of international airlines, who argued that the directive was in breach of *inter alia* principles of customary international law, the Chicago Convention and the Kyoto Protocol.[144] Advocate General Kokott concluded that the allegation that the scheme was extraterritorial was based upon a highly superficial reading of the directive, which did not breach any principle of customary international law.[145] Similarly, the Grand Chamber of the Court of Justice held that it was possible that the directive was liable to create obligations for private actors under EU law.[146] It held that the EU was not bound by the Chicago Convention because the EU was not a party to it, and that the Kyoto Protocol was not unconditional and sufficiently precise. Rather, the EU's directive could be assessed in the light of customary international law but that it did not have the same degree of precision as an international agreement.

The decision has received stringent critique on a variety of fronts. The Court in its decision did not specifically refer to jurisdiction whatsoever despite the rationale for the extraterritoriality of the directive, nor to the global disquiet that it created through its de facto and de jure global reach. Both the Advocate General and Court expressly referenced the role of failed global regulation in the origins of the EU scheme without it being central to their reasoning. It is not clear why the Court chose to adopt such a circumscribed analysis of the effects of customary international law, seemingly in breach of Article 3(5) TFEU.[147]

In the wake of the decision, considerable global opposition emerged to the EU's rules.[148] The EU rules were suspended to allow negotiations to take place within the ICAO.[149] The ICAO thereafter agreed to develop a global market-based mechanism by 2016. Prior to this, the directive has been amended so that only emissions from flights within the EEA fall within it.[150] Notably, however, the EU legislature has sought to *broaden* the EU–ETS legislative techniques to other areas.[151]

144 See C-366/10, *Air Transport Association of America* v. *Secretary of State for Energy and Climate Change*, EU:C:2011:864 [2011], ECR I-000, Opinion of A.G. Kokott, 6 October 2011.

145 Para. 160.

146 Para. 109.

147 For example, Geert De Baere and Cedric Ryngaert, 'The ECJ's Judgment in Air Transport Association of America and the International Legal Context of the EU's Climate Change Policy' (2013) 18 *EFAR* 389, for example 401; see Joanne Scott and Lavanya Rajamani, 'EU Climate Change Unilateralism' (2012), 23 *EJIL* 469; Elaine Fahey and Ester Herlin-Karnell, 'Special Issue: EU law qua global governance law? Deciphering regulatory and constitutional competence between EU environmental law and global governance' (2012), 13 *GLJ* 1147.

148 See 'Developments in the Law – Extraterritoriality' (n. 2).

149 Decision No. 377/2013/EU.

150 Regulation (EU) No. 421/2014 of the European Parliament and of the Council of 16 April 2014 amending Directive 2003/87/EC establishing a scheme for greenhouse gas emission allowance trading within the Community, in view of the implementation by 2020 of an international agreement applying a single global market-based measure to international aviation emissions [2014], OJ L 129 1.

Adjudicating extraterritoriality

The variety of examples canvassed here indicate that there is extensive exploitation of the fluidity of the boundaries of the 'internal' and 'external' of EU law. The EU legislature arguably profits from much uncertainty as to the EU's place beyond the nation state. This is further evidenced by the rising incidence of territory openly being debated in the EU legislative process. An ostensible intention on the part of the legislature to increase regulatory capture in a variety of ways largely goes unchecked. The cases outlined concern diverse scenarios instituted by a member state authority implementing the rules, an outvoted member state and third parties respectively, where the Court's decisions do not generally admit much of a direct role for the participation of third-party interests. They lend support to the view that there is limited merit in such entities contesting the global reach of EU law in this area, where the Court in formations mostly smaller than its Grand Chamber hands down a 'light-touch' review of legislation impugned for its transboundary effects.

One may query indeed whether the EU moved away from an ad hoc instrumentalist engagement with international law, which 'the EU has long professed to set itself against'.[152] However, it is difficult to form a balanced and conclusive view on the compatibility of *all* four examples with public international law principles precisely because of the adjudication techniques employed. The case law suggests that competence is also a significant core principle here, but is one which does not arise 'cleanly' for adjudication. Recent legislation explored here, for example, as to the CRD suggests a possible overlap with the externalisation of the internal market in terms of how the 'external' manifests itself in legislation albeit this has also yet to arise.

The increasing assertions of extraterritoriality are a vivid reminder of the 'acceptance factor' that surrounds the global reach of EU law and the question of its broader social legitimacy. Light-touch review of assertions of the global reach of EU law arguably does little for the acceptance of EU participation in the global legal order. This leads to a consideration next of judicial review of EU participation in international organisations, as a further example of EU global reach through the fluidity of the boundaries of the 'external'.

The shifting boundaries of the global reach of EU law and its adjustication

As this account has outlined, there are increasing forms of the global reach of EU law arising in legislative form, EU action and in case law in a diverse range

151 See Regulation (EU) 2015/757 of the European Parliament and of the Council of 29 April 2015 on the monitoring, reporting and verification of carbon dioxide emissions from maritime transport, and amending Directive 2009/16/EC [2015], OJ L 123 55.

152 See Gráinne de Búrca, 'The ECJ and the International Legal Order: A Re-evaluation' in Gráinne De Burca and Joseph Weiler (eds), *The Worlds of European Constitutionalism* (Cambridge University Press, 2012), 148–49.

of areas. How and why it manifests itself are of much significance. The global reach of EU law often appears triggered by forms of constitutional flexibility and the fluidity of the 'internal' and 'external' in EU law. The fluidity between the 'internal' and 'external' of EU law has been argued here to raise questions as to how to understand the boundaries of the global reach of EU law, along with their nexus. The internal–external regulatory dynamic is one that is still in flux. More significantly, however, it is also one which is attracting increased political attention at national level.

As has been considered here, the externalisation of the internal market, the EU's participation in international organisations and extraterritoriality form three areas that show increased global regulatory capture by the EU through the fluid boundaries of EU global reach. Increased assertions of extraterritoriality suggest that there is much use and even exploitation of the boundaries of the internal and external, profiting from the uncertain place of territory, sovereignty and jurisdiction beyond the nation state. The examples of the externalisation of the internal market and EU participation in international organisations indicate that there is much fluidity to the construct of competence as it pertains to the internal and external. The incidence of such examples is surely likely to increase.

The account has focused upon how the treaties do not formally distinguish with any particularity between internal and external competences of the EU and do not establish any clear 'venue preference'. Accordingly, it is a dynamic of some concern in so far as it generates global reach. There is no formal description of the objectives or mechanics for the externalisation of the internal market in the treaties despite its many manifestations. Moreover, the parameters of the internal and external may even also enable a broad variety of extraterritoriality, although this is not yet evident. Looking more broadly at the issue, the ability of the EU to engage in the global legal order as actual global reach also has very few jurisprudential boundaries or limits. In this regard, as this account has emphasised, global reach may happen in a variety of ways not limited to legislation. The fluidity of external competences is also an important dimension of this account. A literal interpretation of 'reach' has also been argued here to be equally deserving of attention and provides evidence of the Court adjudicating EU participation in the global legal order so as to support 'global reach' with thin legal foundations.

The global reach of EU law is not necessarily just a 'court-centric' idea and, as this account has outlined, has many manifestations. It also brings another dimension to the role of the Court which is understood to have a different view of the telos of external action to the internal dimension. Nevertheless, some of its most common forms are arising more frequently before the Court of Justice. While the relative significance of the Court in developing the external and internal objectives of EU law is argued to differ greatly by some, nevertheless, the Court currently appears as the most frequently invoked check upon the global reach of EU law. This is especially so for EU action taking place within the nexus of the 'internal' and 'external' of EU law. There is limited engagement on the part of the Court with those impugning the authority or legitimacy of EU law, where it has expansive regulatory capture beyond its territory in various examples. The ability of parties to contest the global reach of EU law on its merits is far from apparent and suggests that they do not benefit from any form of meaningful participation as the subjects and objects of this regulatory capture. Similarly, the Member States are also being eclipsed in the evolution of global reach in EU external action. A highly 'confirmatory' or 'rubber-stamping' approach to the actions of the legislator or EU institutions is adopted in the instances surveyed. The case law surveyed indicates that the Court is not willing to engage in intensive review. As a result, current checks upon the EU's executive and legislature acting with global reach appear increasingly inadequate and the subjects and objects of EU law appear less understood than ever.

The nature of EU law may cause its formal and even social legitimacy much 'slippage' as it generates more global reach, exacerbated by minimal checks upon EU institutional actors on the part of the Court. The global reach of EU law as unchecked aggrandisement may score lowly on many fronts, both inside and outside the EU, and is a state of affairs of some concern.

3 The EU as an actor in rule-making

Introduction

The conceptualisation of 'actors' engaging in rule-making – defined here as those who adopt acts, practices and/or standards in the exercise of legal authority – is central to theorising power, autonomy, influence and even legitimacy in rule-making beyond the nation state. It is central to the 'how', the 'who' and the 'where' of such rule-making. However, as Jupille and Caparaso state, there is no consensus in scholarship on what it means to be an actor, despite its centrality to discussions on rule-making, power and influence, across disciplines.[1] This is particularly the case in rule-making beyond the nation state, where the actors may either be fledging or manifold and where the rule-making practices may vary substantially from conventional practices. To view an institution as an actor in their own right remains perhaps an 'unpopular' outlook or even a technically inaccurate one.[2] Legal scholarship is no different and employs formal, limiting criteria to assess what we may frame here loosely as 'actorship' qualities, such as legal personality, legal authority to act and institutional autonomy. They remain heavily rooted in an attachment to the *Trias Politica*.[3] Yet such formalism, if we may call it that, may pose many limitations. Consider those seeking to conceptualise actors

1 More broadly, see Elaine Fahey (ed.), The Actors of Postnational Rule-Making: Contemporary Challenges of European and International Law (Routledge, 2015). On the EU: Christopher Hill, 'The Capability-Expectations Gap, or Conceptualizing Europe's International Role' (1993), 31 (3) JCMS 305; Joseph Jupille and James Caporaso, 'States, Agency and Rules: The European Union in Global Environmental Politics' in Carolyn Rhodes (eds), The European Union in the World Community (Rienner, 1998), 213.

2 See Michael Barnett and Martha Finnemore, *Rules for the World International Organizations in Global Politics* (Cornell University Press, 2004).

3 See, for example, Dan Sarooshi, *International Organizations and Their Exercise of Sovereign Powers* (Oxford University Press, 2005); Richard Collins and Nigel White (eds), *International Organizations and the Idea of Autonomy: Institutional Independence in the International Legal Order* (Routledge, 2011); Jan Klabbers, 'Presumptive Personality: The European Union in International Law' in Marti Koskenniemi (ed.), *International Law Aspects of the European Union* (Martinus Nijhoff/BRILL, 1998), 231; Andrea Bianchi (ed.), 'Relativizing the Subjects or Subjectivizing the Actors? That is the Question' in Andrea Bianchi (ed.), *Non-State Actors and International Law* (Ashgate, 2009).

in international law as 'participants' or those arguing for a departure from an understanding of international legal personality limited to state actors or those cautioning against the celebratory nature of international law scholarship on individuals becoming the subjects of international law.[4] Nonetheless, emerging theories of international politics accord more freedom of action and open up a greater distance between law and other disciplines already existing in lexicon.[5] It is argued here that it is far from a problem of descriptive taxonomy. There are significant legitimacy challenges resulting from ambiguities surrounding the construct of actors, which the present account has demonstrated in Chapters 2 and 7 that the EU exploits in much contemporary rule-making.

One may note how flexible public international law has been to these challenges. For example, it has been willing to accord autonomous international arrangements in multilateral environmental agreements, involving a conference or meeting of parties with decision-making powers, a secretariat and specialist subsidiary bodies, their own lexicon.[6] Yet how malleable is and should our lexicon be for each new actor as part of a system and/or organisation? So should EU law follow this tendency, as a creature of public international law? It has been forcefully argued that to construe international law in overly simplified terms, of subjects and objects, would subject it to a form of 'intellectual prison'.[7] Instead, many call for more elaborate conceptual tools to systematise the lexicon of non-state actors and their role played in contemporary international law.[8] Yet whether the solution lies in relativising the subjects or subjectivising the actors remains contestable.[9]

While the proliferation and pluralisation of actors are concerns of contemporary EU law, there is no agreed definition of an 'actor' under EU law.[10] Instead, a sharp distinction is drawn there between the masters of the treaties and those amenable to judicial review or those with legal personality. This concern is

4 Roslyn Higgins, *Problems and Process: International Law and How We Use It* (Oxford University Press, 1994); Christian Walter, 'International Law in a Process of Constitutionalization' in Janne Nijman and André Nollkaemper (eds), *New Perspectives on the Divide Between National and International Law* (Oxford University Press, 2007); Bianchi (n. 3); Rene Uruena, *No Citizens Here: Global Subjects and Participation in International Law* (BRILL, 2012).

5 Barnett and Finnemore (n. 2); Michael Zürn, 'The politicization of world politics and its effects: Eight propositions' (2014), 6 (1) *EPSR* 47. See Walter Mattli and Ngaire Woods (eds), *The Politics of Global Regulation* (Princeton University Press, 2009) focusing upon on the lack of transparency and accountability of regulatory outcomes at the global level, developed in various case studies, to outline their problematisation of actor conduct.

6 See Ralf Churchill and Geir Ulfstein, 'Autonomous institutional arrangements in multilateral environmental agreements: a little-noticed phenomenon in international law' (2000), 94 *AJIL* 623; Frank Biermann and Bernd Siebenhüner (eds), *Managers of Global Change: The Influence of International Environmental Bureaucracies* (MIT Press, 2009).

7 See Higgins (n. 4).

8 Ibid., Higgins (n. 4).

9 See Bianchi (n. 3).

10 See Matthias Ruffert, 'Personality under EU-Law: A Conceptual Answer towards the Pluralisation of the EU' (2014), *ELJ* 346.

usually framed around the control of discretion or legality control of the powers of burgeoning agencies vis à vis the Commission, the member states and national authorities. Yet whether there are advantages to sustaining or supporting the present approach may be argued to be doubtful. As a result, a permissive approach to the rule-making of the proliferating agencies has been adopted by many – for example, the Court of Justice[11] – where it has laid emphasis upon the importance of highly structured functionality rather than controls per se, even where extensive institutional design has been built up upon thin legal authority.[12] It also reflects the under-developed conceptualisation of institutional balance in contemporary EU law.[13] More generally, the grant of legal personality under EU law has been predominantly accorded to entities such as agencies in a wholly pragmatic rather than conceptual basis.

Pragmatism remains a challenge for the EU and perhaps public international law, as does the malleability of language. For example, consider those who have argued that each piece of international law should be studied as an institution itself, such that the set of institutions comprises a 'continent'.[14] This might be said to be simply unconvincing and lacking rigour.[15] Nonetheless, the burgeoning use of the term 'non-state' actors as a term of art to comprise almost any entity *inter alia* contesting legitimacy, authority or accountability in public international law has followed a similarly pragmatic rather than conceptual path.[16] EU law thus reflects broader trends in rule-making beyond the nation state, but what are and should be the limits of practice is another matter.

The 'bicepheral' stance of the EU in theory and practice is argued here to be excusatory and indulgent of the overreach of EU powers, as exemplified in accounts of the global reach and effects of EU law, discussed in Chapter 2. Behavioural understandings of EU action dominate EU law and governance scholarship – for example, observing its practices, assessing its action and locating its place in a broader global context. In this regard, a closer focus upon how we understand and depict actors in rule-making has resonance with this scholarship.

11 Case C-270/12 *UK* v. *European Parliament* EU:C:2014:18.

12 That is, Article 114 TFEU.

13 See Jean Paul Jacqué, 'The Principle of Institutional Balance' (2004), 41 *CMLR* 383; Case 294/83 *Les Verts European Parliament* ECLI:EU:C:1986:166 [1986], ECR 1339, para. 23–25; Gerard Conway, 'Recovering a Separation of Powers in the European Union' (2011), (2) *ELJ* 320; Ben Smulders and Katharina Eisele, 'Reflections on the Institutional Balance, the Community Method and the Interplay between Jurisdictions after Lisbon' (2012), 31(1) *YEL* 112; Paul Craig, 'Institutions, Power and Institutional Balance' in Paul Craig and Grainne de Búrca (eds), *The Evolution of EU Law* (Oxford University Press, 2011).

14 See Barbara Koremenos, 'The Continent of International Law' (2013), 57(4) *JCR* 653.

15 See Andrea Bianchi (ed.), 'Relativizing the Subjects or Subjectivizing the Actors? That is the Question' *in Non-State Actors and International Law* (Ashgate, 2009).

16 The rise of pragmatism is further evident in recent debates on the possible decline of formal treaties as a mechanism for cooperation in international law; see Joel P. Trachtman, 'Reports of the Death of Treaty are Premature, but Customary International Law may have Outlived its Usefulness' (2014), *AJIL Unbound*: www.asil.org/blogs/reports-death-treaty-are-premature-customary-international-law-may-have-outlived, accessed 23 December 2015.

It comprises a highly 'internal' analytical perspective regarding doctrine and lexicon as outlined above, whereas an external perspective might be said to consider more the formal nature of the EU as a legal actor and its practical effects, which this account considers next.

Accordingly, this chapter assesses the paradoxes and limitations involved in considering the EU as a unified legal actor in the world. It then outlines the evolution of living institutional components and their place within the theory and practice of actors in rule-making. Next, it reflects on the dominance of normative power Europe as a means of understanding the normative dimension to EU action in the world, while the last section assesses pressures upon the 'construct' of actors in rule-making beyond the nation state, from the perspective of organisations as structures, subject matter and operationally.

The EU as a legal actor in the world: riddled with paradoxes and limitations

Even if it is able to collect a Nobel Peace Prize, have its own diplomatic service or have nearly every EU executive actor and agency endowed with a global mandate,[17] the EU does not function as a unitary actor in the world. It does not participate as a state in the global legal order. Although it has 'single legal personality' – i.e. formal authority to act – the EU has a broad range of 'statuses' in international organisations.[18] Sometimes it acts alongside its member states, sometimes it does not. It faces the reality that international agreements cannot be easily renegotiated. And some international organisations cannot easily change their admission rules. While the EU treaties are no obstacle to EU participation in international organisations (e.g. Articles 220 TFEU, 221 TFEU), this contrasts sharply with its treaty-making activities. Yet each instance has its own particularities and history. The EU has been confined in its treaties to specific arrangements for the Food and Administration Organization (FAO), the European Bank for Reconstruction and Development (EBRD), the World Trade Organization (WTO), *Codex Alimentarious* and the Hague Conference of Private International law. It is not a member of the United Nations, International Labour Organization, World Bank, International Monetary Fund or Council of Europe for reasons of sovereignty of the member states as much as the rules of the organisations themselves.[19] And an 'apprehensive' approach towards EU membership within the

17 See Deirdre Curtin, 'Challenging Executive Dominance in European Democracy' (2014), 77 *MLR* 1.

18 Jan Wouters, 'The Institutional Structure of EU External Relations' in Takis Tridimas and Robert Schütze (eds), *Oxford Principles of European Union Law* (forthcoming); Piet Eeckhout, *EU External Relations Law* (2nd edn, Oxford University Press, 2011).

19 See Eeckhout (n. 18); Wouters (n. 18); Jed Odermatt and Jan Wouters, 'Are all international organisations created equally?' (2012), 9 *IOLR* 7; Frank Hoffmeister, 'Outsider or Frontrunner? Recent Developments under International and European Law: On the Status of the European Union in International Organizations and Treaty Bodies' (2007), 44 *CMLR* 41.

UN system exists.[20] Even if it is neither coherent nor optimal, the EU and its member states continue to co-exist and function together, globally. The EU is often referred to as a 'global actor'; such a view of its 'actorness' is not always shared across disciplines, vexed by the structure of the EU and its practices.[21]

These challenges are not limited to the EU in the outside world. Internally, the EU comprises very powerful institutional components that sometimes appear more powerful than the sum of its parts. They are broadly understood as actors engaged in rule-making after the state. Yet doctrinal or formalist understandings of 'actors' engaged in rule-making are unable to capture new manifestations of 'executive' actors widely found in the EU or its powerful and independent judicial components or its transnational parliament.[22] There is a paradox as to the state of the EU: it is an empowered, sophisticated legal actor. Yet it faces as many external and internal hurdles in its development as what is argued here, later to be its embryonic sovereignty evident in the global reach and effects of EU law.

This internal/external dichotomy remains far from academic. For example, the EU regularly makes arguments before the US Supreme Court against the death penalty so as to promote its values.[23] Yet more recently, it made submissions before the US Supreme Court on human rights legislation, as did various EU member states, each arguing for different standards and practices. Such incoherence, divergence but also pragmatism are repeatedly evident in EU rule-making flowing from the internal/external dichotomy. However, the precise theorisation of these practices – linked innately to the EU's role in the world in Article 21 TEU – remains far from certain or complete in legal scholarship.[24] As outlined in Chapter 2, the articulation of the global reach and effects of EU law is notably *not* an actor-specific account. The contemporary formulation of the global reach and effects of EU law does not grapple with the inconsistencies, incoherence and challenges of EU action in the world by articulating the complexities of 'actor'-related questions. Nevertheless, as the case studies pursued in Chapters 4, 5 and 6 demonstrate, the tension between the internal and external in EU law often flows from the autonomy exercised by its actor components.

20 See Wouters (n. 18).

21 Christian Kaunert and Kamil Zwolski, *The EU as a Global Security Actor – A Comprehensive Analysis Beyond CFSP and JHA* (Palgrave Macmillan, 2013); Marise Cremona, Jorg Monar and Sara Poli (eds), *The External Relations of the Area of Freedom, Security and Justice* (Presse Interuniversitaire Europeénne, 2011); Uwe Wunderlich, 'The EU an Actor Sui Generis? A Comparison of EU and ASEAN Actorness' (2012), 50 *JCMS* 653; Henri de Waele and Jan-Jap Kuipers (eds), *The European Union's Emerging International Identity: Views from the Global Arena* (BRILL, 2013).

22 See Deirdre Curtin, 'Challenging Executive Dominance in European Democracy' (2014), 77 (1) *MLR* 1; C-350/12 P *Council* v. *in 't Veld* EU:C:2014:2039, Opinion of A.G. Sharpston, para. 73 on the nature of the EU Executive in this significant decision of the Court on transparency and international relations.

23 *Kiobel* v. *Royal Dutch Petroleum Co.* 133 S.Ct. 1659 (2013); Elaine Fahey, 'On the Use of Law in Transatlantic Relations: Legal Dialogues between the EU and US' (2014), 21 *ELJ* 368.

Living institutional components as 'actors' in rule-making

One means of looking beyond the limits of legal and doctrinal formalism might be to gauge how we have evolved our understanding of the measurement of entities qua institutions. Formalist understandings of those who are 'actors' engaged in rule-making are unable to capture much about EU law-making with many new manifestations of 'executive' actors, its powerful and independent courts or the rise of the European Parliament as a transnational parliament, broadly understood as actors engaged in rule-making after the State.[25] To be sure, some may act with considerably more institutional, social or political legitimacy than others. We may say that formalist criteria and theorisations operate to exclude the acts or practices of institutional entities or components that are part of international organisations who exercise public authority beyond the State, who are not regarded as unitary actors or equivalent to the organisation itself. Yet how do they in reality interact with private associations, unions or certain experts? What is their zone of influence? How do we assess the autonomy of these component parts?

In scholarship on regions and organisations, the phenomena of 'actorness' is of much significance. It embraces less readily evolving organisations or their institutional components, even when they obtain legal personality or legal authority to act – for example, the EU or ASEAN.[26] The criteria remain greatly contested and under development.[27] The criteria of 'actorness' in non-legal scholarship often include *inter alia* the de facto or de jure recognition of its actions, the legal authority to act, its institutional autonomy or distinctiveness

24 Which provides that the EU's action on the international scene is to be guided by respect for the principles of the UN Charter and international law, and that it shall promote multilateralism within the UN framework. See how this is asserted to occur in a comparative judicial context, Gráinne De Búrca, 'International Law before the Courts: the European Union and the United States compared' (2015), *55 Virginia JIL 685.*

25 On the Executive: Deirdre Curtin, *Executive Power of the European Union: Law, Practices and the Living Constitution* (Oxford University Press, 2009). On courts: Karen Alter, *The New Terrain of International Law: Courts, Politics, Rights* (Princeton University Press, 2013); Elaine Fahey, 'The EU Emission Trading Scheme and the Court of Justice: The High Politics of the Indirect Promotion of Global Standards' (2012) *GLJ* 1247; R. Daniel Kelemen, *The Transformation of Law and Regulation in the European Union* (Harvard University Press 2012). On transnational parliaments: Davor Jancic, 'Interactions between the EU and US legal order' in Elaine Fahey and Deirdre Curtin (eds), *A Transatlantic Community of Law* (Cambridge University Press, 2014); Neil Walker, 'Postnational Constitutionalism and Postnational Public Law: A Tale of Two Neologisms' (2012), 3 *TLT* 61

26 Marise Cremona, 'The European Union as a Global Actor: Roles, Models and Identity' (2004), 41 *CMLR* 553; Uwe Wunderlich, 'The EU an Actor Sui Generis? A Comparison of EU and ASEAN Actorness' (2012), 50 *JCMS* 653; Thomas Forsberg, 'Normative Power Europe, Once Again: A Conceptual Analysis of an Ideal Type' (2011), 49 *JCMS* 1183.

27 Eugénia de Conceição Heldt and Sophie Meunier, 'Speaking with a Single Voice: Internal Cohesiveness and External Cohesiveness of the EU in World Politics' (2014), 21 *JEPP.*

and the cohesion between its constituent parts in the formulation of policy.[28] The conventional conceptualisation of the actorness qualities of international organisations thus largely encompasses 'formal' international organisations, less so fledgling or new organisations or their institutional components, irrespective of how powerful they are. As a result, the conventional criteria for actorness sit ill with transnational rule-making practices. The EU in particular poses acute problems of characterisation, even after the acquisition of legal personality, but to label it as sui generis or exceptionalist may not meet the challenge of postnational rule-making.[29]

The rise of transnational parliamentarianism – e.g. the Transatlantic Legislatures Dialogues,[30] the ASEAN[31] or the Arctic Council assemblies – through embryonically formalised contacts and then rule-making initiatives, may indicate 'living' practices of actorness. Courts are largely omitted from theorisations of actorness, even courts that are globally and/or empirically acknowledged to be powerful, independent bodies engaging in rule-making practices, directly or indirectly.[32] Similarly, 'agencification' in regional, national and international legal orders – empowering many independent actors and according them legal personality with increasingly few checks – has little putative relevance because it is outside actorness. And are they appropriately excluded from actorness as a result? These developments are arguably accepted with ease in legal scholarship and even welcomed as evidence of the evolution of transnational law.[33] It can be easily seen how the issue is broader than just semantics. For example, new typologies of what have been labelled as 'quasi-autonomous' actors under EU law have even generated a new lexicon of accountability.[34] While lexicon has provided EU law with relative flexibility and creativity, EU law does not engage with actorness. What remains problematic is that there are highly fixed legal contours to actors in rule-making that do not engage sufficiently with the challenge that actors are a construct.

There are descriptive and normative components to actorness that may appear to sit together uneasily from a legal perspective. For example, do the criteria logically and analytically flow from one another? Who is to judge the criteria?

28 Charlotte Bretherton and Jon Vogler, 'The European Union as a Sustainable Development Actor: The Case of External Fisheries Policy' (2008), 30 *JEI* 401; Carmen Gebhard, 'Coherence' in Christopher Hill and Michael Smith (eds), *International Relations and the European Union* (2nd edn, Oxford University Press, 2011), 101.

29 See Joris Larik, 'From Speciality to a Constitutional Sense of Purpose: On the Changing Role of the Objectives of the European Union' (2014), 63, *ICLQ* 935; Wunderlich (n. 21).

30 See Jancic (n. 25).

31 Wunderlich (n. 21).

32 See Kelemen (n. 25); Alter (n. 25).

33 Jancic (n. 25); Walker (n. 25).

34 Curtin (n. 25); Mark Bovens, 'Analysing and Assessing Accountability: A Conceptual Framework' (2007), 13 *ELJ* 447; Madalina Busuioc, *European Agencies: Law and Practices of Accountability* (Oxford University Press, 2013).

Which of them is most legally, socially or politically authoritative? It raises many other challenging questions for legal scholarship – for example, how do actorness practices impact upon rule-making itself? How has or should legal scholarship responded to the evolution of actorness? And how does and should the attribution of legal personality of an organisation strengthen its actorness vis à vis its institutions and other components? It also raises the issue as to whether there is a distinction between de facto and de jure actorness? If so, is it pragmatic or valid? How to the actors advance the components of actorness through law? And how flexible is actorness? How does and should actorness influence theorisations of legitimacy and accountability?

These matters are addressed more indirectly and practically by the case studies of the interrelationship between internal and external security conducted in Chapters 5 and 6 in particular. They demonstrate in various ways the rising autonomy of institutional actors in EU law. This analysis – largely of descriptive concerns – leads to a consideration of the normative dimension to EU action in the world as a meta-behavioural standard for EU law.

The normative dimension to actors and action

Overview

'Normative Power Europe' (NPE hereafter) is a famous conceptualisation of how the EU acts externally outside its regional territory as a promoter of normative values, borne in non-legal scholarship.[35] It has a particularly dominant influence upon EU legal theory, especially EU external relations law and theory on the depiction of EU action, on its development, projection and practices.[36] Yet, often overlooked is the fact that it was developed as a direct critique on EU *legal* scholars, admonished for failing to acknowledge the high legal standards that the EU was practising and adhering to externally.[37] Although less of a dominant narrative now in other disciplines, its dominance in legal theory raises the question of its ongoing relevance for accounts of the

35 Ian Manners, 'Normative Power Europe: A Contradiction in Terms?' (2002), 40 *JCMS* 235; Ian Manners, 'European Union Normative Power and the Security Challenge' (2006) European Security 405; Ian Manners, 'The European Union as a Normative Power: A Response to Thomas Diez' (2006), *Millennium Journal of International Studies* 167; Ian Manners, 'Normative Power Europe Reconsidered: Beyond the Crossroads' (2006), 13 *JEPP* 182; Johan Galtung, *The European Community: A Superpower in the Making* (Allen & Unwin 1973); Richard Rosecrance, 'The European Union: A New Type of International Actor' in Jan Zielonka (eds), *Paradoxes of European Foreign Policy* (Kluwer, 1998) 15; Chad Damro, 'Market Power Europe' (2012), 19 *JEPP* 682; David Vogel, *Trading Up: Consumer and Environmental Regulation in a Global Economy* (Harvard University Press, 1995).

36 Cremona (n. 21); Laurent Pech, 'The Rule of Law as a Guiding Principle of EU's External Action', CLEER Working Paper 2012/3.

37 Manners, 'Normative Power Europe' (n. 35) 241. Many leading human rights and EU lawyers of the time were the subject of this particular passage.

global reach and effects of EU law. Recent innovations to evolve the EU as a postnational democracy and newer legal provisions to develop its competences as an actor in the global legal order also invite further reflections.[38] NPE envisages the EU acting as a 'Robin Hood' of virtue in its rule-making outside its territory, spreading its values and leveraging its territorial power.[39] It is renowned for its assertion of the salience of what the EU *is* over what the EU does or does not say or do.[40] Subsequent theorisations of NPE evolved the components of the theory around the *transfer* of core elements of the EU's norms, via *inter alia* contagion, information diffusion, procedural diffusion and cultural filters. One may remark that these are processes conducted predominantly *through* and *by* law but without much attention to methodology. They retain a specific relevance for law as a means and end in the depiction of the EU's action in the world.[41]

The portrayal of the 'active' dimension of the EU's role in the global order places the active dimension thereof as part of the narrative overall – for example, portraying the EU as evolving from leader to 'leadiator'.[42] Others similarly depict the EU actively leveraging its normative and market power so as to globalise sectors of regulation – for example, environmental law.[43] However, there are those who contend that the EU exercises its power through an externalisation of its market policies directly and indirectly, particularly with regard to its relationship with the US, and flexibly adjusts its rules accordingly.[44] Other accounts suggest that the EU is a 'power by default' or is a 'hyper regulatory actor' and thus demonstrate similar elliptical challenges.[45] However, such theses tell us little about processes surrounding the operation of legal rules, legal methodology and the relevance of law thereto. Non-legal scholarship on EU external governance arguably remains mired in contestation, descriptively as much as normatively: is the EU acting, leading, causing, setting or just

38 See Deirdre Curtin, *Postnational Democracy: The EU in Search of a Political Philosophy* (Kluwer Law, 1997); Colin Crouch, *Coping with Post-Democracy* (Polity Press, 2004); Jürgen Habermas, *The Postnational Constellation: Political Essays* (MIT Press, 2001); Armin Van Bogdandy, 'The European Lesson for International Democracy: The Significance of Articles 9–12 EU Treaty for International Organizations' (2012), 23 *EJIL* 315.

39 Manners sought to draw from a threefold evaluative template: (n. 37) 'Normative Power Europe' 252.

40 Per Vicky Birchfield, 'Normative Power Europe Framework of Transnational Policy Formation' (2013), 20 *JEPP* 907: 'it is a dialectic of being and becoming'. See Ian Manners and Richard Whitman, 'Normative Power and the Future of EU Public Diplomacy' in Ma'a K. Davis Cross and Jan Melissen (eds), *European Public Diplomacy: Soft Power at Work* (Palgrave Macmillan, 2008).

41 Thomas Forsberg, 'Normative Power Europe, Once Again: A Conceptual Analysis of an Ideal Type' (2011), 49 *JCMS* 1183.

42 Karin Bäckstrand and Ole Elgström, 'The EU's role in climate change negotiations: from leader to "leadiator"' (2013), 20 *JEPP* 1369.

43 R. Dan Kelemen, 'Globalizing EU Environmental Regulation' (2010), 17 *JEPP* 335.

44 Damro (n. 35); Vogel (n. 35).

45 Zaki Laïdi, 'European preferences and their reception' in Zaki Laïdi (ed.), *EU Foreign Policy in a Globalized World: Normative Power and Social Preferences* (Routledge, 2008).

contributing to global governance, in any given policy field, as a security or health or environmental actor, or is it just past its peak?[46] Recent EU legal scholarship has been engaging in similar analytical ellipses, varying between advocating and depicting the EU's action in the world, while adopting arguably a rather blurred 'pinpoint' between the descriptive and normative.[47] It also tends, bravely perhaps, to directly address its concern to the EU's AFSJ, perhaps beginning with rather than dodging the complexity of EU global action in a complex field.

NPE and its many manifestations across subjects may be said to nonetheless possess many shortcomings when it comes to understanding EU action in the world through law, irrespective of the 'spectacles' of the observer. For example, arguably it fails to adequately explain the primacy that the EU places upon external norms in EU rule-making both inside and outside its territory and the complex relationship between them.[48] It cannot explain the spread of legal rules developed by the EU externally then enacted internally, adopted later globally or developed first by the EU with bilateral partners then adopted internally. Nor can it explain the gap between the standards the EU expects externally to those it can impose on its own member states. Moreover, it cannot easily explain the gap between formulations and the enforcement of human rights conditionality in EU trade agreements.[49] While all of these matters may not be conclusively determined here, it serves to emphasise the challenges for legal and non-legal scholarship alike in depicting EU action. The infelicities of NPE for contemporary legal scholarship emphasises the relevance of articulating the 'voice' of law. This is advocated here in this account through the explicit articulation of the legal dimension of the global reach and effects of EU law, as outlined in Chapter 2 and later in the case studies. This leads to an analysis of what it entails for the EU to be charged with 'doing good' in the world pursuant to Article 21 TEU, considering its components, construction and values.

An actor charged with 'doing' good in the world: unpacking the premises

One of the most novel and recent attempts at a depiction of EU global action through law – i.e. in the EU treaties – is to the effect that an actor must 'do' good

46 Damro (n. 35), Vogel (n. 35); Charlotte Bretherton and John Vogler, 'A Global Actor past its Peak?' (2013), 27 *IR* 375.

47 Bart Van Vooren, Steven Blockmans and Jan Wouters (eds), *The Legal Dimension of Global Governance: What Role for the EU?* (Oxford University Press, 2013); Dimitry Kochenov and Fabien Amtenbrink (eds), *The European Union's Shaping of the International Legal Order* (Cambridge University Press, 2013); Wouters (n. 18); Pieter Jan Kuijper, Frank Hoffmeister, Geert De Baere and Jan Wouters, *The EU and International Law* (Oxford University Press, 2013).

48 As will be developed here in Chapter 4.

49 See Bruno De Witte, 'The EU and the International Legal Order: The Case of Human Rights' in Malcolm Evans and Panos Koutrakos (eds), *Beyond the Established Legal Orders – Policy Interconnections between the EU and the Rest of the World* (Hart, 2011), 127.

in the world by practising good global governance pursuant to Article 21 TEU. Article 21 TEU provides that:

> The Union's action on the international scene shall be guided by the principles which have inspired its own creation, development and enlargement, and which it seeks to advance in the wider world: democracy, the rule of law, the universality and indivisibility of human rights and fundamental freedoms, respect for human dignity, the principles of equality and solidarity, and respect for the principles of the United Nations Charter and international law. The Union shall seek to develop relations and build partnerships with third countries, and international, regional or global organisations which share the principles referred to in the first subparagraph. It shall promote multilateral solutions to common problems, in particular in the framework of the United Nations … promote an international system based on stronger multilateral cooperation and good global governance …

There is both a descriptive and normative content to this article, which as a legal standard evokes unparalleled complexity. Writing prior to the advent of Article 21 TEU in the Treaty of Lisbon, Craig and De Búrca, in the 2008 edition of their leading textbook on EU law, witheringly critiqued the depiction of the EU as an actor in the world provided for in the Laeken Declaration, as 'rather self-important and […using] bombastic tones'.[50] Such a viewpoint perhaps demonstrates the challenges felt by legal scholars engaging with the complexity of the factual and normative description of the EU *as an autonomous legal and political actor* in the world. However, there is surprisingly little critique of this standard for EU action.[51] Also, Article 21 TEU may be said to offer little by way of practical legal or political insights into its evolution. The fact that the EU is now legally obliged to act as a 'good' global governance actor in its own treaties suggests much coherence in its practices, organisation and institutional frameworks.

The acquisition of single 'legal personality' by the EU is an important legal formality for authority to act, but has not yet meant that the EU fully participates as a state in the global legal order. International organisations' admission rules and international agreements cannot be easily renegotiated.[52] The international legal order cannot adopt *in toto* for it quickly enough. While the EU is referred to as a 'global actor', this view is not always shared across disciplines or observers of its conduct. Even if neither coherent nor optimal, the EU and its member states continue to co-exist and function *together*, globally. As mentioned above, the EU regularly makes arguments before the US Supreme Court against the

50 Writing in the 4th edition (now in 6th edn): Paul Craig and Grainne De Búrca, *EU Law: Texts, Cases & Materials* (4th edn, Oxford University Press, 2008), 168.

51 See Introduction to Van Vooren, Blackmans and Wouters (n. 47); Joris Larik, 'From speciality to a constitutional sense of purpose: On the changing role of the objectives of the European Union' (2014), 63 *ICLQ* 935.

52 See Wouters (n. 18); Louise van Schaik, *EU Effectiveness and Unity in Multilateral Negotiations: More than the Sum of its Parts?* (Palgrave Macmillan, 2013).

death penalty in the US so as to promote its values, as do the member states, something that it did both before and after the acquisition of legal personality and the advent of an External Action Service. The EU member states often allow the EU to act as lead negotiator in certain organisations, even where the member states themselves have competence.[53] One could surmise that legal incoherence is a default state in this context. The issue remains for legal scholarship to unravel the nature of just what it means to be a legal actor in this context and how it can act through law to pursue its global objectives.

The ambiguous contours of Article 21 TFEU are inescapable as to its worldly ambitions. One may understand the active component thereof involving the EU more than just 'nudging' global behaviour by its action, to draw upon the famous work of Sunstein *et al.*, except that the criteria beyond this are difficult to pinpoint with precision.[54] This is because Article 21 TEU ostensibly includes both active and directional criteria as a normative standard of EU actorship qualities. The issue remains for legal scholarship to unravel and understand the nature and direction of what it means to be a legal actor in this context. Just what is the real and essential direction of EU 'action'? For example, the formula of nudging might include within its ambit both direct and certain indirect actions. It does not necessarily envisage completeness of action. Just as the EU must do good in the world, *attempts* to do good are as valid as actual successes. And yet there remains the niggling ambiguity of 'good' – i.e. is EU drone surveillance and/or its secretive funding actually 'good'?[55] Is the creation of exceptions to internal free movement rules so as to bolster member states excessively burdened by international refugees 'doing good'?[56] A challenge for legal theory is then to capture the outwards and inwards effects of EU action in a manner which is descriptively and normatively accurate. Of course, the challenge of 'description' is not only posed by the EU treaties but also by realpolitik and again, more concretely, by EU secondary legislation and the effects thereof. This is developed in further case studies on inwards and outwards rule-transfer in Chapters 5 and 6, and then more theoretically in Chapter 7.

Pressures on the construct of actors in rule-making beyond the nation state

It is an immense challenge to capture the changing practice of actors within any narrative of rule-making beyond the nation state, not least the global reach and

53 Allan Rosas, 'Exclusive, Shared and National Competence in the Context of EU External Relations: Do Such Distinctions Matter?' forthcoming, on file with the author.

54 Richard Thaler and Cass Sunstein, *Nudge: Improving Decisions About Health, Wealth, and Happiness* (Penguin 2009).

55 See 'EU steps up funding for drone research' (12 February 2014): http://euobserver.com/defence/123098, accessed 23 December 2015.

56 On exceptions to the Schengen Area: see http://ec.europa.eu/dgs/home-affairs/what-we-do/policies/borders-and-visas/schengen/index_en.htm, accessed 23 December 2015.

effects of EU law. Changes to authority structures and the delegation of power also operate in the background with significance in EU rule-making. This account draws from three specific developments in rule-making beyond the nation state in making the proposition that the place of the EU as an actor in rule-making needs to be carefully recalibrated as part of a future research agenda. This perspective begins from the premise that uncertainty surrounds EU rule-making, which it readily exploits. First and foremost, as to *structural and organisational questions*, as adverted to above, there is a movement to reconsider how and why there is an evolving content of actorness – i.e. broadly understood as understandings of organisational unity. The conventional criteria of actorness appear closed to new organisations and rising autonomy of institutional components. From the perspective of legal scholars, there has been much manipulation of the content of legal personality and 'actorship', especially during the EU's financial crisis.[57] Whether it sits ill with the proliferation of actors in the EU remains less explored. Legal scholarship is argued here to benefit from further engagement with actorness as an evolving construct because of its flexibility and willingness to consider change, because it appears instructive. Secondly, as to *subject matter* – the nature of the subject of much of the predominant focus of this book – the EU's AFSJ and specifically security in contemporary times has placed legal and political demands of an exceptional nature upon formal limitations of the nation state. Witness, for example, the head of the EU's internal security delegation negotiating with the US on the NSA affair, paradoxically being formally powerless to deal with matters of internal security in the member states, pursuant to the EU treaties.[58] The post-9/11 era also gave considerably greater force to rule-making beyond the nation state in security out of necessity in the face of ostensibly global challenges. It still has quite a bearing upon contemporary Area of Freedom, Security and Justice (AFSJ) rule-making, as will be demonstrated in Chapter 5. While AFSJ agencies have gradually been regularised in the post-Lisbon period, law and governance practices of such bodies remain fluid.[59] Paradoxically, decentralisation of actors in the AFSJ is also

57 See Ruffert (n. 10); see Curtin (n. 17).

58 See Articles 72 and 73 TFEU. See Commission communication of 27 November 2013 (COM (2013) 0847) on the functioning of the Safe Harbour from the perspective of EU citizens and companies established in the EU, and to the Commission communication of 27 November 2013 on rebuilding trust in EU–US data flows (COM(2013) 0846 'EU–US agreements: Commission reports on TFTP and PNR European Commission' – IP/13/1160, 27/11/2013, http://europa.eu/rapid/press-release_IP-13-1160_en.htm, accessed 23 December 2015. Traditionally, however, for the EU to negotiate with third parties, as Schütze states, it had to fight a 'two-front war' – namely, to negotiate with both a third party and also with the Council: Robert Schütze, *European Constitutional Law* (Cambridge University Press, 2013).

59 See Elaine Fahey, 'Law and Governance as Checks and Balances in Transatlantic Security: Rights, Redress and Remedies in EU–US Passenger Name Records and the Terrorist Finance Tracking Program' (2013), 32 *YEL* 1.

a current theme of contemporary rule-making.[60] Formalism and doctrinalism offer us increasingly less in an age where rule-making beyond the State may take precedence for reasons of political and strategic pragmatism in this context and create new configurations of actors and also authority.[61] This leads to a third issue as to *operational* questions of rule-making beyond the nation state. There are increased calls for the heightened politicisation of international organisations and to increase their transparency and openness, especially in the digital era.[62] This politicisation arguably reflects the rising transfer of authority to such bodies, including the EU.[63] It also gives significance to new methods of accountability, especially in the EU context.[64] This must have a bearing upon our assessment of how organisations as actors evolve and engage in rule-making.

The EU is not unaffected by any of these three developments. On the contrary, it operates as a central case study of note – for actorness, for evolving constructions of security and the politicisation and openness of international organisations. They impact upon the construct of actors in the context and also the view of the EU as an exceptional actor engaging in rule-making. True to its bicepheral character, the EU is exceptional as a *sui generis* construct, but also paradoxically is a core case study of evolution and change. There are compelling reasons to recalibrate our understanding of actors in rule-making by way of a future research agenda. Empirical practice is argued here to yield further insights as to developments in EU rule-making through a series of case studies considered here next.

Conclusions

While there is little consensus on what it means to be an actor, legal doctrine largely employs formal limiting criteria to speak about actors in rule-making. There are many instances, however, of the flexibility of lexicon being used. EU law is a living subject, rooted in pragmatism and flexibility. Yet pragmatism remains a particular challenge. The EU in particular may obtain formal status as

60 See, for example, the proposals for a European Public Prosecutor drawn from a national panel or a European Cybercrime Centre (EC3) to be set up as a 'desk' within Europol: Proposal for a Council Regulation on the establishment of the European Public Prosecutor's Office COM /2013/0534 final, Article 7 or www.europol.europa.eu/ec3, accessed 23 December 2015.

61 For example, on the rise of private actors in security, Simon Chesterman and Angelina Fisher (eds), *Private Security, Public Order: The Outsourcing of Public Services and its Limits* (Oxford University Press, 2009).

62 See Michael Zürn, 'The politicization of world politics and its effects: Eight propositions' (2014), 6(1) *EPSR* 47; see Curtin (n. 17).

63 See also Lisbeth Hooghe and Gary Marks, 'Delegation and Pooling in International Organizations' (2014), *Review of International Organizations*, forthcoming. On courts: Armin Van Bogdandy and Ingo Venzke, *In Whose Name: A Public Law Theory of International Adjudication* (Oxford University Press, 2014).

64 See Jonathan Zeitlin and Charles Sabel (eds), *Experimentalist Governance in the European Union* (Oxford University Press, 2012); Mark Bovens, Robert Goodin and Thomas Schillemans (eds), *The Oxford Handbook of Public Accountability* (Oxford University Press, 2014). See also Bovens (n. 34); Busuioc (n. 34).

an actor in law to act on the global stage but such a view is not necessarily shared across disciplines, even if they paradoxically appear more open to such developments than legal scholarship. Incoherence, divergence and pragmatism are overarching characteristics of EU rule-making on the global stage. Yet the assessment is not necessarily such a gloomy one. On the contrary, an evolving lexicon has been matched by evolving normative standards – for example, a new lexicon of accountability. This chapter has outlined in detail the infelicities and inadequacies of NPE for contemporary EU legal scholarship on rule-making. The global reach and effects of EU law may indeed result in fundamental changes to the seemingly elementary discussion of what it means to be an actor engaged in rule-making.

The case studies developed here feed into these issues individually: for example, in Chapter 6 (cybercrime and cybersecurity) they show evidence of the increasing autonomy of agencies and other actors in the AFSJ, creating tension in external and internal rule-making. Chapter 4 next explores external primacy in rule-making. It examines the role of the EU and the member states in the agreements that the EU promotes in its rule-making. It thus focuses upon the question of unity of action between the internal and external in rule-making. The case study on the global reach and effects of EU law suggests that the transparency of the ambitions of the EU reach externally, and to be tolerated in its external reach as an actor. True to its bicepheral character, the EU is exceptional as a *sui generis* construct but also paradoxically is a core case study of evolution and change. As this book emphasises, the social acceptance and social legitimacy of EU rule-making carries more significance now than ever before. There are compelling reasons to refine our understanding of actors in rule-making by way of a future research agenda.

4 External norm primacy and EU law

AFSJ directives in the post-Lisbon legislative cycle

Introduction

Depicting how the EU 'acts' in the world is not necessarily a straightforward task for any discipline any more, not least for legal scholars. As a descriptive and normative evaluation, it involves many layers of enquiry, but also assumptions and dichotomies that require evaluation. An elementary layer might be said to be the relationship between internal and external rule-making processes through law.[1] Yet even such an elementary layer is not straightforward. It is also ostensibly a multidirectional enquiry, as to its role 'inwards' and its role 'outwards'. Such an enquiry relates to what the EU wants to do externally and how it reflects that internally in practices, processes and rule-making – for example, how the EU acts in the world is the normative dimension, whether the EU's values are adequate internally,[2] how it practises good global governance externally,[3] how consistent the EU is between the internal and external,[4] and how it integrates external

1 The empirical work in this chapter is developed further in Elaine Fahey, 'Joining the dots: external norms, AFSJ directives and the EU's role in the global legal order' (2016), 41 *ELR* 105.

2 For example, Dimitry Kochenov, Andrew Williams and Grainne De Búrca (eds), *Europe's Justice Deficit?* (Hart Publishing, 2014); A. Williams 'Taking Values Seriously: Towards a Philosophy of EU Law' (2009), 29(3), *OJLS*, 549.

3 The external reach of the internal values of the EU have become central concerns of EU law and governance. Cf. Ian Manners, 'Normative Power Europe: A Contradiction in Terms?' (2002), 40 *JCMS* 235. See its most recent incarnations, Chad Damro, 'Market Power Europe' (2012) 19 *JEPP* 682 and from a legal perspective, Anu Bradford, 'The Brussels Effect' (2013), 107 *Northwestern University Law Review*, 1; Joanne Scott, 'Extraterritoriality and Territorial Extension in EU Law' (2014), 62, *AJCL*, 87.

4 On haphazardness: Marise Cremona, 'The European Union as a global actor: Roles, models and identity' (2004), 41 *CMLR* 553; Laurent Pech, 'Promoting the Rule of Law Abroad: On the EU's limited contribution to the shaping of an international understanding of the rule of law' in Fabian Amtenbrink and Dimitry Kochenov (eds), *The EU's Shaping of the International Legal Order* (Cambridge University Press, 2013); the earliest proposals on the future agenda of EU justice have already been subject to extensive critique for its incoherence in its values. House of Lords European Union Committee 13th Report of Session 2013–14, 'Strategic Guidelines for the EU's Next Justice and Home Affairs Programme: Steady as she Goes' (14 April 2014); Steve Peers, 'The next multi-year EU Justice and Home Affairs programme: Views of the Commission and the Member States', *Statewatch:* www.statewatch.org/analyses/no-238-new-jha-programme.pdf, accessed 23 December 2015.

norms in its rule-making.[5] These questions most often arise empirically as to its sensitive and evolving policy field, its Area of Freedom, Security and Justice (AFSJ), newly regularised within EU constitutional processes post-Lisbon. It is a highly process-oriented enquiry, but it is also highly behavioural because it depicts EU action.

This account proposes to consider the output of one instrument of EU AFSJ rule-making through Finnemore and Sikkink's formula of the 'life of norms' in order to gain insights as to recent rule-making practices for the depiction of EU action internally with external effects.[6] Rule-making constitutes a discrete mode of EU action and is understood here in its formalist sense – i.e. of the legislative process. It involves assessing three distinct stages of process and development in rule-making: 'norm emergence', 'cascade' and 'internalisation'. As to the specific stages of the life of norms, Stage 1, *norm emergence*, results from 'persuasion' by a 'norm entrepreneur' or generator, whereby a critical mass of what are termed as 'norm leaders' embrace new norms. Stage 2 involves specific *actions* in the form of 'norm cascades' predominantly through what is termed as socialisation, for reasons of legitimacy, conformity and esteem. Stage 3 involves their *internalisation*, whereby actors specifically conform to those norms and processes through further adoption. In each of these stages, this framework is through law in all of its stages as distinct processes. As a result, the 'life of norms' arguably offers an attractive analytical framework for those seeking to study methodologies for understanding rule-making. It is, however, derived principally from non-legal scholarship and requires certain calibrations to be made.

As a start, by way of a definitional 'throat-clearing' exercise, norms are understood here as both values *and* rules.[7] Values are argued here to underpin rules which are institutionalised and formalised manifestations of norms and, as a result, a broad construction of norms arguably provides both a viable and realistic fit from a legal perspective.[8] Finnemore questioned the disciplinary isolation

5 On the challenges of integration of external norms: see specific case studies such as Christina Eckes, *EU Counter-Terrorist Policies and Fundamental Rights: The Case of Individual Sanctions* (Oxford University Press, 2009); Odran Bures, *EU Counter-terrorism Policy: A Paper Tiger?* (Ashgate, 2011).

6 Martha Finnemore and Katherine Sikkink, 'International Norm Dynamics and Political Change' (1998), 52; *IO* 887; cf. Martha Finnemore, 'Norms, Culture and World Politics: Insights from Sociology's Institutionalism' (1996), 50; *IO*, 325.

7 Norms as values provide a collective understanding of justice and freedom. By contrast, norms as rules differ from values in that they prescribe specific action: see Frederich Kratochwil, *Rules, Norms and Decisions: On the Conditions of Practical and Legal Reasoning in International Relations* (Cambridge University Press, 1990); Christoph Roos and Natasha Zaun, 'Norms Matter! The Role of International Norms in EU Policies on Asylum and Immigration' (2014), 16; *EJML*, 45.

8 Norms within the context of rule-making exercises usually fulfil this dual focus. Norms as shared assessments between many actors raise the question as to how many actors must share an assessment before it is a norm. Because norms involve standards of appropriate or proper behaviour, both subjective and evaluative dimensions are inescapable when discussing norms. See n. 6, Finnemore and Sikkink, 891.

of norm development scholarship because of its universality and lauded the work of legal scholars who began to develop the lexicon of norm entrepreneurs, imitation and norm cascades, initially in *domestic* analogies, to study the evolution of rule-making processes and procedures.[9] Nowadays, it is a formula increasingly used by legal scholars examining rule-making practices *beyond the nation state.*[10] The supranational context of EU rule-making may offer us a wider window of insight into rule-making through the study of the life of norms. EU rule-making now involves a vast array of 'sources,' but it is argued here that their formalist categorisation as mere 'sources' does little justice to them.

This chapter considers how *external* norms – i.e. understood predominantly as instruments of international law, including but not limited to conventions, agreements, treaties, agreements qua norms, 'cascade' and 'internalise' into AFSJ rule-making in seventeen proposed and adopted directives as expressed in their recitals. Recitals offer an explicit and transparent indicator of origin, influence and objective for EU rule-making. In order to take into account the fact that legal instruments rather than policy are studied within this rubric of the life of norms, the account proposes to consider a limited and narrow 'lifespan' of norms within EU rule-making in a specific subject field, the AFSJ, as to directives since the coming into force of the Treaty of Lisbon – i.e. in the 2009–2014 'Stockholm Programme' legislative cycle.[11] It is limited because it is an examination of a short period of time and one type of instrument. Nor is implementation into the national context conducted. As a result, the account assumes that external norms have *already emerged* through their use in international rule-making processes and studies the process of what could be understood as their 'internalisation' within EU law, as norm emergence. It considers what practices and methods are used and in what form, and thus focuses upon the methodology surrounding and interlinking stages one to two of Finnemore's rubric without considering the empirical exercise of stage three. It assesses the relationship between EU rule-making practices and their link to the EU's role in international organisations so as to connect stages one and two.

9 Martha Finnemore, 'Norms, Culture and World Politics: Insights from Sociology's Institutionalism' (1996), 50; *IO*, 325. See n. 6, Finnemore and Sikkink, 893.

10 'Norm promotion' as a search term appears in approximately 600 hits in Westlaw International, 'world legal journals' search (last accessed 23 December 2015). See Jaye Ellis, 'Shades of Grey: Soft Law and the Validity of Public International Law' (2012), 25; *LJIL*, 313; at n. 5: 'Finnemore and Sikkink do not focus on legal norms; nevertheless, their discussion of the life cycle of international norms, at 895 ff., is highly illuminating for discussions of the emergence of international legal norms'. See also Katarina Linos, *The Democratic Foundations of Policy Diffusion* (Oxford University Press, 2013); cf. Julia Black, 'Constructing and Contesting Legitimacy and Accountability in Polycentric Regulatory Regimes' (2008), 2; *Regulation and Governance*, 137.

11 As the EU is at the end of its current legislative cycle and the end of the post-Lisbon transitional period. See Protocol No. 36 on transitional provisions. Cf. The Stockholm Programme – An open and secure Europe serving and protecting citizens [2010], *OJ C*/115, 1–38. Cf. Article 68 TFEU and the role of the European Council predominantly in setting new guidelines for the AFSJ. See European Council Conclusions 26/27 June 2014, *EUCO* 79/14 (Brussels, 27 June 2014).

Much former Third Pillar law took external norms – for example, Council of Europe Conventions – as its overarching inspiration. It is demonstrated here that nowadays external norms are deployed in most of the seventeen directives of the AFSJ's last legislative cycle. Most external norms relate to organisations or agreements that the EU is not a party to, nor are the member states necessarily party to it. Their deployment appears to signify both an 'inwards' and 'outwards' meaning – as benchmarks of rule-making and of openness to international best practice. Nevertheless, the absence of a reference to external norms in contemporary legal instruments can be particularly telling evidence of controversy and constitutional challenges. It is shown here that there are considerable variations in expressions of conformity to external norms and compliance therewith, and are not the basis of systematic study in legal scholarship. Most AFSJ directives are now expressed as minimum harmonisation directives to ensure their compliance with subsidiarity, but this is not always the case, warranting further study. This account shows how external norms offer a means to trace formulations of minimum and maximum harmonisation and their compliance with subsidiarity, which has significant effects upon sovereignty and member state autonomy. There is an increasing tendency to explicitly pin AFSJ law to ECHR case law through a variety of drafting formulations. While CJEU case law suggests that better and more detailed norm promotion is essential, a wide variety of norm promotion practices is evident.

The chapter makes a claim for the benefits of tracing textual methodologies for the study of EU rule-making in the broader scheme of understanding the relationship between internal and external EU action through law.[12] As the object of study, the promotion of norms in AFSJ rule-making reveals much about the evolution of the contours of the AFSJ itself – i.e. the relationship between the 'external' and 'internal', for example, in EU security, of use to many disciplines.[13] It may also assist us to comprehend the evolution of best practice in EU rule-making. The chapter demonstrates that the study of AFSJ rule-making by the EU demonstrates that the use of external norms in EU rule-making is in effect an internalisation of those norms. Yet their use and place in rule-making operates also as an expression of external norms. It is shown how currently the internalisation of external norms is less haphazard than the external expression of norms. The chapter shows how the EU almost always practises

12 To give an example of the nature and value of the study conducted here, international relations scholarship has typically focused upon *internalisation* in the EU's AFSJ rule-making. Such accounts of the EU as 'norm-taker' reflect an inaccurate role separation in rule-making processes, concerned instead with the meta-account of power in rule-making, less attentive to methodology. See Javier Argomaniz, 'When the EU is the 'norm taker': The Passenger Name Records Agreement and the EU's internalisation of US Border Security Norms' (2009), 31 *JEI* 119, 124.

13 Elaine Fahey, 'EU'S Cybercrime and Cyber Security Rule-Making: Mapping the Internal and External Dimensions of EU Security' (2014), 1; *EJRR*, 46; Christian Kaunert and Kamil Zwolski, *The EU as a Global Security Actor* (Palgrave, 2013); Bart Van Vooren, Steve Blockmans and Jan Wouters (eds), *The EU's Role in Global Governance: The Legal Dimension* (Oxford University Press, 2012); Florian Trauner and H. Carrapiço, 'The External Dimension of EU Justice and Home Affairs after the Lisbon Treaty: Analysing the Dynamics of Expansion and Diversification' (2012), 17; *EFAR*, 1.

some form of external norm primacy in directives, but more generally that the EU mainly practises haphazard norm promotion in its rule-making, more as to form than substance. Rule-making practice gives no indicator of international political processes but rather instead, demonstrate EU willingness to set, lead or follow international best practice.

In the first part of the chapter, the account outlines its instrument focus of directives in AFSJ rule-making and details the sample by subject area and by their descriptive characteristics. The next section (1) examines norm promotion practices, (2) considers the expression of legislative self-characterisation (stage one of the 'life of norms') and (3) considers in detail the formulation of 'norm cascade' into EU law (stage two of the 'life of norms'). It focuses in this regard upon the expression of EU–ECHR equivalence in EU legislation. The chapter then assesses stage three in the life of the norms – so-called international 'socialisation' – by examining the role of the EU and its member states in specific organisations and agreements. Thereafter, the final account examines the primacy of external norms as an overall process, by analysing the relationship between form and rationale, followed by conclusions.

Directives in the AFSJ: instruments for change?

Directives in the post-Lisbon legislative cycle

Directives in the AFSJ are a newish and ostensibly distinctive form of rule-making post-Lisbon. None of the treaties is so explicit about this development, nor are they considered to be of tremendous constitutional significance.[14] Nonetheless, they provide room for manoeuvre by member states in this evolving and sensitive field, bearing heavily upon sovereignty, especially in implementation, and worthy of not being so easily overlooked.[15] AFSJ directives post-Lisbon are often expressed as, justified and even legitimised from the perspective of subsidiarity as 'minimum' harmonisation directives.[16] Minimum harmonisation

14 The general regime of legal acts mentioned in Articles 288–294 TFEU applies to measures adopted in the AFSJ. Cf. the regularisation of the AFSJ in Title IV TFEU of the Consolidated Treaties of the European Union. Both standard and specialist textbook accounts of specific constitutional questions of EU law do not devote any space to this instrument – for example, Robert Schütze, *European Constitutional Law* (Cambridge University Press, 2013), 309 ff.

15 See Article 67(1), 69 and 72 TFEU for highly variable expressions of member state autonomy and competence vis à vis AFSJ rule-making. On the relevance of sovereignty from differing perspectives, Richard Rawlings, Peter Leyland and Alison L. Young, *Sovereignty and the Law – Domestic, European, and International Perspectives* (Oxford University Press, 2013).

16 In four of the sixteen directives considered here – for example, Directive 2013/48, recital 54: 'This Directive sets minimum rules. Member States may extend the rights set out in this Directive in order to provide a higher level of protection. Such higher level of protection should not constitute an obstacle to the mutual recognition of judicial decisions that those minimum rules are designed to facilitate. The level of protection should never fall below the standards provided by the Charter or by the ECHR, as interpreted by the case-law of the Court of Justice and of the European Court of Human Rights.'

directives were the norm in pre-Lisbon Third Pillar practice, in form and in substance.[17] They reflected the largely decentralised regulation of AFSJ matters in law, practice and institutional arrangements.[18] However, as will be considered below, the most recent legislative cycle reveals that this is not necessarily always the case and that the EU legislature has also adopted 'maximalist' criminalisation directives, where they have been perceived as necessary.[19]

Neither autonomy nor competence concerns have precluded their adoption in the most recent legislative cycle. Theoretically, a directive is understood to be more suited to having a coordinating rather than a consolidating role.[20] However, a feature of contemporary AFSJ rule-making is that a directive may, as a single instrument, unite a broad range of substantive and procedural issues for the AFSJ in ways not previously possible. Nonetheless, it may still permit, at least theoretically, Member State autonomy – e.g. through implementation or enforcement.[21] AFSJ directives may thus have a 'norm unifying' effect if it can incorporate a patchwork of existing instruments.[22] As Craig has stated, writing in 2010, the 'Member States' willingness to embrace EU intervention over crime at the "macro" level must, however, be balanced by difficulties of realisation at the "micro" level as attested by contestation over the content and passage of particular criminal measures without there being any 'logical inconsistency'".[23] Nonetheless, the legislator post-Lisbon has not necessarily respected the boundaries of this 'logical' inconsistency. Also, while EU directives embody a specific tension within EU law as to form and autonomy, the account here will demonstrate that external norm primacy remains a 'constant' within rule-making practices and perhaps expose how the choice of instrument is sometimes inconsequential. This is evidenced through the unconvincing rationales used to legislate for both maximalist *and* minimalist directives, explored further below.

17 See Stephen Coutts, 'The Lisbon Treaty and the Area of Freedom, Security and Justice as an Area of Legal Integration' (2011), 7; *CYELP*, 87, 103.

18 For example, see the proposal for a decentralised European public prosecutor drawn from national ranks or a European cybercrime centre based as a so-called 'desk' within Europol as evidence of this.

19 See pp. 72–74.

20 Alicia Hinerajos, *Judicial Control in the European Union Reforming Jurisdiction in the Intergovernmental Pillars* (Oxford University Press, 2009), 51.

21 Article 67 TFEU, for example, emphasises respect for the differing legal systems and traditions of the member states. See Valsamis Mitsilegas, *EU Criminal Law* (Hart, 2009).

22 Cf. the European Investigative Order (Directive 2014/41/EU of the European Parliament and of the Council of 3 April 2014 regarding the European Investigation Order in criminal matters: *OJ* L130, 11–36) on the transfer of evidence between member states purports to unify the rules drawn from a Council of Europe convention on mutual assistance in criminal matters and two protocols, the EU Convention on Mutual Assistance, the Framework Decision on the European arrest warrant and the Framework Decision on the execution of orders and freezing of property or evidence. See above, pp. 72–74.

23 Paul Craig, *The Lisbon Treaty: Law, Politics and Treaty Reform* (Oxford University Press, 2010), 372.

The meaning of cascading and 'internalisation' of norms is a specific one in the case of directives in the AFSJ. The degree of manoeuvre as to the external norm in implementation may be largely non-consequential. For example, the specific action to be taken by the member state may not necessarily have an effect upon the original meta-norm. Member State action may relate more to enforcement and compliance rather than standard-setting. Nevertheless, the exercise of tracing rule-making and disentangling the life of norms within this process can improve our understanding of norm interaction in EU law. By examining directives and not regulations or other types of legislation as a new form of legislation arising from the 'mainstreaming' of the AFSJ within the ordinary legislative procedures, the account produced here is a potentially a distinctive one for our understanding of EU rule-making 'top-down'. Further 'bottom-up' research on implementation in the AFSJ and also on regulations therein will be of significance, so as to understand the life of norms further.

The account here next considers the features of AFSJ directives considered.

Overview of subject areas

The instruments of the 2009–2014 legislative cycle examined here as set out in Figure 4.1 can be collected into five distinct themes – namely, accused and victims' rights, fighting serious crime /terrorism, third country nationals/asylum, and immigration and other crime-related fields. Matters related to third country nationals comprise the most numerous of these proposals,[24] while the accused and victims' rights agenda forms a close second thereto.[25] Their numerical

24 That is, Directive 2014/36 on the conditions of entry and residence of third-country nationals for the purposes of seasonal employment [2014], *OJ* L94/375; Proposal for a Directive on conditions of entry and residence of third-country nationals in the framework of an intra-corporate transfer 2010/0209 (COD); Directive 2011/98 on a single application procedure for a single permit for third-country nationals to reside and work in the territory of a member state and on a common set of rights for third-country workers legally residing in a member state [2011], *OJ* L343/1; Directive 2011/95 on standards for the qualification of third-country nationals or stateless persons as beneficiaries of international protection, for a uniform status for refugees or for persons eligible for subsidiary protection, and for the content of the protection granted [2011], *OJ* L337/9; proposal for a directive on the conditions of entry and residence of third-country nationals for the purposes of research, studies, pupil exchange, remunerated and unremunerated training, voluntary service and au pairing COM(2013), 151 final; Directive 2013/32 on common procedures for granting and withdrawing international protection [2013], *OJ* L180/60; Directive 2013/33 laying down standards for the reception of applicants for international protection [2013], *OJ* L180/96.

25 Directive 2010/64 on the right to interpretation and translation in criminal proceedings [2010], *OJ* L280/1, Directive 2012/29 establishing minimum standards on the rights, support and protection of victims of crime, and replacing Council Framework Decision 2001/220/JHA [2012], *OJ* L315/57; Directive 2012/13 on the right to information in criminal proceedings [2012], *OJ* L142/1; Directive 2011/99 on the European protection order [2011], *OJ* L338/2. A Regulation in the Road Map legislative is omitted in this account which only considers directives – that is, Regulation (EU) No. 606/2013 on mutual recognition of protection measures in civil matters [2013], *OJ* L181/4.

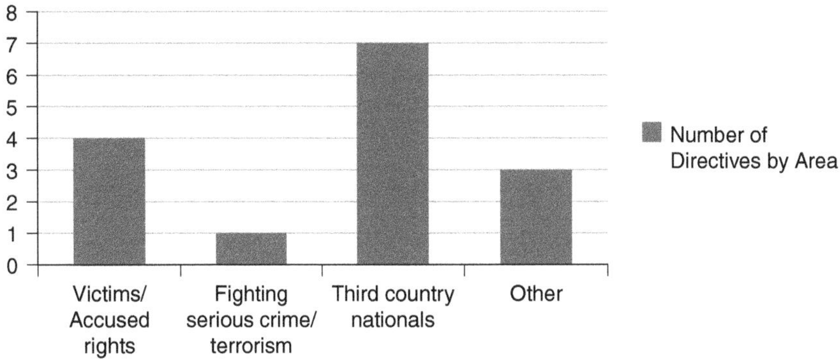

Figure 4.1 Number of directives by area.

concentration in these fields indicates the breadth of the legislative agenda in newer areas of competence as well as its success and its political salience. The selection of directives in these fields indicate a specific concern to afford member state autonomy as to matters traditionally at the heart of member state sovereignty – for example, procedural and substantive criminal law.

On a more practical level, three specific remarks may be made about the subject area of recent AFSJ directives in the last legislative cycle. First, the collection of directives analysed here does not appear to provide a very even implementation of the Stockholm Programme, touching upon only a small number of the themes in the Action Plan to implement the Stockholm Programme.[26] This outcome could indicate that directives were not considered a central instrument of the implementation of the Stockholm Programme post-Lisbon. Nor, as a second point, do they correspond to the priority areas of the AFSJ according to citizens' expectations. The only Eurobarometer special report on security-related themes in the post-Lisbon legislative cycle was publicised in late 2011 on 'Internal Security' commissioned by DG Home Affairs of the Commission, well after the publication date of many of the directives considered here.[27] Last, but not least, they do not necessarily correspond evenly to the split of the portfolios of the work of the two Directorates General of the European Commission tasked with the subject area of the AFSJ, Home Affairs and Justice, perhaps indicating that institutionalisation of portfolios is not necessarily of much practical significance, remaining instead an organisational

26 Delivering an area of freedom, security and justice for Europe's citizens: Action Plan Implementing the Stockholm Programme COM(2010) 171 final. It deployed the themes of ensuring the protection of fundamental rights, empowering citizens, strengthening the European judicial area, ensuring the security of Europe, global Europe and political priorities. The selection of directives is arguably mostly centred upon theme 2 (empowering citizens).

27 Citizens in this survey rated *inter alia* as the most important challenges to security economic and financial crises, organised crime, terrorism and poverty (registering 40, 39, 25 and 24 per cent respectively), Special Barometer 371, *Internal Security* (November 2011).

division only.[28] Future research and time will tell perhaps how precisely the role of directives has been in this period, but their subject spread is nonetheless a factor worthy of reflection.

The account then moves to the substantive exercise of identifying norm promotion in the last legislative cycle in directives.

Overview of 2009–2014 AFSJ directives

The directives and proposed directives of the latest legislative cycle are considered from the perspective of 'descriptive' characterisations followed by more 'analytical' characterisations of what is termed here as norm promotion. Norm promotion is understood to be the active process of the advancement of a norm. Descriptive characterisations include assessing *inter alia* how the directive mentions external norms in its recitals, their place therein and expression, their manner of referencing the Charter of Fundamental Rights and its compliance therewith, its express statements as to the case law of the European Convention on Human Rights, its analysis of studies of the impact of the legislation upon fundamental rights and even the omission of external norms. More analytical characterisations going beyond descriptive categorisations include the general distinctiveness of the legislation compared to other directives in the same field, the comparative analysis of subsidiary, proportionality and charter compliance, and particularly explicit statements of principle as to external norms. This account considers both of these characterisations hereafter for the sake of completeness.

As to their descriptive characterisations, the first and earliest EU criminal law directive enacted post-Lisbon was the Trafficking Directive, which drew from three external norms (UN Convention on the Rights of the Child, the International Labour Organisation Convention and the Convention on the Status of Refugees) and one internal norm, the Charter of Fundamental Rights.[29] Although a purely numerical calculation, this numerical formulation ('three plus one') tends to be in excess of most of the sixteen AFSJ directives thereafter. It raises the issue as to the relevance of norm promotion quantity from the perspective of the legislature, and then other readers, users and interpreters thereof, which is returned to below.

28 The AFSJ portfolio split in the European Commission is as follows: DG Home Affairs holds policy portfolios as to immigration, common European asylum system, organised crime and human trafficking, crisis and terrorism, Schengen, police cooperation, internal security and international affairs. DG Justice holds policy portfolios as to, *inter alia*, fundamental rights, citizenship and free movement, criminal justice, relations with third countries and effective justice.

29 Directive 2011/36 on preventing and combating trafficking in human beings and protecting its victims, and replacing Council Framework Decision 2002/629/JHA [2011], *OJ* L101/1, Recitals 8, 9 – that is, UN Convention on the Rights of the Child and the 2000 United Nations Protocol to Prevent, Suppress and Punish Trafficking in Persons, Especially Women and Children, the 1930 ILO Convention No. 29, concerning forced or compulsory labour and the 1951 Convention relating to the status of refugees – that is, the Geneva Convention.

The life of norms: stage one

EU norm promotion practices in AFSJ directives

In all seventeen directives examined here, *external* norms formed part thereof in thirteen directives. The most usual or dominant form of norm promotion that is evident in the directives is the assertion of compatibility with an *internal* legal source, most usually the Charter of Fundamental Rights (Charter hereafter).[30] By contrast, prior to EU accession to the European Convention on Human Rights (ECHR), certain fundamental rights norm promotion remain classifiable *stricto sensu* as *external* norms for the purposes of this study – for example, ECHR case law.[31] Otherwise, the external norms referred to include the General Agreement on Trade in Services (GATS), Economic Partnership Agreement with the CARIFORUM countries, UN Convention on the Rights of the Child, United Nations Convention on the Rights of Persons with Disabilities, UN Protocol to Prevent, Suppress and Punish Trafficking in Persons, ILO Convention concerning forced or compulsory labour, convention relating to the status of refugees/ Geneva Convention 1951, UN Convention on the Rights of the Child Optional Protocol, Second Optional Protocol on the Sale of Children, Child Prostitution and Child Pornography, Third Optional Protocol to the

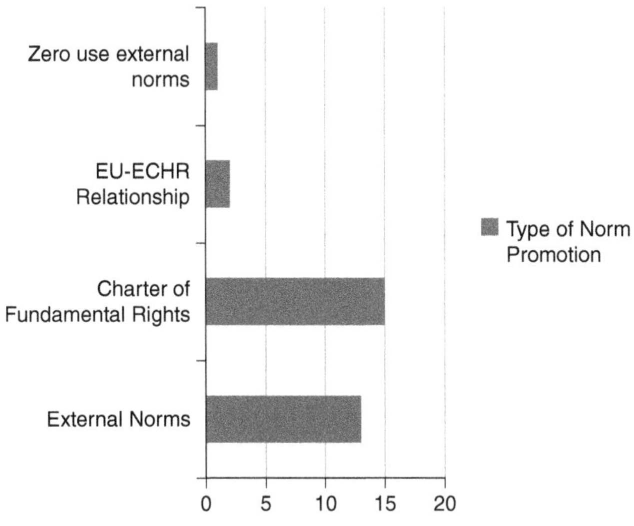

Figure 4.2 Type of norm promotion.

30 Which is on the same level as the EU treaties and now legally binding in Article 6(1) TEU. See Case C-555/07, *Kücükdeveci* v. *Swedex GmbH & Co*, EU:C:2010:21.

31 On the state of EU accession to the ECHR, the aftermath of Opinion 2/13 ECLI:C: 2014:2454 is not dealt with in this account.

Convention on the Rights of the Child on a communications procedure, Convention on the Protection of Children against Sexual Exploitation and Sexual Abuse, and the UN Convention on the Elimination of all Forms of Discrimination Against Women.[32]

While all AFSJ directives deploy the Charter, the strength of the commitment to compliance or mere respect and observance thereof differs considerably in its formulations.[33] And in three directives, a very specific formulation of EU–ECHR case law is provided for,[34] while in two of the directives there are no commitments to external norms whatsoever. For instance, perhaps striking is first the omission of external norm promotion in the proposed Passenger Name Records (PNR) Directive,[35] a controversial AFSJ measure post-Lisbon, proposing surveillance of EU citizen travel within the EU. Notably, it references the infamous EU–US PNR Agreements and PNR agreements with other countries alone and not other external norms.[36] In fact, in this instrument, these policies and their values are expressed with striking brevity. One might say here, then, that there may be a failure of transparency in EU rule-making as to its provenance, through the emasculation of its legislative history. Similarly, with regard to legislative omissions, one might expect legislation on a common set of rights for third country workers to include a wide array of external norms and sources because of its distinctive origins in international law.[37] However, the limited reference to external norms in such instruments appears all the more striking.[38] A failure to expound the normative influences upon EU rules can be inferred to emphasise its originality of controversial origins, its stringency in its original format, its challenges for

32 The specific role of the EU and its Member States in the membership of these norms is considered on pp. 76–77 above.

33 Only in some instances is the 'chain' between the Charter, international law agreements and conventions that the EU or its member states are party to and member state constitutions explicitly articulated. For example, see the exception: Directive 2014/41 regarding the European Investigation Order in criminal matters [2014], *OJ* L130/1, para. 39: 'This Directive respects the fundamental rights and observes the principles recognised by Article 6 of the TEU and in the Charter, notably Title VI thereof, by international law and international agreements to which the Union or all the Member States are party, including the European Convention for the Protection of Human Rights and Fundamental Freedoms, and in Member States' constitutions in their respective fields of application'. As to 'primary law', see art. 6, TEU.

34 As argued by Roos and Zaun, n. 7.

35 Proposal for a directive of the European Parliament and the Council on the use of Passenger Name Record data for the prevention, detection, investigation and prosecution of terrorist offences and serious crime 2011/23 (COD). The European Council called on the Council and Parliament to finalise work on the EU PNR proposal: European Council, 30 August 2014, p. 6, EUCO 163/14, 30 August 2014.

36 Agreements which have generated serious fundamental rights and data protection concerns: see Elaine Fahey, 'Law and Governance as Checks and Balances in Transatlantic Security: Rights, Redress, and Remedies in EU–US Passenger Name Records and the Terrorist Finance Tracking Program' (2013), 32 *YEL*, 368.

37 Roos and Zaun, n. 7.

38 For example, Directive 2011/98 refers only to the Charter of Fundamental Rights (third country workers' rights).

judicial review or its failure to balance fundamental rights concerns appropriately.[39] The work of the legislature here may rightfully generate concern, not least because of the strong objections of, for example, the Fundamental Rights Agency or the Data Protection Supervisor to this particular instrument.[40]

Remaining on the theme of norm omission, one of the most politically controversial measures of the recent legislative cycle worthy of mention is the European Investigative Order (EIO).[41] The EIO is a bold departure from traditional methods of evidence gathering, traditionally conducted through Mutual Legal Assistance. Even though this directive operates ostensibly as a broad patchwork quilt of norms, the only norm referenced in its recitals therein is the Charter.[42] Strikingly, the member states curtailed the European Commission's proposals on evidence gathering in favour of their own instrument through enhanced cooperation. It has received extensive critique for its scope (permitting investigation of any matter in Article 3, with little judicial control, thereby embodying the controversial means by which EU law continues to develop mutual recognition as a core principle.[43] Its controversy might be said to be evident through its establishment from enhanced cooperation, which in turn might be said to necessitate very explicit subsidiary and proportionality commitments. On the contrary, what may be observed therein is a common and prosaic recitation of subsidiarity.[44] This might be said to be a good example of where external norms (for example, ECHR case law) could have provided a useful legitimation template. Arguably, norm

39 Ibid.: cf. limited number of external norms deployed in Directive 2011/98, listing only the Charter in its recitals (31) rather than any labour or migrant-related instrument.

40 Opinion of the European Union Agency for Fundamental Rights FRA Opinion – 1/2011 Vienna, 14 June 2011; Opinion of the European Data Protection Supervisor 25 March 2011, https://secure.edps.europa.eu/EDPSWEB/webdav/shared/Documents/Consultation/Opinions/2011/11-03-25_PNR_EN.pdf, accessed 23 December 2015; Article 29, Working Party on Data Protection Opinion, no. 145 of 5.12.2007.

41 Fn. 32, Directive 2014/41. On its controversy, see EU Observer, 'New EU police investigation co-operation alarms civil liberties watchdogs': http://euobserver.com/justice/30553, accessed 23 December 2015.

42 Council of Europe Convention on Mutual Assistance in Criminal Matters of 20 April 1959 (and its two additional protocols); the Schengen Convention; the 2000 EU Convention on mutual assistance in criminal matters (and its Protocol); 2008 Framework Decision on the European evidence warrant; the 2003 Framework Decision on the execution in the European Union of orders freezing property or evidence (as regards freezing of evidence).

43 Debbie Sayers, 'The European Investigative Order: Travelling without a Roadmap' (2011), Centre for European Policy Studies Brief; Steve Peers, 'The Proposed European Investigation Order: Assault on Human Rights and National Sovereignty', *Statewatch Analysis* (May 2010): www.statewatch.org/analyses/no-96-european-investigation-order.pdf, accessed 23 December 2015; Steve Peers and Emilio De Capitani, 'The European Investigation Order: Shaping a New Approach to Mutual Recognition in Criminal Matters' (22 May 2014): http://theme.wordpress.com/credits/free-group.eu/, accessed 23 December 2015.

44 That is: 'Since the objective of this Directive, namely the mutual recognition of decisions taken to obtain evidence, cannot be sufficiently achieved by the Member States but can rather, by reason of its scale and effects, be better achieved at Union level, the Union may adopt measures in accordance with the principle of subsidiarity as set out in Article 5 of the TEU.'

promotion should be particularly detailed in instruments of enhanced cooperation so as to gain legitimation, given their propensity to generate *inter alia* subsidiarity and proportionality concerns.[45] Judicial practice in the post-Lisbon era appears to give less than subtle indications about the role of the legislator in this regard,[46] creating an impetus for more and better norm promotion.

This leads to the need to reflect beyond descriptive characterisations upon the expression of form, source and substance in legislative method. They reach into broader questions of legislative expression, considered here next, where the more analytical characterisations of directives are considered.

Legislative 'self-characterisations'

While 'law' performs an important communicative function, law is not an agent and cannot speak, lacking personality or personification.[47] Nonetheless, all EU legislation not limited to directives carries strong expressive statements of intent and objective, referred to here as 'self-characterisation'. It entails factual and assertive statements as to the effects of legislation. Transparency and openness might be said to be usual motivating factors in this regard, as well as the amenability of legislation to judicial review. The contemporary era of EU law post-Lisbon is one of strikingly 'strong' judicial review. One may say that several recent high-profile fundamental rights decisions as to data and privacy rights demonstrate how formulations of subsidiarity, proportionality and fundamental rights compliance as communications have never been more important.[48] This in turn generates a distinctive communicative character to the checks and balances taking place between the institutions and how they or their feedback are communicated into the legislative process.

Similarly, while subsidiarity has acquired a heightened constitutional significance in EU law, recent AFSJ directives may not necessarily demonstrate this.[49] Recent AFSJ directives are often expressed as 'minimum' legislation and in turn are self-expressed to be compliant with, respect and promote *inter alia* the Charter and

45 And more recently, their propensity to be litigated: Joined Cases C-274/11 and C–295/11 *Spain and Italy* v. *Council* (unitary patent) EU:C:2013:240; C–209/13 *United Kingdom* v. *Council* EU:C:2014:283 (Financial Transaction Tax).

46 For example, in the data retention litigation.

47 Albeit without defining what law is: see Cass Sunstein, 'On the expressive function of law' (1995), 144; U Penn LR 2021, 2024; but see Matthew Adler, 'Expressive Theories of Law: A Skeptical Overview' (2000), 148 U Penn, LR 1363.

48 For example, see the (unusually) detailed data retention decision, where the ECJ took issue with subsidiarity and proportionality commitments in legislation: Joined Cases C–293/12 and C–594/12, *Digital Rights Ireland and Seitlinger and Others*, EU:C:2014:238.

49 On Protocol No. 2 on the application of the principles of subsidiarity and proportionality being taken seriously by national parliaments, see the high-profile yet numerically limited objections to the right to strike legislation (Monti II) and the Proposal for a Council Regulation on the establishment of the European Public Prosecutor's Office. Subsidiarity compliance practices of the Commission in response to national parliaments may perhaps be criticised for their formalistic and artificial nature.

subsidiarity because of this self-expressed minimalist character.[50] They raise the question about their persuasiveness, reliability and accuracy. Minimalist harmonisation is not the only 'constitutional' characteristic of an AFSJ directive. Thus, a recent directive imposing far-reaching criminal penalties in the area of sexual abuse and exploitation of children explicitly *justifies* its characterisation beyond 'minimalist legislation' because of the exceptionalist treatment that the subject area demands – i.e. it is thus expressly non-minimalist legislation.[51] Yet one may question the legitimacy of this formulation and its compliance with subsidiarity, or at the very least how compelling this is in reality. Beyond this, external norms might have provided for more compelling legitimation thereof.

In a similar vein, another formula for norm promotion in proposed AFSJ directives are self-characterised assertions of its *positive* impact upon fundamental rights.[52] And many other Directives boldly and factually assert compliance with fundamental rights.[53] These assertions are quite striking if we reflect on whether they are bland 'puffs'[54] or more likely to influence judicial views on ECHR equivalence. Is it an important shift in the normative turn of the EU, striving to act as a 'good' global governance actor?[55] Nonetheless, in the era where the CJEU is striking down legislation with greater regularity where fundamental

50 For example, on its minimalist character: n. 25, Directive 2012/29, recitals 6 and 14. See also Directive 2014/42 on the freezing and confiscation of instrumentalities and proceeds of crime in the European Union [2014], *OJ* L127/39, Art. 8 'With a view to fully comply with the Charter of Fundamental Rights, this Article introduces minimum safeguards at EU level.' See also Directive 2013/48, recital 54. On fundamental rights compliance: n. 24, Directive 2011/95 in recital 16: 'This Directive respects the fundamental rights and observes the principles recognised in particular by the Charter of Fundamental Rights of the European Union. … this Directive seeks to … promote the application of Articles 1, 7, 11, 14, 15, 16, 18, 21, 24, 34 and 35 of that Charter …' Cf. n. 35, Proposal for Passenger Name Records Directive, recital 31: 'The Proposal is fully in line with the overall objective of creating a European area of freedom, security and justice …'

51 Directive 2011/93 on combating sexual abuse and sexual exploitation of children, and child pornography, replacing the Council Framework-Decision 2004/68/JHA [2011], *OJ* L 335/1, for example, recital 11: 'This Directive, because it contains an exceptionally high number of different offences, requires, in order to reflect the various degrees of seriousness, a differentiation in the level of penalties which goes further than what should usually be provided in Union legal instruments.'

52 Cf. Proposed Directive of the European Parliament and of the Council on the conditions of entry and residence of third-country nationals for the purposes of research, studies, pupil exchange, remunerated and unremunerated training, voluntary service and au pairing, COM (2013) 151 final: 'This Proposal has positive effects on fundamental rights, as it strengthens third-country nationals' procedural rights and recognises and safeguards the rights of remunerated trainees and au-pairs. In this respect, it is consistent with the … Charter of Fundamental Rights.'

53 Cf. Proposal for a Directive of the European Parliament and of the Council on conditions of entry and residence of third-country nationals in the framework of an intra-corporate transfer, 2010/0209 (COD), recital 27: 'This Proposal complies with fundamental rights … as it recognises and safeguards the principle of equal treatment for intra-corporate transferees and includes procedural guarantees and the right to family life.'

54 A 'puff' is the exaggeration of the strong or desirable feature of an entity or object that is generally not justifiable.

55 Cf. art. 21 TEU.

rights are at stake,[56] the legislature arguably needs to be considerably more cautious about the expression of positive effects upon fundamental rights as self-expressions of norm promotion.[57]

While grand statements as to the benefits of a directive may cause one to doubt the persuasiveness of the character of norm promotion as puff-like, nevertheless norm promotion still goes beyond discussions of the use of legislative history, or *travaux preparatoires*, in so far as it represents the concrete end product of the legislative process. Factual compliance assertions ostensibly encourage a markedly literal approach to legislative interpretation. Such an approach would be the antithesis of judicial practice conducted in EU law for some time.[58] And current trends in judicial review arguably support the significance of rather explicit norm promotion rather than legislative puffs or overly literal constructions. Whether the approaches of the legislature formulating minimalist and maximalist directives, or self-expressed rights compliance, tallies with this in the eyes of the Court of Justice remains to be seen.

One more specific area of the AFSJ and norm promotion for consideration is the formulation of EU–ECHR equivalence, considered in the following section within the idea of 'norm cascades', which form Stage 2 in the life of norms, as part of the phenomenon of socialisation.

Norm cascade into EU law: EU–ECHR 'equivalence' in EU law

The second stage of the life of norms concerns norm cascades. Norm cascades are understood to occur where societies are presented with rapid shifts to new

56 For example, recent decisions of the ECJ in *Digital Rights Ireland and Seitlinger and Others* n. 47; C–131/12 *Google Spain SL, Google Inc.* v. *Agencia Española de Protección de Datos (AEPD), Mario Costeja González* EU:C:2014:317; Case C–362/14, *Schrems* v. *Data Protection Commissioner* EU:C:2015:6.

57 Recital 37: 'This Directive should respect the fundamental rights guaranteed by the Charter of Fundamental Rights of the European Union and by the European Convention for the Protection of Human Rights and Fundamental Freedoms, in accordance with Article 6 TEU.' Cf. see the distinctive difference in emphasis between the EU and member state obligations Directive 2013/33 laying down standards for the reception of applicants for international protection: Recital 9, 'In applying this Directive, Member States should seek to ensure full compliance with the principles of the best interests of the child and of family unity, in accordance with the Charter of Fundamental Rights of the European Union, the 1989 United Nations Convention on the Rights of the Child and the European Convention for the Protection of Human Rights and Fundamental Freedoms respectively' or recital 35: 'This Directive respects the fundamental rights and observes the principles recognised in particular by the Charter ... and to promote the application of Articles 1, 4, 6, 7, 18, 21, 24 and 47 of the Charter and has to be implemented accordingly.'

58 For example, extra-judicially Nial Fennelly, 'Legal Interpretation at the European Court of Justice' (1996), 20 Fordham *ILJ* 656; Miguel P. Maduro, 'Interpreting European Law: Judicial Adjudication in a Context of Constitutional Pluralism' (2007), 1 *EJLS* 1. On the use of *travaux preparatoires*, see their evolution charted by Gerard Conway, *The Limits of Legal Reasoning and the European Court of Justice* (Cambridge University Press, 2012), pp. 255–257. Albeit encouraged more recently in citizen-related case law – for example, data retention decision, supra n. 56.

norms.[59] EU accession to the ECHR and the acceptance of the ECHR acquis may neatly be depicted as a process of norm cascade.[60] A particular formulation of norm promotion of note in recent AFSJ directives is what is described here as 'EU–ECHR equivalence' – i.e. the legislature's efforts to explicitly 'pin' EU law to ECHR norms, case law and standards in EU legislation. The nature of norm promotion has taken a particular semantic turn in one specific field – namely, the accused and victims' rights, a core part of the Stockholm Programme legislative agenda.[61] For example, three directives have been adopted pursuant to the road map for strengthening procedural rights under the objective of strengthening mutual trust between judicial authorities in the area of defence rights (interpretation and translation, victims' rights and information rights).[62] It is commonly said that the directives mark a milestone in EU integration inspired by ECHR case law – for example, on access to a lawyer. Certain directives of this package have recently been mirrored or even developed further in various member states' courts, thereby functioning as a threshold.[63] Nonetheless, there are certain variants in EU–ECHR equivalence clauses in these directives and, accordingly, these directives are worthy of note.

The latest directive on the information rights of the accused establishes its core principle on the basis of ECHR law – for example, 'The right to information about procedural rights, which is inferred from the case-law of the European Court of Human Rights, should be explicitly established by this Directive' – and contains highly specific equivalence provisions.[64] For example, it provides that '[t]he provisions of this Directive that correspond to rights guaranteed by the ECHR should be interpreted and implemented consistently with those rights, as interpreted in the case-law of the European Court of Human Rights'.[65] It may be contrasted against considerably more nuanced variants of this in later road-map directives, such as the directive on the right of access to a lawyer provided that the conditions in which suspects or accused persons are deprived of liberty 'should fully respect the standards set out in the ECHR ... and in the case-law

59 Cass Sunstein, 'Social Norms and Social Rules' (1995) *John M. Olin Law & Economics Working Paper* No. 36 (2D Series): www.law.uchicago.edu/files/files/36.Sunstein.Social_0.pdf, accessed 23 December 2015, especially citations at n. 16.

60 Per Finnemore and Sikkink. These processes often involve studying how processes induce norm breakers to be norm followers: 902. The present account does not attempt such a study, assuming that all EU member states cannot be presumed to be such norm breakers. M. Finnemore, *National Interests in International Society* (Cornell University Press, 1996).

61 The so-called 'Roadmap' Procedural rights in criminal proceedings Luxembourg (23 October 2009) 14828/09: http://ec.europa.eu/justice/criminal/criminal-rights/index_en.htm, accessed 23 December 2015. Communication from the Commission to the European Parliament, the Council, the Economic and Social Committee and the Committee of the Regions *Strengthening victims' rights in the EU* COM(2011), 274 final.

62 See the accused and victims' rights directives, supra n. 25.

63 For example, on access to a lawyer: *Salduz* v. *Turkey* Application No. 36391/02 [2008], *ECHR* 1542; *Cadder* v. *Her Majesty's Advocate* [2010], UKSC 43 (UK Supreme Court).

64 Directive 2012/13, recital 18.

65 Ibid., recital 42. See similarly Directive 2010/64, recitals 32 and 33.

of the Court of Justice ... and the European Court of Human Rights'.[66] Recent AFSJ case law before the Court of Justice underscores the caution suggested here on statements of equivalence. Take, for example, the recent case of *Baláž*, where Advocate General Sharpston was confronted with considering a particular Austrian Court and whether it was a Court with jurisdiction within the meaning of Framework Decision 2005/214/JHA, having been previously so found to be a tribunal within the meaning of Article 6(1) ECHR by the European Court of Human Rights itself.[67] Instead of following directly the clear conclusions of the ECHR, Advocate General Sharpston sought to leave the final determination of the question to the member state Court. While *Baláž* relates to pre-Lisbon legislation, it neatly demonstrates how direct statements of 'equivalence' may not permit sufficient space for the operation of judicial discretion – for example, within the preliminary reference procedure. This is precisely the danger of 'pinning' EU law directly to ECHR law in legislation. There remains at the time of writing some concern over future formulation of the 'rebuttable presumption of equivalence' in case law on the relationship between the EU and ECHR legal orders,[68] against the backdrop of the development of the EU–ECHR Accession Agreement.[69] Arguably, the legislature should tread with caution in its efforts to procure 'norm cascades' here through statements of equivalence.

These considerations of the analytical features of the directives necessitate further reflection on how best to understand EU norm promotion. The next section thus considers the place of so-called 'socialisation' within the life of norms. It assesses the place of the EU and its member states in specific organisations and agreements that it promotes. It is followed by analysis of the relationship between form and rationale of norm promotion in directives.

Stage two of the life of norms: 'international socialisation'

The role of the EU and its member states in external norms promoted in EU law

The second stage of the theorisation of the life of norms, 'norm cascade' involves the broader process of the 'socialisation' or acceptance of a norm into, for example, a legal order. When others are persuaded to support normative change and there is an inducement to adhere to a norm, then a norm cascade occurs. Actors, usually Member States, are understood to become exposed to common norms, procedures

66 Recital 2013/48, recital 29.

67 Case C–60/12 *Marian Baláž* EU:C:2013:733, Opinion of Advocate General Sharpston 18 July 2013 (as to the *Unabhängiger Verwaltungssenat*). This line of argument is nowhere to be found in the decision of the Court of 14 November 2013.

68 From a vast literature, see Vicky Kosta, Nikos Skoutaris and Vassilis Tzevelekos (eds), *The EU Accession to the ECHR* (Hart, 2014); Paul Grägl, *The Accession of the European Union to the European Convention on Human Rights* (Hart, 2013); On rebuttable equivalence, see *Bosphorus Hava Yollari Turizm ve Ticaret Anonim Sirketi* v. *Ireland* (App. No. 45036/98) Judgement of 30 June 2006, ECtHR 20005–VI.

and a way of doing things, whereby they incorporate them. The process of exposure and thereby socialisation can be constructed through EU actors as norm entrepreneurs through social interpretation, common projects and social learning. As Koops states, both forms of socialisation are integral to understanding the Europeanisation of member state policies.[70] Socialisation does not just mean norm diffusion and can relate to common concrete projects.[71] The integration of norms as socialisation may be theoretical, institutional or operational and it is this broad focus which is deployed here to consider the overall process taking place.

Should the EU adequately promote the external norms/instruments to the same degree within the legislative process as the international political process so as to institutionally socialise its operation? And should AFSJ directives over any other form of instruments be any different? The instruments promoted in the seventeen directives considered here thus include two specific 'internal' norms and the remainder are analysed here as 'external' norms: thus, the convention on mutual assistance in criminal matters between the member states of the European Union[72] or the European Social Charter 1961[73] are EU-specific instruments and are thus classifiable as 'internal' instruments. By contrast, the 'external' norms as referred to here, found in all other AFSJ directives, include the General Agreement on Trade in Services (GATS),[74] Economic Partnership Agreement with the CARIFORUM countries,[75] European Convention for the Protection of Human Rights and Fundamental Freedoms,[76] UN Convention on the Rights of

69 Which does not explicitly detail as much: Fifth Negotiation Meeting Between The CDDH Ad Hoc Negotiation Group and the European Commission On The Accession of the European Union to the European Convention On Human Rights 47+1(2013)008rev2 Strasbourg, 10 June 2013 Final report to the CDDH, www.coe.int/t/dghl/standardsetting/hrpolicy/Accession/Meeting_reports/47_1(2013)008rev2_EN.pdf, accessed 23 December 2015. An opinion from the Court of Justice sought pursuant to art. 218(11) TFEU by the Commission, on whether the Draft Accession Agreement is compatible with the constituent treaties of the European Union is still pending (Opinion 1/14).

70 The evolution of the AFSJ is understood here to some extent as a form of Europeanisation of Member States justice policies. Cf. Joachim Koops, *The European Union as an Integrative Power: Assessing the EU's Effective Multilateralism towards NATO and the United Nations* (VU Press, 2011), 215.

71 On the EU as an integrative power, see Koops, ibid., p. 213.

72 28 parties, member states of the European Union: http://eur-lex.europa.eu/legal-content/EN/ALL/;ELX_SESSIONID=z61PThcWYbLtpq8wyGpN90VSqn1byQwqV21Vq9R0kQGCK2X9DJGc!-694022248?uri=CELEX:42001A1121%2801%29, accessed 23 December 2015.

73 47 parties, 28 EU member states' governments signatory hereto, being members of the Council of Europe: http://conventions.coe.int/Treaty/en/Treaties/Html/163.htm, accessed 23 December 2015.

74 159 members, all 28 EU MS members, EU a member, all members of the WTO are signatories to the GATS: www.wto.org/english/docs_e/legal_e/26-gats.pdf, accessed 23 December 2015.

75 43 parties, 27 EU MS except Croatia, EU a member: http://ec.europa.eu/world/agreements/prepareCreateTreatiesWorkspace/treatiesGeneralData.do?redirect=true&treatyId=7407, accessed 23 December 2015.

76 The governments' signatory hereto, being members of the Council of Europe, 28 EU Member States (MS), http://conventions.coe.int/treaty/en/treaties/html/005.htm, accessed 23 December 2015. As amended by the Lisbon Treaty, art. 6(2) TEU provides that the European Union 'shall accede' to the Convention for the Protection of Human Rights.

the Child,[77] United Nations Convention on the Rights of Persons with Disabilities,[78] UN Protocol to Prevent, Suppress and Punish Trafficking in Persons,[79] ILO Convention Concerning Forced or Compulsory Labour,[80] Convention Relating to the Status of Refugees/Geneva Convention 1951,[81] UN Convention on the Rights of the Child Optional Protocol,[82] Second Optional Protocol on the Sale of Children, Child Prostitution and Child Pornography,[83] Third Optional Protocol to the Convention on the Rights of the Child on a Communications Procedure,[84] Convention on the Protection of Children Against Sexual Exploitation and Sexual Abuse[85] and the UN Convention on the Elimination of All Forms of Discrimination Against Women.[86]

A number of the agreements, treaties or conventions used by the EU in AFSJ directives have not been ratified by all of the member states themselves.[87] Nonetheless, the vast majority of external norms involve all member states as parties and contrariwise, the EU is not a party itself to many of the instruments used. The role of the EU as an organisation has been suggested to be highly exceptional and successful within certain international rule-making processes – for example, at the UN Convention on Disabilities, where it succeeded in exporting its governance norms.[88] It demonstrates the relevance of norm promotion for the study of global governance. Nevertheless, take the example of the UN

77 194 Parties, all EU MS are parties: https://treaties.un.org/pages/ViewDetails.aspx?src=TREATY&mtdsg_no=IV-11&chapter=4&lang=en, accessed 23 December 2015.

78 147 parties, all EU MS are parties, EU is a party: https://treaties.un.org/Pages/ViewDetails.aspx?src=TREATY&mtdsg_no=iv-15&chapter=4&lang=en, accessed 23 December 2015.

79 159 parties, 27 EU MS are parties, except Czech Republic, EU is a party: https://treaties.un.org/Pages/ViewDetails.aspx?mtdsg_no=XVIII-12-a&chapter=18&lang=en, accessed 23 December 2015.

80 177 parties, all EU MS are parties: www.ilo.org/dyn/normlex/en/f?p=1000:11300:0::NO:11300:P11300_INSTRUMENT_ID:312174, accessed 23 December 2015.

81 145 parties, all EU MS are parties: https://treaties.un.org/Pages/ViewDetailsII.aspx?&src=UNTSONLINE&mtdsg no=V~2&chapter=5&Temp=mtdsg2&lang=en#Participants, accessed 23 December 2015.

82 First Optional Protocol on the Involvement of Children in Armed Conflict, 155 parties, all EU MS are parties: https://treaties.un.org/pages/ViewDetails.aspx?src=TREATY&mtdsg_no=IV-11-b&chapter=4&lang=en, accessed 23 December 2015.

83 167 parties, all EU MS are parties, https://treaties.un.org/Pages/ViewDetails.aspx?mtdsg no=IV-11-c&chapter=4&lang=en, accessed 23 December 2015.

84 11 parties, 5 EU MS are parties: https://treaties.un.org/pages/viewdetails.aspx?src=treaty&mtdsg_no=iv-11-d&chapter=4&lang=en, accessed 23 December 2015.

85 31 parties, 18 EU MS are parties: www.conventions.coe.int/Treaty/Commun/ChercheSig.asp?NT=201&CM=1&DF=&CL=ENG, accessed 23 December 2015.

86 188 parties, all EU MS are parties: https://treaties.un.org/Pages/ViewDetails.aspx?src=TREATY&mtdsg_no=IV-8&chapter=4&lang=en, accessed 23 December 2015.

87 As outlined in all of the preceding footnotes. More generally, see Jan Wouters, 'The Institutional Structure of EU External Relations' in Takis Tridimas and Robert Schütze (eds), *Oxford Principles of European Union Law* (forthcoming); see also Pieter Jan Kuijper, Jan Wouters, Geert De Baere and Thomas Ramopoulos, *The Law of EU External Relations Cases, Materials, and Commentary on the EU as an International Legal Actor* (2nd edn, Oxford University Press, 2015).

88 Grainne De Búrca, 'The EU in the Negotiation of the UN Disability Convention' (2010), 35 *ELR* 174.

Convention on the Rights of the Child, which features extensively in recent AFSJ directives, which the EU is not a party to.[89] Should its use and place in AFSJ directives necessarily have any formal significance? Arguably, there is little by way of causal links between norm promotion in AFSJ directives and international political processes to conclude that 'active' international socialisation takes place. The EU's membership thereof is not necessarily of legal significance in AFSJ directives. However, conversely, EU law appears to remain extremely open to the integration of external norms and processes of socialisation, irrespective of its status in international organisations and irrespective of the desire to respect member state sovereignty or autonomy or enforcement through the vehicle of a directive. It may underscore the aesthetic qualities of norm promotion practices as sometimes practised by the EU. More generally, it also indicates the clear primacy of external norms in AFSJ rule-making and EU openness to both following and leading international practice. However, beyond this, without studying a broader array of legislation or the implementation of a directive in all the member states, further conclusions are difficult to draw but will also form a useful area of future study.[90]

The next section considers further the relationship between form and rationale in norm promotion, and the primacy of external norms in rule-making practice.

Assessing the primacy of external norms in EU rule-making: from form to rationale

The present account reveals thus many inconsistencies in rule-making practice but also certain rule-making patterns in the socialisation process of external norms into EU rule-making; nonetheless, they are largely questions of form. Moving beyond form to rationale, three specific features thereof are hypothised here. First, it may be said that 'strong' over 'weak' assertions of norm promotion (detail, length, listing of multiple concerns, broad justifications, compliance assertions) tend to take place in areas of particular sensitivity between Member States and the EU, as to their innately cross-border or transnational character – for example, the directive on minimum standards for the victims of crime, or the Trafficking Directive. Second, 'detailed' over less 'detailed' formulations of norm

89 See n. 24, Directive 2013/33 (International protection); Directive 2013/32 (international protection); Directive 2012/29 (victims' rights); Directive 2011/95 (international protection); Directive 2011/93 (sexual abuse and sexual exploitation of children and child pornography).

90 Non-legal scholars argue that EU law frequently reaches for external norms such as the UN International Convention on the Protection of all Migrant Workers and their Families and the Council of Europe Convention on the legal status of migrant workers, albeit which most EU states are not party to, because of their asserted 'robustness'. See n. 7, Roos and Zaun, 61–62. In order to measure the *impact* of international norms, international relations scholars have argued that their robustness can be measured, as to their specific, definition, binding force, coherence under domestic law and international law and understanding among actors. However, to measure such impact from a legal perspective would arguably amount to a much larger study of case law, legislation, policy and doctrine that goes beyond the scope of the exercise conducted here.

promotion might include, for example, specificity, length, multiple ECHR article references, impact assessment references referring in detail to stakeholders' assertions, and tend to explicitly express the avoidance of externalities – i.e. with regard to external legal orders or beyond the EU – for example, in the directive on translation and interpretation rights or information rights for the accused. Yet, for example, while instruments such as the Passenger Name Records Directive (PNR) may extensively assess its impact upon stakeholders during the legislative process,[91] it simultaneously omits a detailed engagement with its external norms in its current form. Third, the expression of more external rather than fewer internal norms tends to be couched in areas where the EU acts as a 'leader' in best transnational practices – for example, in the Directive on Trafficking.

However, what the promotion of norms in EU legislation actually reveals remains the overarching question. For all of its haphazard qualities, this account has revealed a consistent commitment to the primacy of external norms in EU law, even in an era of more internal legal instruments for fundamental rights at its disposal. For example, the approach of the EU legislator itself appears somewhat 'scattergun', by haphazardly referencing the Charter, the treaties and national constitutions in new directives. The relationship between the justificatory nature of legislation and their specific external influences remains strikingly non-systematic. And the *impact* of instruments rather than their provenance might appear the dominant concern in EU rule-making instruments so as to satisfy Charter, fundamental rights and proportionality concerns, albeit aesthetically. Yet the advent of directives in the AFSJ surely raises manifold issues of discretion and even sovereignty. The provenance, ambitions and objectives of directives arguably require more careful and consistent formulation, in an era where norm promotion specificity and transparency have become more essential.

The opposite of haphazard practice might be standardisation or systematisation and that this might be argued to be a more laudable focus of AFSJ rule-making. However, there may be shortcomings to EU standardisation of practice in rule-making. For example, efforts on the part of the EU to systematise the EU's integration of internal and external norms appear often more cosmetic or aesthetic than substantive. After the entry into force of the Treaty of Lisbon, the EU Commission Treaties Office sought to systematise transparently all EU agreements with a bilateral or multilateral dimension by categorising the use by the EU of human rights 'evolution' and territorial clauses.[92] In doing so, it sought to bring transparency to the EU's external reach through law. Such categorisations, however imperfect, constitute useful tools so as to understand the nature of EU

91 COM(2011) 32, final, 6.

92 Treaties Office, Database of the European External Action Service: http://ec.europa.eu/world/agreements/viewCollection.do?fileID=67962, accessed 23 December 2015.

rule-making practices. And while there is much merit to such transparency, such typologies may reveal diverse and haphazard practices, inspired more by aesthetic 'transparency' than by more substantive ideals.

The study of AFSJ rule-making by the EU demonstrates that the use of external norms as part of EU rule-making is in effect an *internalisation* of those norms. Yet their use and place in rule-making operates also as an expression of *external* norms. The present work reveals that there are considerable variations in the detail of expression, strength of compliance and number of instruments and values promoted. They indicate haphazardness of form over substance in rule-making practice. The haphazardness commonly spoken of as to EU norm promotion practices is shown here not necessarily to pertain to standards but rather to form and practice. Nonetheless, this is not to trivialise textual expressions. Banal compliance assertions in legislation as to any individual instrument may have a detrimental impact upon jurisprudence in the longer term. Similarly, ill-expressed or overly detailed statements on the relationship between internal and external legal orders may also be less than beneficial in the future. Norm promotion in AFSJ directives offers a particular perspective on the development of the EU as a legislator and actor in the world, signifying a very clear gap between legislative, political and perhaps even judicial processes that may yet prove problematic. Tracing norm promotion offers a broader methodology to view how the EU evolves as an organisation. Currently, the internalisation of external norms is less haphazard than the external expression of norms. The EU in the main consistently strives for best practice and for standard-setting. However, exceptions to practice remain and are very revealing as to controversies in the area of the AFSJ. Banal compliance assertions may, of course, result from heavy proceduralisation of the legislative process, and this remains ripe for further explanation.

Tracing the promotion of norms in AFSJ rule-making reveals much about the evolution of the shifting contours of the AFSJ itself. It offers specific insights into the evolving relationship between the 'external' and 'internal' in the AFSJ. More broadly, tracing textual methodologies provides evidence of the evolution of practice. It offers a clear demarcation of the evolution of the EU itself. From the perspective of the social acceptance of its rules, its attempts to co-opt third countries and international organisations into its rules, as explored in detail in Chapter 2, may carry less force as a result. This may be more acute in the Area of Freedom, Security and Justice than in other fields, and is explored in Chapters 5 and 6.

Conclusions

This chapter has considered two central themes – one being the operation of contemporary norm promotion in legal instruments of the AFSJ and the other being the character of directives in the AFSJ as an instrument in the last legislative cycle. In doing so, the chapter has attempted to make two broader methodological claims. First, tracing norm promotion practices has been shown to be insightful for our understanding of this legislative cycle as much as the development of EU rule-making itself. It has further demonstrated that the EU mainly practises haphazard norm promotion in its rule-making and how the EU almost always practises some form of external norm primacy in directives. These practices give no indicator of international political processes but rather instead, demonstrate EU willingness to set, lead or follow international best practice.

Second, the chapter has demonstrated how many possible risks run through the haphazard formulations of norm primacy in rule-making. One of the most serious risks of the haphazardness of the formulation of values in the AFSJ is their non-consequential effects. Their variable expression in legislation runs the risk that legislation which necessitates literal understandings of norm promotion may get overlooked or will not be adequately promoted in practice, inside or outside courtrooms. Another risk is that the formulation of norm promotion may have unintended consequences or imprison judicial actors in a manner which is artificial or inflexible. For example, it may go beyond the letter of the instrument itself, putting specific emphasis on one core value over another. The two claims made demonstrate how internal and external rule-making practices require 'joined-up scrutiny' so as to understand the evolution of the EU and its rule-making practices in the evolving field of the AFSJ.

5 Tracing transatlantic rule-transfer

Introduction

The European Union (EU) Internal Security Strategy of the first post-Lisbon legislative cycle and its implementation strategy were striking for their legal taxonomy of 'internal security'.[1] Notably, it included many EU–US Justice and Home Affairs (JHA) measures in its midst, including the EU–US Passenger Name Records (EU–US PNR) Agreements and EU–US Terrorist Financial Tracking Programme (EU–US TFTP) agreements.[2] Moreover, it alluded to the success of the EU–US Cyber Security and Cyber Crime Working Group (WGCC) in delivering results so as to warrant further *and related* internal EU rule-making.[3] Far from being fortuitous or gratuitous references in a text, there are many EU security policies currently being pursued which have clear 'imprints' of EU–US policies – for example, an EU PNR[4] and an EU TFTS,[5] mirroring EU–US PNR and EU–US TFTP. Put another way, EU 'internal' security readily embraces 'external' transatlantic security but similarly EU security rules under development may be said to demonstrate the migratory effects of EU–US legal rules by way of some form of rule transposition or 'rule-transfer,' as defined and developed in this account.[6] The EU has sought to establish a global approach for

1 Commission Communication, 'First Annual Report on the implementation of the EU Internal Security Strategy' COM(2011) 790; Commission Communication, 'The EU Internal Security Strategy in Action: Five steps towards a more secure Europe' COM(2010) 673 final.

2 First Annual Report, p. 4: EU–US PNR; pp. 6–7: EU–US Cybercrime and cyber security; and on p. 16: EU–US TFTP. Agreement between the United States of America and the European Union on the use and transfer of Passenger Name Record Data to the United States Department of Homeland Security of 17 November 2011; [2012], *OJ* L 215/5; agreement between the European Union and the United States of America on the Processing and Transfer of Financial Messaging data from the European Union to the United States for the purposes of the Terrorist Finance Tracking Program [2010], *OJ* L195/5.

3 First Annual Report, p. 6.

4 Commission, 'Proposal for a Directive on the use of Passenger Name Record data for the prevention, detection investigation and prosecution of terrorist offences and serious crime', COM(2011) 32.

5 Commission Communication, 'A European terrorist finance tracking system available options' COM(2011) 429 final.

EU PNR rules, after having signed similar agreements with Canada and Australia which had certain inconsistencies and differences with the EU–US PNR rules. The 'global approach' of the EU here is an ambitious but 'inwards–out' one, where the EU hopes that third countries will opt into its standards and that they will then become global standards. It faces new challenges from the EU judicial branch in recent case law, considered below.

Returning to the transatlantic agreements, transatlantic security cooperation received its most prominent rule-making impetus after the September 2001 (9/11) terrorist attacks, when a raft of EU–US Justice and Home Affairs Agreements were enacted.[7] Rule-making from this particular period may be considered to demonstrate the limitations of mutual recognition of each other's legal order or the shortcomings of adequacy presumptions in law.[8] Even if the impetus for terrorism legislation in the transatlantic context has abated, the effectiveness of transatlantic rule-making has been lauded as a reason to engage in transatlantic 'rule-convergence', in data protection. Moreover, this rule-making has inspired the EU to engage in 'replica' rule-making of policies, programmes and agreements.[9] Transatlantic security rule-making has generated high-profile challenges on legal competence and transparency grounds, heightening its controversial character.[10] Current EU–US cooperation in counterterrorism and

6 These terms are discussed further in Ch.1.

7 See Marise Cremona, 'Justice and Home Affairs in a Globalised World: Ambitions and Reality in the tale of the EU–US SWIFT Agreement', Institute for European Integration Research, Working Paper No 4/2011; Elaine Fahey, 'Law and Governance as Checks and Balances in Transatlantic Security: Rights, Redress and Remedies in EU–US Passenger Name Records and the Terrorist Finance Tracking Program' (2013), 32 *YEL* 1; Marieke de Goede, 'The SWIFT affair and the Global Politics of European Security' (2012), 50 *JCMS* 214.

8 See Fahey, ibid. and also Gregory Shaffer, 'Reconciling Trade and Regulatory Roles: The Prospects and Limits of New Approaches to Transatlantic Governance through Mutual Recognition and Safe Harbor Agreements' (2002), 9 *CJEL* 29.

9 For example, Commission, 'Proposal for a Directive on the use of Passenger Name Record data for the prevention, detection investigation and prosecution of terrorist offences and serious crime' COM(2011), 32; Commission Communication, 'A European terrorist finance tracking system available options' COM(2011), 429 final.

10 See Valsamis Mitsilegas, 'Transatlantic Counter-terrorism Cooperation and European Values: the Elusive Quest for Coherence' and Juan Santos Vara, 'Transatlantic Counter-terrorism Agreements on the transfer of personal data: a test for democratic accountability in the EU' in Elaine Fahey and Deirdre Curtin (eds), *A Transatlantic Community of Law: Legal Perspectives on the Relationship between the EU and US Legal Orders* (Cambridge University Press, 2014), Chapters 14, 15. See Valsamis Mitsilegas, 'EU–US Co-operation in Criminal Matters post-9/11: Extradition, Mutual Legal Assistance and the Exchange of Police Data' (2003), 8 *EFAR* 515; Valsamis Mitsilegas, 'The External Dimension of EU Action in Criminal Matters' (2007), 12 *EFAR* 471; Kristin Archick, 'EU–US Cooperation Against Terrorism' (2012), *Congressional Research Service* 7–5700; Patryk Pawlak (ed.), 'The EU–US security and justice agenda in action' (EUISS Chaillot Paper, 2012); Theodore Georgopoulos, 'What Kind of Treaty-Making Power for the EU? Constitutional problems related to the conclusion of the EU–US Agreements on Extradition and Mutual Legal Assistance' (2005), 30 *ELR* 191; William Gilmore, 'The External Dimension of EU Action in Criminal Matters' in Maria Fletcher, Robin Loof and William Gilmore (eds), *EU Criminal Law and Justice* (Edwin Elgar, 2008), 150.

security includes diverse and particular areas such as *inter alia* EU–US Cybercrime and Security, Counter Violent Extremism (CVE) cooperation, foreign fighters' cooperation and explosives security.[11] Future areas of EU–US criminal law cooperation envisaged include *inter alia* victims' rights and hate crimes. They explicitly take cognisance of EU legislative developments, as well as the process of reform of EU agencies underfoot – e.g. Europol, Eurojust, etc.[12] This demonstrates the vibrancy of the cooperation and its evolving character, as well as the challenging relationship between the 'external' and 'internal' for the EU. The outbreak of the NSA surveillance saga in the midst of the rule-making processes has operated to place EU citizens' fundamental rights and data protection centrally in *all* rule-making of the EU with the US, from trade to security. It caused the European Parliament to vote to suspend all EU–US data transfer agreements.[13] By contrast, the EU–US Justice and Home Affairs Ministerial meeting in late 2013 stressed the importance of developing the EU–US negotiations on a data protection agreement, referencing the work of the EU–US ad hoc working group on the NSA surveillance saga.[14] Nonetheless, the recent decision of the Court of Justice as to the Data Retention Directive suggests that the consequences and practices of rule-transfer are of much significance, striking down Directive 2006/24/EC mainly on proportionality grounds.[15] Some now suggest EU–US agreements providing for systemic and indiscriminate storage of personal data fundamentally contradict the basis of this judgment and that EU rule-making variants of these agreements are similarly contradictory.[16]

11 Summary of Conclusions of the EU–US JHA Ministerial Meeting (18 November 2013) Council doc. 16682/13. See also the European External Action Service overview of transatlantic cooperation in justice and home affairs: http://eeas.europa.eu/us/sector_en.htm, accessed 23 December 2015.

12 Ministerial JHA meeting (n.11).

13 European Parliament resolution of 23 October 2013 on the suspension of the TFTP agreement as a result of US National Security Agency surveillance (2013/2831(RSP)). See Nicolaj Neielsen, 'EU–US Counterterrorism pacts at risk over snooping affair' *EUObserver.com* (5 July 2013); 'MEPs raise suspension of EU-US bank data deal', *LIBE Press release* (24 September 2013): www.europarl.europa.eu/news/en/news-room/content/20130923IPR20604/html/MEPs-raise-suspension-of-EU-US-bank-data-deal, accessed 23 December 2015.

14 EU–US Justice and Home Affairs Ministerial Meeting of 18 November 2013, Council 16418/13, 18 November, 2013; 'Report on the Findings by the EU Co-chairs of the Ad Hoc EU–US Working Group on Data Protection', Council doc. 16987/13, 27 November 2013; European Commission, 'Rebuilding Trust in EU–US Data Flows' COM(2013), 846 final.

15 In Joined Cases C-293/12 and C-594/12, *Digital Rights Ireland and Seitlinger and Others* EU:C:2014:238; cf. C-131/12, *Google Spain SL, Google Inc.* v. *Agencia Española de Protección de Datos (AEPD), Mario Costeja González* EU:C:2014:317; Case C-362/14 *Schrems* v. *Data Protection Commissioner*, EU:C:2014:317.

16 'There are fundamental compatibility problems, in particular when it comes to undifferentiated bulk data collection and transfer of flight passenger and bank data to the US', 8, 71, in Franziska Boehm and Mark D. Cole, 'Data Retention after the Judgement of the Court of Justice of the European Union' (Report: The Greens/European Free Alliance) Münster/Luxembourg, 30 June 2014: www.statewatch.org/news/, accessed 23 December 2015. Nicolaj Neilsen, 'Scrapped EU surveillance law throws doubt on US data agreements', *EUObserver.com* (24 July 2014): http://euobserver.com/justice/125089, accessed 23 December 2015.

The legal influences or imprints of transatlantic security upon the EU internal legal order raise important questions of legal taxonomy. EU internal security rules appear to bear tangible influences from transatlantic security with regard to nomenclature, objectives and methods. Moreover, an EU PNR and an EU TFTS ostensibly appear to impact more intrusively on individual rights than comparable EU–US measures. In some instances, the adequacy of the existing transatlantic rules themselves is difficult to assess. Fundamental rights commitments and concerns become more central to the EU rules emerging than their transatlantic counterparts but still remain significantly influenced by the transatlantic rules. There is little jurisprudence from courts or tribunals in the EU or US on EU–US rules in this area and the extent then to which one can assess legal safeguards or remedies in either the transatlantic or emerging internal EU rules remains complex. On account of its possible implications for individual rights and reviewability, the legal impact of transposing transatlantic legal measures upon internal EU security law is worthy of attention itself. However, the precise detail of these measures is far from certain or complete. Thus, a straightforward legality analysis of the measures cannot be conducted per se. Transatlantic 'imprints' upon EU internal security law may also be described as an exportation and importation of legal values through mutual recognition which is largely incomplete. This forms a perspective from which to view the EU internal security rules emerging and is adopted in this account. It is argued here that the transposition of transatlantic justice and home affairs measures, from EU–US PNR and EU–US TFTP into EU law, raises many questions about appropriate legal standards and safeguards for individual rights. It shows how rule-transfer in this field is fraught with challenges and uncertainties about the legal norms evolving.

As a result, there is a question then as to the appropriate *legal* methodology to employ so as to capture legal issues of transatlantic imprints upon EU law. The analysis of 'imprints' or influences and effects upon a legal order is possibly a legal, political and sociological question at the least – i.e. as to why and how the values of EU–US policies have come to infiltrate EU internal security law. There is a considerable literature on the external dimension of the Area of Freedom, Security and Justice (AFSJ), wherein transatlantic relations lie, in a range of disciplines, which takes a harsh view of legal scholarship in this field.[17] A broad range of theoretical approaches are enumerated as to the external dimension to the AFSJ, such as Europeanisation, external governance, new institutionalism, security governance, foreign policy analysis, critical policy perspectives and critical security perspectives.[18] In this enumeration of techniques, legal perspectives on external AFSJ

17 Helena Carrapiço and Florian Trauner, 'The External Dimension of EU Justice and Home Affairs after the Lisbon Treaty: Analysing the Dynamics of Expansion and Diversification' (2012), 17 *EFAR* 1, Table 1.

18 Ibid.

developments are criticised for being limited to the rule of law or legality analysis. This account purports to capture and analyse this rule-transfer by tracing a specific case study which encapsulates the exportation and importation of values into EU law and which also functions as a global standard for the EU, initially at least.

This chapter explores select areas of transatlantic imprints on EU security rules, first examining the operation of rule-transfer and then considering the question of importation and exportation of values via EU law as well as the context of mutual recognition in transatlantic security agreements. An analysis of two transatlantic agreements and their impact upon and link to internal EU security rules is set out in the next section. The final section considers the mooted 'global approach' of the EU to PNR, followed by Conclusions.

Depicting the process of EU rule-transfer

Overview

As outlined in Chapter 1, the transposition of legal rules is a concept which is an elementary part of member states' obligations of membership of the European Union – for example, through the vehicles of directives. Transposition in this sense depicts a process as well as a legal phenomenon of EU law. However, the nuances of bilateral rules being 'developed' or 'evolved' into internal EU rules is argued here not to be adequately captured by the perhaps mundane legal term of transposition. Another means to depict the developments of the present account might be as a form of rule-transfer. Rule-transfer is understood in this sense as a means or process by which legal rules are adopted in other legal orders. As outlined in Chapter 1, it is a term deployed in non-legal scholarship on governance and policy development, but it has a distinctive legal component, given that it depicts legal rules and/or legislative measures.[19] There is an emerging *legal* scholarship on *actual* rule-transfer from the EU legal order to the US legal order, which suggests that it is far-reaching and widespread, but without deploying the terminology of rule-transfer. Thus, the so-called 'Brussels effect' is the subject of recent US-based scholarship, assessing the perceived 'spillover' effect of EU regulatory standards on US rules in the realm of *inter alia* genetically modified foods, data privacy standards and chemical safety rules.[20] Equally, accounts consider the extent to which EU legal rules being actually transplanted or physically replicated in the US is increasing – for example, the transposition of EU environmental standards in California, Boston and Maine.[21] These (legal) accounts conceptualise

19 See, for example, its use without any formal definition by Frank Schimmelfennig and Ulrich Sedelmeier, 'Governance by conditionality: EU rule transfer to the candidate countries of Central and Eastern Europe' (2004), 11 *JEPP* 669.

20 Anu Bradford, 'The Brussels Effect' (2012), 107 *NULR* 1; Joanne Scott, 'From Brussels with Love: the Transatlantic Travels of European Law and the Chemistry of Regulatory Attraction' (2009), 57 *AJCL* 897.

the *actual* transfer of rules from the EU to the US. The phenomenon considered here of EU–US policies being transposed into EU law where they were not previously, in forms similar to or progressed further, based upon EU–US rules, appears thus distinctive. Internal EU security does not exhibit the same character – for example, as single market policies (as depicted in the 'Brussels effect', for example), displaying more complex legal, constitutional and structural characteristics as part of the AFSJ. Moreover, rule-transfer may bear some similarities to the concept of a legal transplant, a principle of comparative law, where a rule is transplanted into another legal order, different from its country of origin.[22] Here the transatlantic origins of the rules being transposed into EU law is neither a 'clean' nor simple division from its 'owner'. Thus, these accounts of rule-migration or rule-transfer have not tended to capture precisely the developments depicted here, nor its consequences for EU law. There is a body of *non-legal* scholarship demonstrating the diffusion of values from the EU to the US legal order, focusing more upon the reasons for this diffusion rather than the process itself, which is not couched in terms of rule-transfer or less still transposition.[23]

Importing and exporting legal values via EU law

Rule-transfer cannot be viewed as an isolated scientific exercise and requires a multifaceted range of approaches for it to be understood. At a more abstract level, it reflects the transfer of values between legal orders. The adoption of transatlantic measures in EU law, particularly in a more stringent format, may be evidence of the highly fluid importation and exportation of values. Thus, the EU frequently *imports* values and norms and itself acts often as a model for values.[24] However, EU value importation through law is far from uncontroversial. For

21 Scott (n. 20).

22 A term coined by Patrick H. Glenn, *Legal Traditions of the World* (4th edn, Oxford University Press, 2010).

23 See, for example, Mark Pollack and Gregory Shaffer, *When Cooperation Fails: The International Law and Politics of Genetically Modified Foods* (Oxford University Press, 2009); David Bach and Abe Newman, 'The European regulatory state and global public policy: micro-institutions, macro-influence' (2007), 14 *JEPP* 827; David Bach and Abe Newman, 'Self-Regulatory Trajectories in the Shadow of Public Power: Resolving digital dilemmas in Europe and the United States' (2004), 17 Governance 387; Wynn Rees and Richard Aldrich, 'European and US Approaches to Counterterrorism' in Ronald Tiersky and Erik Jones (eds), *Europe Today: A Twenty-First Century Introduction* (3rd edn, Rowman & Littlefield, 2007), 437–64. Cf. see the (legal) account of Schaffer to similar effect: Gregory Shaffer, 'Globalisation and social protection: the impact of EU and international rules in the ratcheting up of US data privacy standards' (2000), 25 *YJIL* 1.

24 Marise Cremona, 'Values in EU Foreign Policy' in Malcolm Evans and Panos Koutrakos (eds), *Beyond the Established Legal Order: Policy Interconnections Between the EU and the Rest of the World* (Hart, 2011) 275–317, 285: the European Convention on Human Rights or the Geneva Convention on the status of refugees are examples of the former; the evolution of the legal order of ASEAN might represent the latter. See also Marise Cremona, 'The European as a Global Actor: Roles, Models and Identity' (2004), 41 *CMLR* 553.

example, there is a view that in the realm of terrorist financial transactions the EU has largely adopted international law measures wholesale, critiqued as an unduly blind absorption.[25] However, the use of international norms in internal EU policy-making in the realm of counterterrorism is clearly far from unprecedented and not unprincipled. The normative reasons for such adoption are usually well intentioned – for example, high standards and a desire to establish international-level compliance.[26] The theme of the *exportation* of EU values has a very broad interpretation and considerable span of subject areas beyond security.[27] For example, all forms of EU trade agreements contain value commitments and value exportations but they are controversial and have been haphazardly applied.[28] Legal scholarship asserts across a broad range of subject areas that there is much fluidity and uncertainty concerning the importation and exportation of values in EU law. Seen in this light, the fluid transposition of transatlantic rules into EU law seems entirely comprehensible or, at the least, similarly fluid.

Mutual recognition and transatlantic relations in justice and home affairs

The context and nature of the phenomenon of the impact of transatlantic rules on the EU legal order is similarly relevant. Transatlantic relations represent a tricky balance of powers in the domain of security rule-making, where the EU has jointly agreed to particular value commitments, similarly entered into by the US but with differences in practical enforcement thereof (outlined above in greater detail), distinguishing this, for example, from unilateral obligations in trade agreements included at the behest of the EU. Transatlantic relations represent a tricky balance of powers, where the EU has *jointly agreed* to particular value commitments, similarly entered into by the US. Legal scholarship has engaged with this phenomenon of the balance of powers in transatlantic relations in security more readily than rule-transfer. Many have provided accounts mapping specific imbalances or unevenness of the rule-making between the EU and US legal orders in the post-9/11 period as considered here.[29] This specific context renders any effort to subsequently transpose transatlantic standards, de facto and de jure, into EU law all the more challenging. As developed above, transatlantic security rules

25 See Oldrich Bures, *EU Counterterrorism Policy: A Paper Tiger?* (Ashgate, 2011).

26 See, for example, Martin Scheinin (ed.), 'European and United States Counter-terrorism Policies, the Rule of Law and Human Rights', EUI RSCAS Policy Papers (RSCAS PP 2011/03).

27 See also Sonia Lucarelli and Ian Manners (eds), *Values and Principles in EU Foreign Policy* (Routledge, 2006).

28 The EU has suspended agreements on fundamental grounds only in a minority of instances: see Bruno De Witte, 'The EU and International Legal Order: The Case of Human Rights' in Evans and Koutrakos (eds), *Beyond the Established Legal Orders: Policy Interconnections Between the EU and the Rest of the World* (Hart, 2011), 127, 143. See also Cremona (n. 24).

29 Cremona (n. 24); De Witte, ibid.; Fahey (n. 7).

derived from the post-9/11 period are perceived to have emanated from a peculiarly complex legal and political context. While a future problem, the legal review of the emerging EU internal security law with its origins in EU–US relations remains problematic. Evidently, the appropriate place for redress, justiciability and fundamental rights generally in security rules is far from settled. The phenomenon of rule-transfer possibly adds a significant dimension to our understanding of transatlantic relations outside the bilateral context and proximity between the legal orders of the EU and US. It is suggested here that it warrants being part of a future research agenda, one which is only canvassed here rather than developed. It indicates a richer context to transatlantic relations *outside* the strictly bilateral context, but one also in need of close analysis and reflection, especially in security.

The legal form of rights, redress and remedies in such rule-making is indicative of a particular imbalance of powers in transatlantic relations in this period, borne out in many accounts.[30] A particular agreement may be underpinned by formulations of mutual recognition of each other's legal order: access to it and assumed and expressed similarities. Mutual recognition in justice inevitably involves the acceptance of aspects of the content and form of the legal system of another legal order. This phenomenon has proven to be particularly complex among the EU Member States themselves, where mutual recognition in justice is recognised as having both substantive and procedural components.[31] However, the imbalance evident overall arguably reflects the impossibilities of actual transatlantic mutual recognition in justice.

While it constitutes more than a merely legal question, legal scholarship has engaged with this complex phenomenon of the balance of powers in transatlantic relations. For example, Cremona and De Witte have provided accounts mapping specific imbalances in power resulting from the EU–US PNR and SWIFT agreements.[32] Moreover, lawyers suggest that there has been an imbalance

30 See further Fahey (n. 7); Mitsilegas (n. 10) Chapter 14. On reciprocity and its limits, see Gregory Shaffer, 'Reconciling Trade and Regulatory Roles: The Prospects and Limits of New Approaches to Transatlantic Governance through Mutual Recognition and Safe Harbor Agreements' (2002) 9 *CJEL* 29; Valsamis Mitsilegas, 'Constitutional Implications of Mutual Recognition in Criminal Matters in the EU' (2006) 43 *CMLR* 1277; Bruno De Witte, 'Too Much Constitutional Law in the European Union's Foreign Relations?' in Bruno De Witte and Marise Cremona (eds), *EU Foreign Relations Law: Constitutional Fundamentals* (Hart, 2008), 11.

31 See Shaffer (n. 30); see Mitsilegas (n. 10).

32 Marise Cremona, 'Justice and Home Affairs in a Globalised World: Ambitions and Reality in the Tale of the EU–US SWIFT Agreement', Institute for European Integration Research, Working Paper No. 4/2011; Bruno De Witte, 'Too Much Constitutional Law in the European Union's Foreign Relations?' in Bruno De Witte and Marise Cremona (eds), *EU Foreign Relations Law: Constitutional Fundamentals* (Hart, 2008), 11; Elaine Fahey, 'Of One Shotters and Repeat-Hitters: A Retrospective on the Role of the European Parliament in the EU–US PNR Litigation' in Bill Davies and Fernanda. Nicola (eds), *EU Law Stories* (Cambridge University Press, forthcoming); Elaine Fahey, 'Reviewing High Politics: Global Governance and the Justiciability of EU–US Relations before the Court of Justice of the European Union' (2012), Amsterdam Centre for European Law and Governance, Working Paper on Postnational Rulemaking, 2012–03.

in powers in transatlantic security rule-making, an adverse one from an EU perspective.[33] They also depict the initial phase of rule-making in EU–US relations in the realm of data transfer and counterterrorism law as arising predominantly from a desire to clarify legal uncertainty, rather than a particular commitment to fundamental rights or EU values generally.[34] This specific context renders any effort to de facto and de jure transpose transatlantic standards into EU law all the more challenging and problematic. Even if possibly *explicable* on account of the fluidity of the exportation and importation of values in EU law, transatlantic security rules have emanated from a peculiarly complex legal and political context. The legal review of the emerging EU internal security law with its origins in EU–US relations remains challenging on account of the uncertainty of assessing the appropriate place for redress, justiciability and fundamental rights generally in security rules which display complexity and imbalances in terms of their values and context.

An analysis of the key features of the transatlantic rules in two select fields alongside their developing EU counterparts is conducted next, focusing specifically upon the operation and safeguards of transatlantic rules.

Tracing the 'external' in the 'internal': assessing the EU PNR and the EU TFTS

There are many significant and high-profile and perhaps even controversial EU–US agreements in the area of justice and home affairs.[35] A more complete or comprehensive account of all such agreements or EU–US security cooperation is not provided here on grounds of space, but is outlined elsewhere in a rich and extensive literature across disciplines. Instead, the account which follows is a selective examination of the legal similarities, differences and relevant normative questions surrounding the impact of recent transatlantic security rules upon two specific recent EU measures proposed. Passenger Name Records (PNR) and the Terrorist Financial Tracking Program (TFTP) are the most high-profile and recent of these EU–US JHA agreements outlined above. Accordingly, the account begins with an analysis of the most recent transatlantic measures adopted

33 Ibid.

34 Cremona (n. 24).

35 Otherwise, agreements not considered here include the agreement between the United States of America and the European Police Office of 6 December 2001, European Council, 14581/01, 6–7 December 2001; supplemental agreement between the Europol Police Office and the United States of America on the exchange of personal data and related information of 20 December 2002; EU–US Extradition Agreement *OJ* L 181/27, 19 July 2003, which entered into force on 1 February 2010; EU–US Agreement on Mutual Legal Assistance *OJ* L 181/34, 19 July 2003, which entered into force on 1 February 2010; US–Eurojust Cooperation Agreement of 6 November 2006. See Mitsilegas, 'EU–US Co-operation in Criminal Matters post-9/11: Extradition, Mutual Legal Assistance and the Exchange of Police Data' (n. 10) 515. For a recent overview, see Archick (n. 10).

in this area – the Second EU–US PNR Agreement and the Second TFTP Agreement – explicitly omitting a lengthy background analysis of EU–US cooperation for reasons of space, and contrasts them with EU measures in development or under proposal.

The second-generation EU–US Passenger Name Records (PNR) Agreement

The most recent EU–US PNR Agreement was concluded in 2011 and was endorsed by a majority of the European Parliament in 2012.[36] It constitutes the so-called Second Generation EU–US PNR and has a defined duration to run for seven years – i.e. until 2019.[37] It was intended to represent, a decade after 9/11, an *improved* agreement with the US to transmit air passenger data to the US, PNR, in the name of fighting serious crime and terrorism. However, while it evolved on the basis of the putative success of first-generation EU–US PNR,[38] second-generation EU–US PNR remains largely similar in form and in substance to first-generation EU–US PNR. Earliest concerns about the legality of first-generation EU–US PNR rules arose in 2004 in relation to the 'pull' extraction of data in PNR databases by US law enforcement officials, in relation to whether the exercise of US sovereign power of European Community territory (as it then was) was lawful.[39] EU–US rules thus eventually developed because consent to the action was required as a matter of law – i.e. European consent to US 'pull' extraction was required. The rules emerging represented a response to EU 'rule of law' concerns rather than specific EU–US 'value commitments'.[40] First-generation EU–US PNR was subjected to two 'joint reviews' by the EU and US in 2005 and 2010, concluding that the US had not misused data[41] and to one adverse decision

36 See n. 2.

37 The 'Second Generation' PNR terminology is taken here from official EU documents – e.g. JHA External Relations Trio programme, Council doc. 12004/11.

38 Agreement between the European Community and the United States of America on the processing and transfer of PNR data by Air Carriers to the United States Department of Homeland Security (DHS), Bureau of Customs and Border Protection ([2004], *OJ* L 183/ 83, and corrigendum at [2005], *OJ* L 255/168); agreement between the European Union and the United States of America on the processing and transfer of Passenger Name Record (PNR) data by air carriers to the United States Department of Homeland Security (DHS) (2007, PNR Agreement) [2007], *OJ* L 204/18.

39 See the account of Cremona (n. 7).

40 Commission Staff Working Paper, 'An EC–US Agreement on Passenger Name Record', SEC (2004), 3.

41 Commission Staff Working Paper of the Joint Review of the implementation by the US Bureau of Customs and Border Protection of the Undertakings set out in the Commission Decision 2004/535/EC of 14 May 2004, COM(2005) final; Report on the Joint Review of the implementation of the Agreement between the EU and US on the processing and transfer of Passenger Name Record data by air carriers to the US Department of Homeland Security, 8–9 February 2010 (Brussels, 7 April 2010).

of the Court of Justice striking it down on legal base grounds.[42] A provisional seven-year agreement was concluded in 2007 to replace the earlier agreement, which De Witte outlines as a significantly worse legal bargain for the EU, wherein the US availed of the renegotiation to extend data retention periods from over three years to fifteen years.[43] The European Parliament sought to postpone its approval vote on the 2007 agreement, deploying its powers accorded to it in the Treaty of Lisbon which came into force in December 2009, seeking a global strategy on external PNR with the US, Canada and Australia from the Commission, which emphasised fundamental rights, better redress and effective legal safeguards.[44] Thereafter, negotiation of a revised EU–US PNR Agreement followed suit.

Overall, the most notable legal developments in second-generation EU–US PNR in comparison with first-generation EU–US PNR are the explicit references to data protection, the shortened dormant retention periods, the guarantees concerning the onwards transfer of data and the enumerated rights of redress.[45] More specifically, the second-generation agreement predominantly now provides for a 'push' system in Article 15, generally perceived as more compatible with data protection rights. 'Push' and 'pull' remain far from quirky descriptors but rather the defining legal objectives of EU–US agreements to obtain and extract legal data. However, rather significantly, a 'pull' system is provided for in exceptional circumstances in Article 15(5).[46] Article 4 limits the use of the data to transnational crime of a serious nature and represents a significant ostensible limitation or legal protection. However, its detailed and complex definition suggests that interpretation of these criteria will be significant. Article 4 also appears ripe to generate inconsistent domestic interpretations in the EU and US legal orders respectively. It is notable that legal remedies in the form of redress and review are expressed in many various ways throughout the agreement: spanning access to information (Article 11), correction and rectification remedies (Article 12) and redress (Article 13). Article 8(1) provides for 'active' data retention periods of five years and a 'dormant' retention period of ten years in Article

42 Joined cases C-317/04 and C-318/04 *European Parliament* v. *Council and Commission* ECLI:EU:C:2006:346.

43 Agreement between the European Union and the United States of America on the processing and transfer of Passenger Name Record (PNR) data by air carriers to the United States Department of Homeland Security (DHS) (2007, PNR Agreement) [2007] *OJ* L 204/18. See De Witte (n. 30) 11.

44 Resulting in the 'Communication from the Commission on the Global Approach to Transfers of Passenger Name Record (PNR) Data to Third Countries' COM(2010) 492.

45 See Article 29 Data Protection Working Party, 'Pull-Push' Version, 21 March 2007. 'Push' denotes the transmission of data by airline carriers, while 'pull' denotes the extraction of data by the Department of Homeland Security.

46 The EU had sought assurances from the DHS on the onwards transfer of data to third countries and for the role of data protection experts in the review process of the agreement: Council doc. 16981/11.

8(3), shorter than the periods provided for in an earlier draft, but nonetheless still extremely lengthy. They appear to raise questions concerning their compliance with the recent data retention directive decision.

Moreover, there is a certain hollowness to the redress contained in the agreement, given the many procedural obstacles found to exist in seeking redress both in the EU and US.[47] Most obviously, for example, the inability of EU citizens to rely upon provisions of the US Privacy Act of 1974, limited as it is to US citizens, is a deliberate and significant omission from the expressed list of Acts under which individuals may seek redress in Article 13(3).[48] While the Commission was keen to portray the new agreement as improving data protection and also fighting crime and terrorism coextensively, there had been much discontent with a previously leaked version earlier in 2011 which the latest version does not substantially differ from.[49] These issues render transposition into EU law problematic, given the difficulty of assessing the adequacy, effectiveness and success of EU–US PNR. Nevertheless, the EU and US have recently reached an agreement on a data protection 'umbrella agreement', expressly striving for a high level of protection.[50] Moreover, an agreement reached with Canada in 2014 has been referred by the EP to the Court of Justice on the basis of its possible non-compliance with the Data Retention Directive decision, substantially similar to the EU–US PNR Agreement.[51]

An EU directive on the use of Passenger Name Record (PNR) data

An EU directive on the use of Passenger Name Record (PNR) data for the prevention, detection, investigation and prosecution of terrorist offences and

47 See the report and US case law cited by Gerrit Hornung and Franziska Boehm, 'Comparative Study on the 2011 draft Agreement between the US and the EU on the use and transfer of Passenger Name Records to the US Department of Homeland Security' (14 March 2012): http://janalbrecht.eu/wp-content/uploads/2012/03/PNR-Study.pdf, accessed 23 December 2015.

48 The Act of 1974 provides in U.S.C. § 552a: '(a) Definitions: (2) the term, 'individual', means a citizen of the United States or an alien lawfully admitted for permanent residence'.

49 Valentina Pop, 'Unhappy MEPs to approve passenger data deal' *EUObserver* (11 November 2011): http://euobserver.com/justice/114252, accessed 23 December 2015. A leaked opinion from the European Commission appeared to indicate that it harboured significant reservations about an earlier version, which suggested that it was not compatible with fundamental rights: European Commission Legal Service, 18 May 2011, sjf (2011) 603245, leaked by the Civil Liberties Organisation, *Statewatch*: www.statewatch.org/news/2011/jun/eu-usa-pnr-com-ls-opinion-11.pdf, accessed 23 December 2015. Articles 4 and 8, limiting the type of data to be transmitted and the length of the data retention were the two substantive changes from the earlier version.

50 See http://europa.eu/rapid/press-release_STATEMENT-15-5610_en.htm.

51 A PNR agreement was signed by the EU Council of Ministers and Canada on 25 June 2014 and referred by the EP to the Court of Justice in November 2014: Opinion 1/15, pending. An agreement from 2006 remains in place.

serious crime was proposed in early 2011.[52] The directive met thereafter with considerable critique on fundamental rights grounds, which has more recently abated.[53] The directive explicitly shares the nomenclature and form of EU–US PNR rules. The directive would apply to air carriers flying into and out of EU member states and applies to unverified passenger data which can be sent to *inter alia* other member states and third countries, and self-evidently has a far-reaching application. The possibility of monitoring EU internal flights was proposed by the UK as part of its Olympic Games security strategy and did not meet with much vociferous opposition, instead evolving into a legal position which would be adopted by the Council.[54] The European Parliament LIBE Civil Liberties Committee rejected the Commission Proposal in April 2013 on proportionality grounds.[55] The first EU PNR proposed directive provided that all passengers flying in and out of the EU would have to provide key data which can be checked against national watch lists. Notably, in introducing the measure, the Commission sought to emphasise its invocation of the data protection guarantees explicitly provided for in the EU treaties post-Lisbon.[56] The directive provided in Articles 8 and 9 that Member States would set up competent authorities to act as a Passenger Information Unit to collect the data from air carriers, with limited processing and case-by-case transfer powers for thirty days and then retention powers for five years. The data would thus be used proactively, in real-time and also reactively. Article 10 provides that member states should provide for dissuasive, effective and proportionate penalties against air carriers acting in breach of

52 Commission, 'Proposal for a Directive on the use of Passenger Name Record data for the prevention, detection investigation and prosecution of terrorist offences and serious crime', COM(2011) 32; EU–PNR Commission Staff Working Paper Impact Assessment COM (2011) 32 final.

53 Opinion of the European Union Agency for Fundamental Rights on the Proposal for a Directive on the use of Passenger Name Record (PNR) data for the prevention, detection, investigation and prosecution of terrorist offences and serious crime (COM(2011) 32 final) FRA Opinion – 1/2011 Vienna, 14 June 2011; Report of Meijers Committee, the Standing Committee of experts on international immigration, refugee and criminal law on Directive on the use of PNR data for the prevention, detection, investigation and prosecution of terrorist offences and serious crime (COM(2011) 32, Utrecht, 21 June 2011). The EU summit (30 August 2014) demanded the proposed EU–PNR law be rushed through by the end of the year. Special Meeting of the European Council Conclusions, EUCO 163/14.

54 Note 'From UK Delegation To Delegations' Council doc. 6359/11. 'Countries rally behind UK on EU Flight data collection', *Euractiv* (12 April 2011): www.euractiv.com/infosociety/countries-rally-uk-eu-flight-dat-news-504007, accessed 23 December 2015. Council doc. 9103/11 (15 April 2011). See the UK's plans in the broader context: http://news.sky.com/story/1327860/terror-plans-more-details-on-air-passengers, accessed 23 December 2015.

55 See the so-called Kirkhope Report, by MEP Timothy Kirkhope 2011/0023 (COD), 14 February 2012: www.europarl.europa.eu/meetdocs/2009_2014/documents/libe/pr/891/891415/891415en.pdf, accessed 23 December 2015.

56 Article 8 Charter of Fundamental Rights (privacy); Article 16 TFEU (data protection).

the directive, which poses challenging questions with regard to enforcement. Article 17 explicitly provides that the feasibility of including internal flights within the scope of the directive would be considered by the Commission. This demonstrated the extent to which the UK's position, which is highly invasive from a fundamental rights perspective, has become central to emerging EU policy.[57] Fundamental rights guarantees are highly detailed in the directive, guaranteeing *inter alia* in Article 11 rights of access, rectification, erasure and blocking and the right to compensation. Much concern had been expressed in the Council about the proportionality of the measures.[58] The so-called Kirkhope Report of the EP on the directive proposal (named after its rapporteur) released in 2015 tabled a new draft text. Notably, while limiting *inter alia* the data retention periods and providing for stronger data protection provisions, it nonetheless offered support for the inclusion of intra-EU flights, despite fears that it would lead to pan-European surveillance.[59] However, the EP also questioned the sustainability of a PNR system in the light of the decision of the Court of Justice in its Data Retention decision and made recommendations accordingly for compatibility, views which were incorporated into its approval of draft EU rules in July 2015.[60]

The Charlie Hebdo, Paris, and Brussels atrocities recently, have again revived the salience of an EU PNR directive. Several Member States, particularly the UK, have meanwhile been developing their own PNR systems, albeit with considerable variations. This has led for calls for harmonisation in the form of an EU PNR system as a means to prevent divergent data collection systems developing. The Article 29 Working Party in 2015 still asserted that the directive had yet to be justified in terms of its necessity and was likely to seriously undermine provisions of the Charter – e.g. Articles 7 and 8.[61] The Commission at the time of writing had recently maintained that the EU PNR directive maintained sufficient safeguards so as not to fall foul of the data retention decision.[62] This was followed by the EP's approval of new EU PNR rules

57 Marie Hynes, 'Proposal for a Directive on the use of Passenger Name Record data for the prevention, detection, investigation and prosecution of terrorist offences and serious crime', *Statewatch Analysis* (March 2011): www.statewatch.org/analyses/no-126-eu-pnr.pdf, accessed 23 December 2015.

58 See Council doc. 11392/11.

59 LIBE Committee Rapporteur (Kirkhope Report), Draft Report on the Proposal for a Directive of the European Parliament and of the Council on the use of Passenger Name Record Data for the prevention, detection, investigation and prosecution of terrorist offences and serious crime (17 February 2015).

60 European Parliament resolution of 11 February 2015 on anti-terrorism measures (2015/2530(RSP)).

61 Article 29, Working Party Letter to the LIBE Committee on EU PNR (19 March 2015).

62 Letter from the Commission to the President of the European Parliament (March 2015), leaked on Statewatch.org: http://statewatch.org/news/2015/mar/eu-com-eu-pnr-letter.pdf.

with considerable safeguards – for example, as to transparency and the exclusion of intra-EU PNR.[63]

Ostensibly, much effort has been made to meet the legal concerns generated by EU–US PNR. EU PNR shares many similarities with EU–US rules: its nomenclature (PNR), its data retention objectives, its use of agents (airlines) and its retention provisions. However, the *scope* of the proposed directive and the extent to which it appears far-reaching is its most outstanding feature. The development of an EU PNR ostensibly providing for the negation of the freedom to travel within the EU without surveillance indicates that internal EU security law may be becoming marginally more intrusive on individual rights in its objectives and scope than comparable EU–US security measures. Overall, the development of an EU PNR influenced by EU–US PNR seems characterised by an effort to learn from earlier controversies but nonetheless, these commitments cannot emasculate the far-reaching nature of the EU rules proposed or their clear hallmarks of transatlantic origins that remain far from flawless or faultless.

The second EU–US Terrorism Financial Tracking Program (TFTP SWIFT) Agreement

The agreement between the EU and US on the processing and transfer of financial messaging data from the EU to the US (also known colloquially as the 'SWIFT' Agreement or the Terrorism Financial Tracking Program (TFTP hereafter)) is the second transatlantic agreement considered here.[64] The legal objectives of EU–US TFTP are to prevent, investigate, detect and prosecute terrorist financing, pursuant to Article 1, by means of providing exclusively to the US Treasury data stored in the territory of the European Union. There are many legal curiosities to the nature of TFTP, not least its legal evolution from soft law to hard law and its exclusive legal goals according specific authorisation to a sovereign agent of the US government.[65] It arose out of a controversy concerning the US secret access to the Belgian-based Society for Worldwide Interbank Financial Telecommunications (TFTP), uncovered by the *New York Times* and the Agreement has placed specific contours on the legality of the data extraction, use and transfer.[66] A further explanation of the nature and form of TFTP may be gleaned from such soft law

63 The EU legislative process on an EU PNR data collection system had taken a dramatic turn at the time of writing due to the EP's approval of new draft EU PNR rules in July 2015: www.europarl.europa.eu/news/en/news-room/content/20150714IPR81601/html/Passenger-Name-Records-MEPs-back-EU-system-with-data-protection-safeguards. See Opinion 5/2015 of the European Data Protection Supervisor (24 September 2014), finding that 'the essential prerequisite for a PNR scheme … is still not met in the Proposal' (III.9).

64 Agreement between the European Union and the United States of America on the processing and Transfer of Financial Messaging data from the European Union to the United States for the purposes of the Terrorist Finance Tracking Program [2010], *OJ* L 195/5.

65 See Cremona (n. 7) for a complete account.

66 See the accounts of De Goede (n. 7).

'representations' undertaken by the US, published in the official journal in 2006 in the form of a letter from the US Department of Treasury, stating that 'TFTP contains multiple, overlapping layers of governmental and independent controls to ensure that the data, which are limited in nature, are used strictly for counterterrorism purposes'.[67]

An EU–US agreement reached in 2009 was vetoed by the European Parliament in 2010, again exercising its powers of approval accorded by the Treaty of Lisbon, pursuant to Article 218 TFEU.[68] Judicial remedies and fears of bulk transfers were reported to be the basis of the concerns warranting the rejection of the agreement.[69] A second SWIFT agreement was reached in 2010 and entered into force the same year. Similar to the EU–US PNR agreement, rights of access to the data transmitted under the agreement or rights to ascertain whether data has been transmitted in breach of the agreement and rights to seek rectification, erasure and blocking are provided for in Articles 15 and 16. An EU citizen seeking rectification, erasure or blocking must complain to their national supervisory authority who in turn transmits the request to the privacy officer of the US Treasury. Article 17 provides that information transmitted must be accurate and provides for measures to be taken to prevent and discontinue erroneous reliance on inaccurate data. Moreover, the agreement provides *inter alia* that any person who considers his or her personal data to have been processed in breach of this agreement is entitled to seek effective administrative and judicial redress regardless of nationality or country of residence, in Article 18. The adequacy of this redress remains thorny, particularly for EU citizens who remain excluded from litigating the US Privacy Act of 1974.[70] The role of the US Treasury remains problematic as to how it should facilitate a judicial review of its decisions, especially for EU citizens.

In this regard, how secrecy impacts upon this specific process in particular remains especially problematic. The European Police Office, Europol, an embryonic EU agency, has a central verification function of US requests for data, pursuant to Article 4 there. It classifies most TFTP information as secret, inhibiting reviews thereof.[71] Reviews to date conducted of the operation of the TFTP agreement by the EU and US, Europol itself and the Europol Joint Supervisory Body (JSB), the latter as the ultimate layer of oversight, suggest

67 European Council, press release, 'Processing and protection of personal data subpoenaed by the Treasury Department from the US based operation centre of the Society for Worldwide Interbank Financial Telecommunication (SWIFT)' C/07/157 Luxembourg, 28 June 2007, 11291/2/07 REV 2 (Presse, 157).

68 See Adriana Ripoll-Servent and Alex MacKenzie, 'The European Parliament as norm taker? EU–US relations after the SWIFT Agreement' (2012), 17 *EFAR* 71.

69 'MEPS hail historic rejection of SWIFT deal', *Agence Europe* (13 February 2010).

70 See Valentin Pfisterer, 'The Second SWIFT Agreement between the European Union and the United States of America – An overview' (2010), 11 *GLJ* 1173, Section E.

71 A fuller discussion of the evolution of Europol is not conducted here.

that claims of the effectiveness of the TFTP are very complex to assess.[72] Earliest reviews found that data-processing provisions had been breached. Recent reviews indicate that the US was increasingly providing more information to substantiate requests but that the amount of data transferred remained unclear. However, a 2012 report of the Europol JSB identified progress in the processing of data, while nonetheless revealing that Europol had never refused a US request for data. While a fuller discussion of these particular review processes is outside the scope of the present work, suffice to say that in these circumstances, it becomes very difficult to assess the propriety and adequacy of the safeguards in the TFTP so as to warrant the development of a replica or mirror-like EU system.

A European Financial Tracking System (EFTS)

The EU–US TFTP agreement explicitly provided in Article 11(1) of the agreement for the future legal cooperation of the US with the EU in the event of the EU adopting a 'more targeted' internal transfer of data system, expressed to be an 'equivalent' system. Thus, there is now a proposal for a European Financial Tracking System (EFTS),[73] which employs linguistic terms and key policy concepts similar to EU TFTP, but its 'systemised' title beyond a mere 'programme' suggests a more entrenched or long-term approach. At the time of writing, an EU TFTS remains still under development. The express legal objectives of the system are the protection of data transferred, alongside the combating of terrorist financing, although they remain uneasy bedfellows in security rules however they are expressed.[74] US media portrayed the EU TFTS as an effort to curb the role of the US rather than a free-standing EU initiative.[75] However, a Communication from the Commission in 2011 expressed the effectiveness, success and the existing appropriate implementation of EU–US TFTP as found by its review procedures to be the predominant reason for the adoption of an EU TFTS.[76] It remains difficult to assess the accuracy of this assertion for reasons outlined above, concerning the review mechanism. The financing of terrorism through the proceeds of cash and non-traceable means remains a major hurdle to surmount when considering its effectiveness.

72 Pursuant to Article 13 thereof: see report on the inspection of Europol's Implementation of the TFTP Agreement, conducted in November 2010 by the Europol Joint Supervisory Body, Report No JSB/Ins. 11-07 (Brussels, 2011); Europol Press Statement, 'Europol JSB inspects for the second year the implementation of the TFTP Agreement' (Brussels, 14 March 2012).

73 Communication from the Commission to the European Parliament and Council – A European terrorist finance tracking system available options COM(2011) 429 final.

74 Ibid.

75 James Kanter, 'Europe Tries to Curb U.S. Role in Tracking Terrorists' Funds', *New York Times* (13 July 2011): www.nytimes.com/2011/07/14/world/europe/14terror.html? r=0, accessed 23 December 2015.

76 Communication from the Commission (n. 73) 2.

The intrusive nature of the system upon fundamental rights was later outlined in the Communication as a reason to evaluate its need.[77] Subsequently, the Council sought to reflect further on the actual need for an EU system.[78] The cost of the introduction of such a system also appears to deter its development at this point.[79] Nonetheless, the nature of the proposal suggests that a particularly stringent system remains possible, which could surpass the EU–US equivalent in terms of its stringency, employing its core legal objectives and essential form. However, as with an EU PNR, a concern for fundamental rights and proportionality remains increasingly more significant in the development of an EU policy. The abandonment of the pursuit of a TFTS could provide evidence of the unsatisfactory balance of powers in EU–US security rule-making. However, the same concerns have not halted the development of an EU PNR.

The global approach to EU PNR rule-making

The transatlantic case study aside, the EU signed several international PNR agreements with Canada and Australia, negotiated on a case-by-case basis. They resulted in provisions on rules for carriers and data protection which were not necessarily coherent.[80] The EU predicts that the number of such agreements is likely to increase in the near future, so there is a need to set out general standards, content and criteria for them.[81] The EU has proposed that an EU law approach is

77 Ibid.

78 Council doc. 13204/11, Questions in relation to the Commission Communication on TFTS.

79 See Archick (n. 10) 8.

80 See House of Commons European Scrutiny Committee (4 September 2013), '22 EU PNR Agreement with Canada', 22.20: 'We have previously questioned whether the recent crop of PNR Agreements with Australia, the United States of America and, now, Canada, strike the right balance between civil liberties, data protection and security. We also question whether the principles expounded in the Commission's 2010 Communication, 'On the global approach to transfers of Passenger Name Record (PNR) data to third countries', are genuinely universal and being applied consistently. We note, for example, that the data retention period ranges from five years in the proposed Agreement with Canada to fifteen years in the PNR Agreement with the United States of America, and that the Agreement with Australia prohibits the processing of sensitive data, whereas the Agreements with Canada and the United States authorise it in exceptional circumstances. We are disappointed that the Minister does not address these anomalies, which are all the more surprising given that the purposes for which PNR data may be collected and processed are broadly the same under all three Agreements': www.publications.parliament.uk/pa/cm201314/cmselect/cmeuleg/83-xiii/8327.htm, accessed 23 December 2015.

81 The second EU–Australia PNR agreement entered into force on 1 June 2012. This agreement was preceded by an agreement signed in 2008; Agreement between the European Union and Australia on the processing and transfer of Passenger Name Record (PNR) data by air carriers to the Australian Customs and Border Protection Service OJ L 186/4 (14 July 2012); in 2014, the EU and Canada signed a new agreement on the processing and transfer of Passenger Name Record (PNR) data by air carriers to the Canadian competent authorities to replace the existing agreement from 2006. Council doc. 10940/14 Brussels, 25 June 2014. Cf. 'Commission Decision of 6 September 2005 on the adequate protection of personal data contained in the Passenger Name Record of air passengers transferred to the Canada Border Services Agency', *OJ* L 91/49. Peter Hobbing, 'Tracing Terrorists: The EU–Canada Agreement in PNR Matters' CEPS Special Report/September 2008: www.ceps.eu/files/book/1704.pdf, accessed 23 December 2015.

more desirable as a rule-making solution for PNR but one which advocates a 'global approach'. Empirically, the Commission has charted a rise in third countries asking for PNR data from the EU because of increasing international terrorism, recent technological changes and the facilitation of mass transit with expedition.[82] However, New Zealand, South Korea, Saudi Arabia, South Africa and Japan are also all using or testing PNR data but have not yet entered into agreements with the EU.[83] The Commission has thus recently argued that a multilateral approach – e.g. a mandate to negotiate an international convention – would take too long, be too uncertain and would allow any country to join and result in lower data transfer standards than under EU law and that as a result, EU law was preferable.[84] The EU expressly seeks the uploading of its rules and for many new third country partners to emerge. The EU 'expects' much. It advocates, in particular, that non-EU countries should apply various basic principles for the protection of personal data and that modalities of transmission should be standardised.[85] It is thus asserting ostensibly high rule-making standards and stringent commitments to fundamental rights and the rule of law. The manner by which the EU purports now to advocate a global approach to PNR is a noteworthy development in rule-making on account of the manner by which the EU has acquired its norms in this field and absorbed them internally. It is a vivid example of the multifaceted directions of rule-transfer and the porousness of the internal and external in contemporary rule-making. Whether the EU will succeed is another matter. The focus in this account is not necessarily upon the desire of the EU to 'upload' its standards but rather the methodological questions arising in rule-making within this case study. Later, this book considers instances of contentions that EU law is *preferable* to international law, where those arguing in support of such a proposition deploy arguments of a variety of hues to make the same claim as the Commission in this case.[86] As will be argued later, to express this much as a descriptive development is a challenging one on account of the methodological issues arising within the case study.

The global approach to EU rule-making is predicated upon historical perception – i.e. the perceived success of its rules in this field. It is also predicated on social perception – i.e. the perceived acceptance and transferability of its rules,

82 Ibid.

83 Ibid. 4.

84 European Commission, 'Roadmap Legislative proposal and Communication on the transfer of passenger data to third countries 10/2013'.

85 'Communication from the Commission of 21 September 2010 on the global approach to transfers of Passenger Name Record (PNR) data to third countries' COM(2010) 492 final. That is, that the method of transmission, based on the 'push' system; limited transmission; non-obligatory collection of additional data.

86 For example, Anne Thies and Bruno de Witte, 'Why Choose Europe? The Place of the European Union in the Architecture of International Cooperation', in Steven Blockmans, Bart van Vooren, and Jan Wouters (eds), *The Legal Dimension of Global Governance: What Role for the EU?* (Oxford University Press, 2013) 23.

even in the face of controversy following from the highly controversial absorption of external rules. It arguably constitutes a form of direct externalisation of EU rules, one which is of course replicated in various ways in other areas of EU rule-making. Nonetheless, the normative questions surrounding its legitimacy and democratic standards remain. The EU's efforts to place 'best practice' in data transfer principles within the global approach follow many years of piecemeal efforts to improve EU–US rules through governance mechanisms, especially forms of experimental governance.[87] Their impact may be said to be modest and to have resulted in few improvements. The labelling of the global approach here by the EU as a 'strategy' carries with it the intentional ambitions of the EU as a global actor. It is, however, distinctive from the global ambitions as expressed in, for example, internal market policies,[88] in so far as it is an inwards–out strategy rather than an outwards–in one – i.e. it tries to co-opt others rather than to spread its rules more indirectly, almost by contagion. The global approach faces new challenges from the EU judicial branch. According to the recent Data Retention Directive CJEU decision, systemic and indiscriminate storage of personal data contradicts the tenets of the ruling.[89] This puts any form of PNR system, however reformed or modified, in conflict with the CJEU decision, not least the transatlantic agreement.

The exercise of tracing transatlantic rule-transfer provides an insight with which to view the global reach and effects of EU law and the precariousness of the internal and external which the EU readily manipulates. This particular case study demonstrates that it is not a fully complete architecture within which to view EU rule-making. Nonetheless, as a methodology to break down evolutions in rule-making, it is clear and insightful and a means to put 'daylight' upon even highly controversial forms of EU rule-making.

Conclusions

EU internal security rules look set to adopt replica rules of measures found in EU–US relations, both in substance and in form. The effectiveness of EU–US relations has been deployed extensively to spur EU rule-making, yet the ability to gauge this is problematic. The question emerges as to how the CJEU would review the EU internal security rules emanating from EU–US relations. The origins of EU internal security law in transatlantic measures remains of much significance for reasons of legality, and also more broadly, for justiciability. Justiciability is the judicial review of legal measures and the conditions for that review. Major justiciability concerns arguably surround EU–US agreements in

87 See Fahey (n. 7).

88 As outlined in Chapter 2.

89 See C-293/12 and C-594/12, *Digital Rights Ireland and Seitlinger and Others*, ECLI:EU:C:2014:238. See also Case C-362/14 *Schrems* v. *Data Protection Commissioner* ECLI:EU:C:2014:317.

JHA, given the highly limited nature of the redress and unusual dependence upon US law for its realisation, which the author has detailed elsewhere.[90]

The Court of Justice of the European Union (CJEU) has yet to formally consider the legal effects of EU–US JHA measures, which adds to the uncertainty surrounding the appropriateness of the transatlantic imprints upon EU security rules. In its leading decision on the legal basis of the EU–US PNR, where the Court struck down the EU–US PNR agreement on competence grounds,[91] the result of the decision was that the EU had, in the words of De Witte, 'to beg the US' to sign a similar agreement on marginally preferable terms to the US.[92] Notably, the Court did not examine fundamental rights questions, attracting considerable critique as a result.[93] The imminent accession of the EU to the European Convention on Human Rights may place an additional onus upon the CJEU to scrutinise security rules with fundamental rights implications. The European Court of Human Rights has recently shown a willingness to review secretive CIA action in Europe and has not shied away from a review of high politics.[94] While there is little by way of quantity in the case law of the Court of Justice on transatlantic relations,[95] recent litigation before the Court of Justice on the transparency of the negotiations of transatlantic relations initiated by a member of the European Parliament has been successful.[96] A pending CJEU Opinion 1/15 on the EU–Canada PNR agreement may alter matters significantly. Such litigation has the capacity to define the legal contours of transatlantic relations more neatly and possibly provide further understanding of the legal implications of rule-transfer as depicted here.

EU 'internal' security readily embraces 'external' transatlantic security but similarly EU security rules under development may be said to demonstrate the migratory effects of EU–US legal rules by way of some form of rule transposition or 'rule-transfer', as defined and developed in this account. The transposition of transatlantic justice and home affairs measures, from EU–US PNR and EU–US TFTP into EU law, raises many questions about appropriate legal standards and safeguards for individual rights. It shows how rule-transfer in this field is fraught with challenges and peculiarities. Internal security law appears to readily embrace

90 See Fahey (n. 32).

91 See joined cases C-317/04 and C-318/04, *European Parliament* v. *Council and Commission* ECLI:EU:C:2006:346.

92 See De Witte (n. 30).

93 Grainne Gilmore and Jorrit Rijpma, 'Annotation of Joined Cases C-317/04 and C-318/04 *European Parliament* v. *Council and Commission*' (2007), 44 CMLR 1081.

94 E.g. *El-Masri* v. *Former Yugoslav Republic of Macedonia* Application No. 39630/09 (ECtHR, 13 December 2012).

95 See Elaine Fahey, 'The Court of Justice as a Global Governance Actor in EU–US relations' (2012), 25(2) EUSA Review 6.

96 C-350/12 P *Council* v. *in 't Veld* ECLI:EU:C:2014:203 [2014] ECR I- 000, where the applicant sought with success annulment of the Council's decision to refuse full access to documents 11897 of 9 July 2009 on an Opinion of the Council's Legal Service as to the TFTP Agreement.

an external component in the form of transatlantic relations. In turn, the imprints of transatlantic relations upon internal security rules indicate another complex layer for analysis. The account here has shown how the stringency of the measures arising as transatlantic legal imprints should be of some concern in the absence of a clear understanding of the adequacy of operation and safeguards of transatlantic rule-making. Moreover, the origins of the EU internal security rules remains of much significance to understanding how the resulting rules themselves should be reviewed. The EU has sought to establish a global approach for EU PNR rules and to set best global practice. However, its efforts to place 'best practice' in data transfer principles within the global approach follows many piecemeal efforts to improve EU–US rules. This approach now faces distinct challenges from the CJEU. According to the recent Data Retention Directive CJEU decision, systemic and indiscriminate storage of personal data contradicts the tenets of the ruling. This possibly jeopardises any form of PNR system, however reformed or modified, in conflict with the CJEU decision, not least the transatlantic agreement. Rule-transfer has been shown here to provide a means with which to view the global reach and effects of EU law, and the precariousness of the internal and external which the EU readily manipulates. This case study demonstrates that it is not a fully complete architecture within which to view EU rule-making. Nonetheless, as a methodology to break down evolutions in rule-making, rule-transfer provides transparency as to the operation of highly controversial rule-making.

6 The EU's cybercrime and cybersecurity rule-making

Introduction

The relationship between internal and external policies, powers and competences of the EU is both a descriptive and normative challenge, as has been explored here. This is especially so in the Area of Freedom, Security and Justice (AFSJ). This chapter approaches the internal/external relationship in one case study in a regulatory field.[1] EU security, as one specific element of the AFSJ, impacts significantly upon individuals and generates many questions of the rule of law, legal certainty and fundamental rights, and is not so easily captured as a regulatory exercise.[2] Regulation often takes into account external and internal limitations of institutional environments and its actors, but this is not dispositive. For example, the EU's internal security strategy has aimed to target the most urgent security threats facing Europe, such as organised crime, terrorism, cybercrime, the management of EU external borders and civil disasters – seemingly 'outwards–in',[3] while the 'European Security Model' outlines an interdependence between internal and external security in establishing a 'global security' approach with third countries.[4] There is thus a descriptive challenge of

1 The chapter draws from Elaine Fahey, 'The EU's Cybercrime and Cyber-Security Rule-Making: Mapping the Internal and External Dimensions of EU Security' (2014), 1 *EJRR* 46. See generally, Florian Trauner, 'The internal-external security nexus: more coherence under Lisbon?' (EUISS Occasional Paper No. 89, March 2011): www.iss.europa.eu/uploads/media/op89_The_internal-external_security_nexus.pdf, accessed 23 December 2015; Florian Trauner and Helena Carrapiço, 'The external dimension of EU justice and home affairs after the Lisbon Treaty: analysing the dynamics of expansion and diversification' (2012), 17 *EFAR* 5.

2 See, most famously, François Ewald, 'Two Infinities of Risk' in Brian Massumo (ed.), *The Politics of Everyday Fear* (University of Minneapolis Press, 1993), 221; Massimo Fichera and Jens Kremer (eds), *Law and Security in Europe: Reconsidering the Security Constitution* (Intersentia, 2013), especially Chapter 7. As a result, see its 'absence' from 'highly effective' risk-regulation – for example, Julia Black and Robert Baldwin, 'Really responsive risk-based regulation' (2010), 32 *Law and Policy*, 181.

3 Communication from the Commission to the European Parliament and the Council of 22 November 2010, 'The EU Internal Security Strategy in Action: Five steps towards a more secure Europe', COM(2010) 673 final, not published in the *Official Journal.*

4 Council of the European Union, document 5842/2/10, REV 2, 'Towards a European Security Model'.

deciphering what is external versus internal as much as a normative challenge concerning their interrelationship. This phenomenon is evident in EU rule-making in the area of cyber policies, as a contemporary case study of the process of rule-making in both internal and external security as well as providing an insight into their specific relationship in its formulation as regulation. Cyber regulation inherently necessitates multi-level risk regulation, employing international and supranational components and local enforcement. It is thus readily portrayed as fragmentary, multi-sourced and ostensibly unfocused not least because of its external and internal components but also because it involves new and emerging technologies and *restrictive* regulation.[5]

At the end of the life-cycle of the Stockholm Programme, the previous governing policy document of the EU's Area of Freedom, Security and Justice (AFSJ),[6] a Cyber Security Strategy for the EU was unveiled, along with a supporting directive and also a Cybercrime Directive.[7] It purported to launch an EU rule-making process, trailing cooperation by the EU with the US in cybercrime and cybersecurity in existence for over two years.[8] And even though modernisation of an EU cybercrime law or any form of over-arching cybercrime policy has only recently materialised, a new 'quasi-institution' had already been created in advance.[9] The absence of and consequent publicised delay in creating an EU cyber framework was the subject of much critique, inside and outside the EU institutions, despite an asserted 'rising incidence' of cyber attacks and espionage.[10] The link between the EU's external and internal rule-making in cybercrime and cybersecurity is explicit in the rule-making process itself. For example, the implementation of the EU Internal Security Strategy explicitly referenced the success and effectiveness of the EU–US cybercrime and Cyber Security Working Group (WGCC) as a reason to pursue EU internal cybercrime rule-making.[11]

5 Julia Black, 'Decentring regulation: understanding the role of regulation and self-regulation in a "post-regulatory" world' (2001), 54.

6 European Council, 'The Stockholm programme — an open and secure Europe serving and Protecting citizens' [2010], *OJ* C 115/01.

7 European Commission, 'Cyber-security Strategy of the European Union: An Open, Safe and Secure Cyberspace' JOIN (2013), 1 final. It was met with calls for its urgent implementation by defence officials: see Council doc. 7847/13. The directives are analysed in more detail in S. 1.

8 Council of the European Union, 'EU–US Summit, Joint Statement', Council doc. 16726/10, 3; Presidency Conclusions of the Cybercrime Conference Budapest Conclusions Budapest, 13 April 2011.

9 The EU Cybercrime Centre, based within an existing agency, Europol ('EC3'): European Commission, 'Tackling Crime in our Digital Age: Establishing a European Cybercrime Centre', COM(2012), 140 final.

10 For example, 'Parliament demands single EU voice on cyber-security'. *EUobserver* (13 June 2012): http://euobserver.com/creative/116606, accessed 23 December 2015. Contrariwise, attacks against the Commission and the EEAS in 2011 resulted in cybersecurity reportedly being considered as a priority by the then Polish, Danish and Cypriot trio of presidencies of the Council.

11 European Commission, 'First Annual Report on the Implementation of the EU Internal Security Strategy', COM(2011), 790; European Commission, 'The EU Internal Security Strategy in Action: Five steps towards a more secure Europe', COM(2010), 673 final.

The EU's Cyber Security Strategy similarly places emphasis upon the US as the EU's lead partner.[12] The European Agenda on Security for 2015–2020 now places cybercrime as one of the three most pressing threats to security.[13]

There is a specific relationship between the taxonomy of cybercrime and cybersecurity. Questions of its taxonomy presuppose particular commitments to the rule of law and fundamental rights, as well as the character of the regulatory processes and the existence of particular risks. The taxonomy or definitional separation of cybercrime from cybersecurity in rule-making is widely criticised and apparent in many legal orders and systems.[14] But it is usually of more concern to legal rather than other scholarship on rule of law and fundamental rights grounds. The Council of the EU has decided that cybercrime is the more pertinent of the two concepts in order to focus the regulatory process.[15] A comprehensive legal definition of 'cybercrime' for EU law is not yet found in secondary law. Instead, the content of the Council of Europe Convention on Cybercrime – i.e. understood here as external norms – is proposed to form the basis for EU rule-making in cyber policies, internally *and* externally.[16] Conceptually, cybercrime may be defined both narrowly, to include offences against computer data and systems, but also more broadly, to include offences committed with the help of computer data and systems.[17] By contrast, cyber-security usually relates to four major societal threats – crime, cyberwar, cyber terrorism and espionage.[18] The Council of Europe Convention adopts a broad perspective on cybercrime but is much criticised for its overbroad content,[19] its lack of provision for cross-border enforcement and its obligations imposed upon Internet Service Providers,[20] and it does not purport to regulate cybersecurity. Nonetheless, as it is the most far-reaching multilateral agreement on cybercrime in existence, purporting to harmonise national legislation procedurally and substantively, its suitability as a pan-Europe source of regulation may be questioned. Its relative 'age' raises the question as to whether its view of risk regulation, its empirical basis and the exponential rise in use of the Internet since its enactment has rendered it outdated. As a result, the failure of many EU Member

12 Cyber Security Strategy (n. 7), 15.

13 European Commission, *The European Agenda on Security*, COM(2015), 185 final, 2.

14 For example, David Thaw, 'The Efficacy of Cybersecurity Regulation' (2013), 30, *Georgia State University Law Review*. See Susan Brenner and Bert-Jaan Koops (eds), *Cybercrime and Jurisdiction: A Global Survey* (Asser Press, 2006).

15 'Informal Justice and Home Affairs Ministers' Meeting, Cyber Security Issues, discussion paper (18–19 July 2013, Vilnius).

16 European Treaty Series (ETS), No. 185, Budapest, 23 September 2001.

17 See Jonathan Clough, *Principles of Cybercrime* (Cambridge University Press, 2010).

18 Joseph Nye, 'Cyber Power', Belfer Center for Science and International Affairs Working Paper, May 2010, 16: http://belfercenter.ksg.harvard.edu/files/cyber-power.pdf, accessed 23 December 2015.

19 It categorises cybercrime in four sets of categories in Articles 2–13: offences against the confidentiality, integrity and availability of computer data, computer-related offences, content-related offences and offences related to intellectual property rights. It is applicable to any crimes for which it is necessary to collect evidence in electronic form – that is, not just to cybercrimes: Article 14(2)(c).

States to ratify it in tandem with a massive change of EU competences in the field since its enactment makes its centrality to the rule-making process somewhat unconvincing.[21] The reduction of cybercrime has been prioritised as a regulatory goal for the EU in its rule-making on cybercrime and cybersecurity.[22] This ostensibly entails the adoption of a 'law and order' approach, one which heightens the need for a holistic, systematic and transparent framework for the regulation of cyber policies.

There are major regulatory advantages in developing in particular the *external* component of cyber regulation. Rule-making between the EU and US legal orders in security has a broad range of regulatory subcomponents, including to enable EU–US trade, spurring global rule-making for the Internet and combating cyber-related criminal activities. In turn, it has clear implications for data protection and privacy, which featured initially only *tangentially* in the EU's cyber rule-making with the US. The outbreak of the NSA surveillance saga in the midst of the rule-making processes has operated to place EU citizens' fundamental rights and data protection centrally in *all* rule-making of the EU with the US. It also operated to cause the European Parliament to vociferously call into question a range of existing EU–US security agreements – i.e. external EU security.[23] However, the NSA surveillance has also operated paradoxically to reignite EU–US negotiations on a data protection framework and alter the regulatory components and trade-offs of this external rule-making.[24]

It is argued here that it is noteworthy that although the EU gives primacy to external norms – i.e. the Council of Europe Cybercrime Convention, in both its contemporary internal and external rule-making in security, it produces very different regulatory results despite the commonality of the norms used. Nor has it produced particularly comprehensive, systematic or conceptually transparent processes in either forum. Differences between external and internal rule-making processes may be explicable because of the on-going 'regularisation' of the AFSJ into ordinary EU law. On the other hand, the evolution of EU criminal law suggests that such a framework should be more holistic, sophisticated and rights

20 Although, on its enforcement provisions, it is argued that the Convention can be read to permit direct interaction between law enforcement and ISPs. This was the subject of review by the Council of Europe in 2013; see also Jack Goldsmith, 'The Internet and the Legitimacy of Remote Cross-Border Searches' (2001), 1, *Chicago Legal Forum*, 103; Maria Grazie Porcedda, 'Transatlantic Approaches to cyber-security and cybercrime' in Patryk Pawlak (ed.), 'The EU–US Security and Justice Agenda in Action' (30 December 2011), EUISS Chaillot Paper, No. 127: www.iss.europa.eu/uploads/media/cp127_EU-US_security_justice_agenda.pdf, accessed 23 December 2015.

21 Opinion of the European Data Protection Supervisor of 14 June 2013 on the Cyber Security Strategy and Directive: https://secure.edps.europa.eu/EDPSWEB/edps/Consultation/OpinionsC, accessed 23 December 2015.

22 Informal Justice and Home Affairs Ministers Meeting (n. 15).

23 European Parliament resolution of 23 October 2013 on the suspension of the TFTP agreement as a result of US National Security Agency surveillance (2013/2831 (RSP)).

24 See Council of the European Union, 'Joint Press Statement following EU–US Justice and Home Affairs Ministerial Meeting of 18 November 2013 in Washington', Council doc. 16418/13.

dependent. However, the character of EU internal regulation in particular necessitates a schema to formulate and regulate risk holistically, which does not yet exist.

Accordingly, this account examines how the distinction between external and internal security in contemporary EU law manifests itself and, in particular, how the EU relies upon external norms. The account also maps the evolution of the rule-making processes themselves. The chapter examines first, the evolution of the instruments of the EU's internal regulation of cybersecurity and cybercrime in the EU Cyber Strategy, its supporting directive along with the development of a cybercrime directive. Second, it examines the development of EU internal rule-making and, third, assesses rule-making between the EU and US in cybercrime and cybersecurity and its relationship to internal EU rule-making, as well as its regulatory impact, followed by conclusions.

Mapping EU internal rule-making

The account begins by mapping the *definitional* nature of the regulatory components and legal tools of EU internal rule-making in both cybercrime and cybersecurity, prior to conducting an analysis of the *substantive formulation* of the regulatory structure. The account thus examines, first, the nature of EU cybersecurity, as the 'first in time' legislative component of EU cyber regulation.

The EU Cyber Security Strategy

The EU's strategy for cybersecurity was finally published in early 2013 and it follows many less than successful or complete policy initiatives in this area. These include a proposal for a Networks and Information Policy in 2001, soft law strategies and various programmes, instruments and policies on so-called Critical Infrastructure, policies that did not establish binding legal obligations upon the operators of critical infrastructures.[25] This reliance upon soft law to regulate cyber risk has been overtaken. Cybersecurity is depicted in the EU's strategy as referring to 'the safeguards and actions that can be used to protect the cyber domain, both in the civilian and military fields, from those threats that are associated with or that may harm its interdependent networks and information infrastructure'.[26] This generates three definitional questions concerning cyber risk. First, the relationship of cybersecurity and confidentiality of information with data protection matters is ostensibly of much significance from the type of harm formulation but

25 See Commission Communication, 'Network and Information Security: proposal for a European Policy Approach', COM(2001) 298; Commission Communication, 'Strategy for a Secure Information Society', COM(2006) 251; Commission Communication, 'Protecting Europe from large-scale cyber-attacks and disruptions: enhancing preparedness, security and resilience', CO(2009) 14; Council Directive 2008/114/EC on the identification and designation of European critical infrastructures and the assessment of the need to improve their protection [2008], *OJ* L 345/75.

26 Cyber Security Strategy (n. 7), 3.

is not reflected in the strategy or its legal tools, discussed next. Second, its definition presupposes the relevance of militarisation to it conceptually. The militarisation of cyber offences is perceived to be a distinctive feature of cybersecurity particularly in the US and accordingly, there is much debate concerning the application of international law relating to war on cyber attacks.[27] While the text of the Council of Europe Convention itself does not mention terrorism, a listed activity on the website of the Council of Europe is cyber-terrorism.[28] However, the strategy does not appear to be substantively motivated by or governed by such concerns as to risk overall. Third, the strategy describes cybercrime to include a range of different criminal activities, not precisely as in the Convention, only approximately so.[29] Its definition of cybercrime has generated infelicities in its taxonomy, infelicities that have prompted much critique and which impact upon its overall formulation of an over-arching framework for risk.[30]

The strategy purports to pursue five strategic priority areas which include, first, that 'achieving cyber resilience' is to be pursued by legislation, in particular by means of a directive on Networks and Information Security (NIS), discussed in detail next. An NIS would require member states to designate at national level competent authorities for NIS, who would in turn cooperate with each other at EU level and private actors would also report to NIS competent authorities. Soft law measures, including awareness-raising exercises, key elements of transatlantic cooperation, form part of this specific first strategic target, similar to the EU–US WGCC, discussed below.[31] In respect of the second priority, that of 'drastically reducing cybercrime', it is this priority which has become the focus of EU rule-making both internally and externally. The strategy urges Member States who had not yet ratified the Council of Europe Cybercrime Convention to do so, which is also similar to the EU–US WGCC. In respect of the third priority, that of 'developing cyber defence policy and capabilities under the Common Security and Defence Policy', it provides that the High Representative would invite the Member States and the European Defence Agency to develop an EU cyber defence policy, seeking to complement the work of the North Atlantic Treaty Organisation (NATO). With regard to the fourth priority, the development of the industrial and technological resources for cyber security, it sought to promote a single market for cybersecurity products, including voluntary EU certification and public–private platforms for the evolution of NIS solutions.[32] With regard

27 See Prepared by the International Group of Experts at the Invitation of the NATO Cooperative Cyber Defence Centre of Excellence, *Tallinn Manual on the International Law applicable to Cyberwarfare* (Cambridge University Press, 2013).

28 The EU Counterterrorism Coordinator is a participant in the EU–US cooperation.

29 Strategy, n. 7, 3 – i.e. where computers and information systems are involved either as a primary tool or primary target, comprising traditional offences, content-related offences and offences unique to computers and information systems.

30 See Opinion of the European Data Protection Supervisor (n. 21).

31 Ibid., 7.

32 Ibid., 13.

to the fifth priority, the development of a 'coherent international' cyberspace policy for the EU, the EU would work more closely with international organisations such as the Council of Europe, the OECD, NATO and ASEAN,[33] in addition to its cooperation with the US, described as 'particularly important'. Nevertheless, the strategy states that while the EU would launch international initiatives to promote global cooperation, *it would not call for the creation of new international legal instruments.*[34] Instead, the Convention would remain the model for drafting *national* cybercrime legislation and would also be a model for international cooperation. With regard to 'roles and responsibilities', the strategy explicitly states that EU 'supervision' is not the answer because cyber incidents do not stop at the borders of the digital economy and society.[35] Institutionally, the strategy envisions overall a division of labour between the areas of (1) Network and Information Systems (NIS), (2) law enforcement and (3) defence,[36] involving a vast range of actors but notably excluding national data protection authorities.

Before analysing the substantive formulation of risk within the strategy, the account turns next to examine the directive introduced to support the strategy.

Legal tools of EU rule-making in cybersecurity: obligations upon market operators

While the strategy is partially centred upon defence, it is based upon a minimum harmonisation directive, which proposes to provide for a high common level of Network and Information Security across the Union (NIS).[37] It purports to establish a cooperative network mechanism for information exchange and to impose binding obligations upon public administrators and market operators of critical infrastructures. Competent national authorities are to be designated at national level,[38] which will be the focal point for cross-border cooperation, assisted by CERT teams in the Member States.[39] These authorities and the Commission will form a so-called permanent network for cooperation, exchanging and circulating information.[40] Moreover, national authorities will monitor the application of the

33 But notably not including the UN.
34 Emphasis supplied, ibid. 15.
35 Ibid., 17.
36 The Commission European Network and Information Security Agency (ENISA), the Computer Emergency Response Team (CERT EU), national networks of competent authorities responsible for NIS, and 'EP3R', the entity which partners the public and private sector (i.e. NIS globally), EC3, the European Police College (CEPOL) and EuroJust (i.e. law enforcement); the EEAS and the European Defence Agency (i.e. defence), CERT, NIS Competent Authorities (i.e. NIS), cybercrime units (i.e. national law enforcement) and national defence and security authorities (i.e. defence).
37 European Commission, 'Proposal for a Directive concerning measures to ensure a high common level of network and information security across the Union', COM(2013) 48 final.
38 Ibid., Article 6.
39 The latter pursuant to Article 7, said to act under the supervision of the competent authority.
40 Ibid., Article 8.

directive at national level and provide, similar to the Commission, early warnings on certain types of incidents, which may result in all competent authorities having to agree a coordinated response. Where an incident emerges, the Commission may adopt delegated acts.

The legal basis for the directive is in Article 114 TFEU, in the form of a minimum harmonisation directive, and this specific choice of legal basis merits attention. The directive provides that divergences in NIS regulations in the member states would constitute obstacles to trade in the event of no EU action being taken, resulting in the objectives being better achieved at EU level.[41] The NIS is thus connected to cross-border trade in so far as the strategy contends that the resilience of information systems is essential to the smooth functioning of the internal market. Nonetheless, the nature of the legal obligations created for the national authorities in the directive is 'light-touch' harmonisation – i.e. through information exchange networks.

The directive as originally proposed placed very onerous obligations upon national administrators and public network operators to identify and manage risk. Article 14(2) required 'market operators' and public administrations to notify the NIS competent authority of 'incidents' which have a 'significant' impact on the security of the core services they provide.[42] However, as the European Data Protection Supervisor has stated, the definition of 'market operator' was insufficiently clear as expressed in Annex II, as is the definition of 'incident' and 'significant impact'.[43] The EP notably made extensive amendments, especially to the scope of such definitions.[44] The use of Article 114 TFEU poses an interesting contrast with the EU's external rule-making with the US discussed below, where neither obstacles to trade or trade conflicts, nor obligations on market operators form any explicit relevance in the rule-making. On one hand, this could be said to demonstrate the lack of symmetry between the internal and external rule-making. On the other hand, trade conflicts and obligations on market operators largely constitute questions relating to enforcement which are conducted at local level, rendering their absence from external rule-making justifiable.

Another legal tool used in the Cyber Security Strategy is the 'mainstreaming' of cybersecurity policies into *inter alia* EU external relations law and policy.[45] 'Mainstreaming' constitutes a complex fusion between a policy instrument, a

41 COM(2013) 48 (n. 37), 8.

42 Small and medium-sized enterprises are excluded: Article 14(8); the obligations only apply *within* the EU. See Annex II. This contrasts with the extensive *voluntary* programme provided for in the recent US Cybersecurity Executive Order.

43 He criticises in particular its compliance with data protection obligations (Directive 95/46/EC of the European Parliament and of the Council of 24 October 1995 on the protection of individuals with regard to the processing of personal data and on the free movement of such data [1995], *OJ* L 281/31) and the obligations incumbent upon microenterprises: Opinion (n. 21), 16–17.

44 www.europarl.europa.eu/sides/getDoc.do?pubRef=-//EP//TEXT+TA+P7-TA-2014-0244+0+DOC+XML+V0//EN&language=EN, accessed 23 December 2015.

45 Strategy, n. 7, 15.

rule-making strategy and norm embedded within EU law and policy.[46] Its actual success or relevance to all areas of EU policy is perhaps patchy after over a decade of its existence, given the unlikelihood of producing practical results if 'everything' must be taken into account. The deployment of mainstreaming as a legal tool is revealing as it constitutes an explicit effort to engage with the amorphous divide between external and internal aspects of security rule-making. In the end, however, it is difficult to view mainstreaming as anything other than a convoluted tool. One may say that this in fact exposes well the challenges of marrying the external and internal in rule-making, especially one based upon a commitment to the primacy of external norms.

The account next examines the content of EU internal rule-making in cybercrime.

Cybercrime: third-generation EU criminal law

The substantive legal content of EU cybercrime law has evolved in a piecemeal form, among a plethora of legal instruments, actual and proposed, and has been conceived apart from cyber security. EU cybercrime 'law' per se is a relatively recent legislative phenomenon, ostensibly beginning with the Framework Decision on attacks against information systems in 2005.[47] However, there is still no commonly agreed definition of cybercrime in EU law or no specific cybercrime directive. Instead, the ratification of the Convention has been advocated by most EU institutions for some time, entailing that it has consistently prioritised external norms in its rule-making.[48] The Framework Decision provided for the criminalisation of online and offline conduct, along with serious penalties and jurisdictional rules, focusing upon individual wrongdoing, but constituting only a minimal or limited harmonisation of laws, so much so that several member states sought to rely upon existing legislation in place by way of satisfaction of the approximation requirements, yet generating some level of regulatory disparities with which the Commission expressed its dissatisfaction.[49] Later policy sought a broader policy framework for cybercrime, including increased law enforcement cooperation, public–private partnerships and international cooperation, which eventually resulted in a proposal to repeal and update the provisions of the Framework Decision.

46 Specifically in the area of EU Gender Equality law, whereby Article 8 TFEU mandates the integration and promotion of equality between men and women in all areas of EU policy. See also the mainstreaming of basic values into the legislative process. For example, it is a central tool of the European Pact for Gender Equality, 2011–2020.

47 Council Framework Decision 2005/22/JHA of 24 February 2005 on attacks against information systems [2005], *OJ* L 69/ 67.

48 See, for example, report from the Commission to the Council based on Article 12 of the Council Framework Decision of 24 February 2005 on attacks against information systems, COM(2008), 448 final; Council Conclusions concerning an Action Plan to implement the concerted strategy to combat cybercrime, 3010th General Affairs Council meeting (Luxembourg, 26 April 2010).

49 See Valsamis Mitsilegas, 'Area of Freedom, Security and Justice, including Information Society Issues' in Julia Laffranque (ed.), 'FIDE Congress XXV Reports: General Report, 40–41' (Tallinn, Estonia, 2012); Commission Communication, 'Towards a general policy on the fight against cybercrime' COM(2007) 267 final.

A directive adopted in late 2013 (hereafter the Cybercrime Directive) places emphasis in particular upon a strategy to fight *new* methods of creating cybercrime – for example, large-scale 'botnets' – i.e. networks of computers with a cross-border dimension.[50] It purports to criminalise access to systems, systems interferences and data interference, with penalties from two to five years. It provides for an ostensibly unwieldy procedure in Article 12, whereby a member state must inform the Commission where it wishes to take jurisdiction over offences *outside* its territory. An earlier version of the Cybercrime Directive has been criticised for its vague legal obligations and its over-criminalisation, especially of 'small-scale' hackers.[51] The Commission has invoked Eurobarometer surveys on cybercrime referencing the legal uncertainty surrounding protections for consumers making online payments to warrant the use of so-called 'third generation' EU criminal law.[52] However, in this regard, in contrast to the Framework Decision, it is not necessarily a superior regulatory instrument. As a directive, disparities inherent in its implementation practices may cause its provisions to be unevenly interpreted across the member states, which seems undesirable from the perspective of regulating risk holistically. It is worth noting that a 'comprehensive' vision of EU cybercrime law was mooted at the launch of the directive by the Commission to include provision for financial cybercrime, illegal Internet content, the collection, storage and transfer of electronic evidence, as well as more detailed jurisdiction rules, in the form of 'comprehensive' legislation operating in parallel with the Convention, with non-legislative measures. It is a formulation of cybercrime law which has yet to materialise and emphasises the non-holistic vision of risk, with regard to its instruments.

Turning, then, to the infrastructure of EU cybercrime,[53] the establishment of a new dedicated Cybercrime Centre was later proposed by the Council and became a key component of the EU Internal Security Strategy and also the

50 Botnets are a network of computers infected by a virus which can be activated without the users' knowledge to attack information systems on a large scale. See Directive 2013/40/EU of the European Parliament and of the Council of 12 August 2013 on attacks against information systems and replacing Council Framework Decision 2005/222/JHA 2013, [2013], *OJ* L 218/8. See its previous draft: COM(2010) 517 final.

51 For example, the UK stated that it would opt into the directive, on the basis that it explicitly states that it will not change existing EU competence. See 'United Kingdom Report' in Valsamis Mitsilegas (ed.), 'Area of Freedom, Security and Justice' (n. 49) 655–81. See also European Parliament, LIBE briefing, June 2012, 2010/0273.

52 European Commission Press Release, 'Cybercrime: EU citizens concerned by security of personal information and online payments' IP/12/751, 9 July 2012. On so-called post-Lisbon Third Generation EU Criminal law and its relationship to the internal market, see Massimo Fichera, 'Criminal Law Beyond the State: The European Model' (2013), 19 *ELJ* 174.

53 The Council in 2008 began plans to institutionalise cybercrime in EU law with the development of so-called 'platforms', a national alert 'platform' and a European 'platform', convergence points of national platforms within the competence of Europol: Justice and Home Affairs Council Conclusions, Council doc. 14667/08, 8–10. See draft Council Conclusions on a Concerted Work Strategy and Practice Measures against cybercrime, Council doc. 15569/08.

implementation of the Stockholm Programme.[54] An EU 'Cybercrime Centre' (the so-called 'EC3') was officially launched in 2013, which is based within Europol ostensibly as a 'desk' thereof.[55] It is a deliberate structural addition to the AFSJ within an agency, portrayed as desired by Europol itself, when much effort is being spent upon 'communautarising' AFSJ agencies, not least Europol itself.[56] This renders its purported 'quasi-institutionalisation' difficult to comprehend.[57] The centre is stated to have four core functions, acting as a European focal point in fighting cybercrime, operationally fusing information and informing Member States of threats. The innovation of the centre was intended to be as to the latter, that it would adopt a 'cross-community approach' – i.e. it would exchange information beyond the law enforcement community, would develop a common standard for cybercrime reporting and would assume the collective voice of cybercrime investigation. However, these functions largely constitute 'information exchange', overlapping with Europol's current mandate.[58] Its establishment prior to the development of an overarching legal infrastructure in cybercrime and cybersecurity provides evidence of the piecemeal evolution of EU internal policies to regulate cyber risk. This leads to a more substantive discussion of the nature of risk within the EU's internal rule-making.

The character of internal EU rule-making

The Cyber Security Strategy, its related directive and the Information Systems Directive present three distinct issues for consideration – namely, the problematisation of EU 'cyber risk' and its management in cyber regulation, including its incidence to warrant regulation; second, its relationship to the multi-stakeholder construction of the regulatory paradigm in EU law and policy and, third, the place of rights-based understandings of cyber regulation – for example, data protection and privacy.

54 See Action Plan Implementing the Stockholm Programme, COM(2010) 171 final, 34.

55 See (n. 11), 3. See its website: www.europol.europa.eu/content/megamenu/european-cybercrime-centre-ec3-1837, accessed 23 December 2015. It is not a 'functionally autonomous' body similar to the European External Action Service.

56 For e.g. as to Europol, Eurojust, ENISA and a European Public Prosecutor's Office, pursuant to Articles 85 and 86 TFEU.

57 'Europol wants to host EU cybercrime centre', *EUobserver* (14 November 2011): http://euobserver.com/cyber/114259, accessed 23 December 2015. At the launch of the centre, Europol was asserted to have previously lacked sufficient resources to gather information from a broad range of sources and to have lacked the capacity to deal with requests from law enforcements agencies, the judiciary and the private sector.

58 A point not considered in much detail in the Feasibility Study for a European Cybercrime Centre, RAND Corporation, 2012, prepared for the European Commission. Notably, Interpol representatives with sit on its board and Interpol will reportedly launch its own Cybercentre in 2015. While non-duplication of EU rules with international rules are aims of the EU, international cooperation is a function of the centre.

First, the problematisation of cybercrime as a regulatory subject is more acutely disputed than cybersecurity, although they overlap considerably even in such literature. As Wall states, there is much confusion about the risks posed by cybercrime and the consensus that it exists.[59] Few national level prosecutions, fuelled by reports of a high rate of cybercrime activity render it problematic. Added to this is the role of external malware unconnected to the Internet – for example, Stuxnet via a USB key – yet also commonly problematised as a form of cyber risk warranting regulation. The rising incidence of both cybercrime and security risks are depicted in the strategy as the reason to warrant regulation qua criminalisation. Such an assertion of 'incidence' relies heavily upon the thesis as made by, for example, ENISA arguing that cybercrime is rarely reported as a chronically underreported crime, with a significant impact upon individual users.[60] It is an assertion as to risk regulation which appears empirically untestable and relies on this absence of knowledge for far-reaching regulatory choices. However, the knowledge relied upon in the EU strategy and the directive for the existence of risk emanates from an extremely limited and disparate range of asserted incidents, despite accepting a rising incidence of harm – so limited, in fact, that little effort is made in the formulation of harm to actually distinguish acts of nature (e.g. flooding), external devices and actual attacks on IT infrastructures.[61] In its launch of the strategy and directive, the Commission described 'facts' about the existence of cybersecurity drawn from *inter alia* Symantec and McAfee studies, two leading market actors in a specific sector with specific financial interests in the establishment of cyber harm, as well as a Eurobarometer poll, Eurostat figures and data from the World Economic Forum.[62] The Commission outlined as a factual assertion that there were an estimated 150,000 computer viruses in circulation every day, although not specifying the global nature of the harms or the relevance of the EU territory to the risk asserted to exist. Similarly, the data of the World Economic Forum or Symantec and McAfee do not in reality establish the existence of harm to warrant the EU to regulate and instead appear strikingly non-specific formulations of the incidence of risk. The LIBE Committee of the European Parliament has condemned the over-criminalisation

59 David Wall, *Cybercrime: The Transformation of Crime in the Information Age* (Polity Press, 2007); see also David Wall, 'Cybercrime and the Culture of Fear: Social Science fiction(s) and the production of knowledge about cybercrime' (2008), 11; *Information, Communications and Society*, 861, writing of a 'series of myths', 862.

60 'Cyber security incidents rarely reported: EU Agency', *Euractiv* (27 August 2012): www.euractiv.com/specialreport-data-protection/eu-agency-cyber-security-inciden-news-514465, accessed 23 December 2015, citing an ENISA report ('Cyber Incident Reporting' (August 2012)), mentioning 51 notifications of 'large' incidents by regulators.

61 'Cybersecurity incidents are increasing at an alarming pace': Strategy, 3; Impact Assessment Strasbourg, 7 February 2013, SWD(2013) 32 final, 12–14. Cf. Annegret Bendiek and Andrew Porter, 'European Cyber Security Policy within a Global Multistakeholder Structure' (2013), 18 *EFAR* 155.

62 European Commission Press Release, 'EU Cybersecurity plan to protect open internet and online freedom and opportunity' IP/13/94, 7 February 2013.

of cybercrime, as much as its disproportionate over-criminalisation in the Cybercrime Directive, in the light of its ineffectiveness.[63] Yet it is not a viewpoint shared across the institutions. For example, the character of cybercrime as a daily nuisance and potential threat has been invoked by the Commission to warrant higher cybercrime penalties.[64] The impetus towards criminalisation has been fuelled by those seeking urgent implementation of the strategy's defensive components, still in the absence of a defined basis of the specific risk to be defended against. As a result, the problematisation of cyber risk appears inadequate, under-theorised and not ripe for a large-scale regulatory framework.

A second consideration is that the regulatory structure of the strategy problematises it as a multi-stakeholder exercise. It emphasises the emergent actor structure of cybersecurity, which transcends national, international, transnational and private actors, both internally and externally.[65] It is, of course, essential to have 'stakeholders' involved in the construction of this form of institutional design, given that industry, users and specialist stakeholders are often best placed to identify new risks. There are many means to enrol such actors within regulatory systems as part of management and service delivery, which reflects broader questions of the fragmentation and hybridity of governance.[66] It is cost-effective to enrol industry into the enforcement of regulation. But whether it is adequate as a regulatory framework for higher-risk forms of regulation is not so certain. Such a framework may become opaque if the firms do not disclose their risk management regimes and may not reveal new risks. The need to have so many partners involved may be explained as part of the knowledge building of rule-making in a complex field, although its complexity raises questions as to its efficacy, as much as its transparency and institutional design. Sharing powers and tasks across actors within regulatory regimes may reduce its effectiveness.[67] This remains an acute challenge for the formulation of risk within the strategy and the NIS directive. One may remark upon the surprisingly small number of stakeholders consulted by the Commission as to the NIS despite the legal obligations of the end product, which calls into question how 'multi-actor' the framework is in reality.[68]

The strategy and NIS directive appear to consider cyber regulation less systematically or holistically than comparable multi-stakeholder regulatory exercises – for example, in EU banking and finance regulation instruments,

63 See n. 51.

64 DG Home Affairs, European Commission, on 'Cybercrime': http://ec.europa.eu/dgs/home-affairs/what-we-do/policies/organized-crime-and-human-trafficking/cybercrime/index_en.htm, accessed 23 December 2015.

65 See Bendiek and Porter (n. 61).

66 See Julia Black, 'Enrolling actors in regulatory systems: examples from UK financial services regulation' (2003), PL 63.

67 See generally Black and Baldwin (n. 2).

68 See COM(2013) 48 final; SWD(2013) 32 final, 2. 'EP3R' is described as the device where the private sector was consulted and a public online and written consultation conducted yielded 179 responses, including from public authorities and NGOs, p. 7. The manner of portraying this procedure is not particularly explicit or detailed.

discussed further below. In this regard, regulation is proceeding in the absence of quantifiable harms or an empirically testable and consistent definitions of cybercrime and cybersecurity. In turn, the dominance of the multi-stakeholder approach appears to lack legitimacy and accountability. From the perspective of national authorities, member state administrative bodies participating in EU-wide networks, with or without EU supervision, are not a new phenomenon of EU law and policy: they are more prevalent in the area of utilities regulations, fundamental rights or data protection, where precise obligations have been imposed upon the member states within a broader framework.[69] From the perspective of private actors, industry and/or market operators, the use of Article 114 TFEU seems to be deployed disproportionately – i.e. oriented towards the regulatory objective of placing a significant burden upon private operators within a less than holistic framework.

The third substantive consideration is that the strategy and its directive expressly propose to create an open Internet and online forum for freedom of expression. However, one can observe that the most telling omission in its regulatory infrastructure is in respect of data protection and citizen rights, both substantively and in its institutional infrastructure. It makes, for example, no provision for the role of Data Protection Authorities to control or police the use of data within the networks of actors collaborating in both the strategy and directive, as voiced by the European Data Protection Supervisor.[70] Similarly, one can note that information-sharing obligations are not couched explicitly in a 'citizen-centric' manner, instead acting as a relevant consideration 'after the fact'. In this regard, it is important to note that the strategy was released prior to the NSA surveillance saga which has unfolded, which may yet ameliorate this concern and leads to the question of the relationship between the internal and external regulatory processes.

The account accordingly turns to examine the external rule-making of the EU with the US in the area of cybercrime and cybersecurity.

The EU's external cyber rule-making: EU–US working group in cybercrime and cybersecurity (WGCC)

Overview

Rule-making in the areas of cybercrime and cybersecurity between the EU and US constitutes the first major transatlantic cooperation in security for a decade. It lacks the counterterrorism impetus attached to previous transatlantic

69 See Bruno De Witte, 'New Institutions for Promoting Equality in Europe: Legal Transfers, National Bricolage and European Governance' (2013), 60 *AJCL* 49, 58 (nn. 28 and 29).

70 Opinion of the European Data Protection Supervisor of 14 June 2013 on the Cyber Security Strategy and Directive: https://secure.edps.europa.eu/EDPSWEB/edps/Consultation/OpinionsC, accessed 23 December 2015.

cooperation.[71] It also takes place in the post-Lisbon context, after which the EU has been granted single legal personality for the EU and competence for its pursuit of the regulation of criminal law, pursuant to Article 82 TFEU and Article 83 TFEU, operating as an entirely new legal background. It forms a specific area of cooperation worthy of attention because of its particular relationship with internal EU rule-making in this area and its regulatory output.

While the EU–US WGCC group was established after the EU–US summit in November 2010, the origins of this cooperation date back to the Joint EC–US Task Force on Critical Infrastructure Protection a decade earlier,[72] and at about the same time, the Council of Europe Cybercrime Convention was adopted, which now forms a central legal element of EU–US cooperation similar to the EU rule-making.[73] EU–US negotiations on a data protection framework agreement also began in early 2010 but appear to have stalled for some time.[74] The EU–US cooperation goals are predominantly in four areas, including (1) to expand cyber incident management response capabilities jointly and globally, (2) to broadly engage the private sector using public–private partnerships, sharing good practices with industry and to launch a programme of joint awareness raising activities, (3) to remove child pornography from the Internet and (4) to advance the international ratification of the Convention by the EU and Council of Europe member states and to encourage pending non-European countries rapidly to become parties.[75] The first Cyber Atlantic exercise in 2011 kicked off a programme of joint cyber-attack exercises, to culminate in a fully fledged EU–US cybersecurity exercise in 2014.[76] The activities of the WGCC were to be conducted in four expert subgroups consistent with the four fields of work of the WGCC,[77] which include a broad network of governmental, agency and institutional actors. Public workshops and meetings have been conducted in 2011 and 2012 as part of the rule-making exercise and one of the hallmarks of this cooperation might be said to be

71 See Elaine Fahey, 'Law and Governance as Checks and Balances in Transatlantic Security' (2013), 32 *YEL* 1. See also on transatlantic rule-making, Elaine Fahey and Deirdre Curtin (eds), *A Transatlantic Community of Law: Legal Perspectives on the Relationship between the EU and US legal orders* (Cambridge University Press, 2014).

72 European Commission, 'Creating a safer Information Society by improving the security of information infrastructures and combating computer related crime': COM (2000), 890 final.

73 It entered into force on 1 July 2004 and was drafted by the Council of Europe member states and Canada, Japan, South Africa and the US.

74 Until recently. See 'European Commission seeks high privacy standards in EU-US data protection agreement', IP/10/609, 26 May 2010. See the press release from 4 April 2013: www.justice.gov/opa/pr/2013/April/13-ag-382.html, accessed 23 December 2015. The LIBE committee of the European Parliament was debriefed on the negotiations in February 2013: LIBE(2013)0220_1.

75 EU–US Working Group on cybersecurity and cybercrime, Concept Paper, 13 April 2011. Annex I. It set a deadline for ratification before the 10th Anniversary celebration of the Convention in 2011.

76 See Commissioner Cecilia Malmström, 'Next step in the EU–US cooperation on Cyber security and Cybercrime', SPEECH/13/380, 30 April 2013.

77 Concept paper (n. 75) 6.

its efforts to initiate transparency and public participation, despite the highly diverse range of stakeholders involved in cyber policies.[78]

The WGCC is expressed to be an 'outreach' model to other countries or international organisations with similar cyber issues and, from the outset, it seems apparent that the WGCC had 'global' rule-making objectives, specifically the advancement of the Council of Europe Convention.[79] This has been an objective of EU rule-making for some time. In 2008, the European Commission suggested that its redrafting or modernisation had become unachievable yet nonetheless since then promoted both international and EU ratification.[80] The WGCC Group mentions specific countries to be 'encouraged' to become parties to the Convention, countries within and outside the EU.[81] In 2012 and 2013, there were still a number of EU member states 'resisting' ratification on various grounds at the time of writing.[82] This context emphasises how the legal objectives of the EU–US cooperation are globally oriented. Similarly, another expected goal of the EU–US cooperation includes the endorsement of EU–US 'deliverables' in cybercrime by the Internet Corporation for Assigned Names and Numbers (ICANNs), the controversial US-based organisation responsible for managing and coordinating the Domain Name System (DNS), engaging in significant postnational rule-making.[83] Further evidence of the nature of the 'global' objectives of the rule-making is provided by the minutes of a 2011 meeting of EU–US Senior JHA officials, where it was stated that the EU and the US would work together in the UN to avoid dilution of the body of international law on cybercrime.[84] One may remark that the European Commission was seeking global cybersecurity policies even before its own EU-level policy had been conceived.[85] Moreover, in advance of the adoption of the Cyber Security Strategy, the European Parliament in 2012 advocated an EU framework on cybersecurity, with a view to the policy being 'brought up' at G8 and G20 level.[86] The goals

78 For example, holding open workshops for a broad range of private and public actors and publishing the lists of all of the participants: www.enisa.europa.eu/activities/Resilience-and-CIIP/workshops-1/2012/eu-us-open-workshop, accessed 23 December 2015.

79 Notably, the US is not a member of the Council of Europe but took part in the drafting of the Convention and has signed and ratified it domestically: see Elaine Fahey, 'On the Use of Law in Transatlantic Relations: Legal Dialogues Between the EU and US' (2014) 21 *ELJ* 368.

80 Proposal for a directive on attacks against information systems and repealing Council Framework Decision 2005/222/JHACOM(2010) 517 final, 2.

81 Concept Paper (n. 75) 4.

82 See the ratification table at: http://conventions.coe.int/Treaty/Commun/ChercheSig.asp?NT=185&CM=&DF=&CL=EN , accessed 23 December 2015.

83 WGCC Concept Paper (n. 76) 3. However, IANN appears increasingly eager to interact publicly with the Internet governance community: see www.icann.org/en/news/announcements/announcement-07feb13-en.htm, accessed 23 December 2015.

84 Council of the European Union, 'Summary of Conclusions of the EU–US JHA Informal Senior Officials Meeting of 25–26 July' Council doc. 13228/11, 3.

85 Cf. European Commission, 'Critical Information Infrastructure Protection – Achievements and next steps: towards global cyber-security' COM(2011) 163 final.

86 See n. 10.

of the WGCC suggest that they will lead eventually to the adoption of a global-like cyber policy or, at the very least, global standard-setting, through their promotion of the primacy of external norms. The ambitious nature of the globally ambitious and externally oriented rule-making *externally* contrasts with the policies pursued by the EU *internally*, as a far more modest rule-making process. By contrast, it can be said that this internal rule-making compares less than favourably with the EU's external rule-making, appearing instead piecemeal and less ambitious, in its failure to regulate holistically, transparently and systematically.

In the same period as the publication of the EU Cyber Security Strategy, the US president signed executive orders providing for rules on cybersecurity for the US, couched in a dense framework of administrative law which accords considerable discretion to officials of the Department of Homeland Security.[87] The difference in cybersecurity approaches between the two legal orders has been suggested to create major regularity challenges for companies operating in the EU and US with the voluntary approach to the US contrasting with the compulsory approach provided for by the EU.[88] The US cybersecurity approach instead involves private actors at all stages of rule-making and enforcement, although the comparative study of EU and US regulation is frequently cautious concerning the outcomes and explanations of policy convergence and divergence.[89] The WGCC does indeed appear eclipsed by such differences in regulatory developments in the respective legal orders, although such an analysis is premature in the light of other regulatory developments discussed next.

This leads to the next section, which considers the substantive impact of the EU's external security rule-making.

The regulatory impact of the EU–US WGCC

Contemporary events surrounding EU–US relations suggest that the regulatory impact of the EU–US cooperation is manifold, affecting EU–US rule-making in many areas – i.e. external security – but is also relevant to EU internal security. Thus, it arguably has both direct and indirect impacts of significance. Its direct regulatory impact is set to be the broad adoption of global standards on cybercrime in the guise of a Council of European Convention. Equally, the deliverables of the EU–US cooperation on Internet domains are set to be adopted by

87 Executive Order 13636, 'Improving Critical Infrastructure Cybersecurity', Federal Register 78, No. 33 (19 February 2013). See the 'Comprehensive National Cybersecurity Initiative', which employs commercial and government technology to engage in threat-based decision-making: www.whitehouse.gov/issues/foreign-policy/cybersecurity/national-initiative, accessed 23 December 2015. See also 'The 2013 Cyber-security Executive Order: Overview and Considerations for Change', Congressional Research Service 7-5700 R42984 (1 March 2013).

88 See 'EU, US go separate ways on cybersecurity' *Euractiv* (5 March 2013); Bendiek and Porter (n. 61).

89 See, more generally, Jonathan Wiener, Brendon Swedlow, James Hammitt, Michael Rogers and Peter Sand, 'Better Ways to Study Regulatory Elephants' (2013), 2 *EJRR* 311.

ICANN and possibly then globally. As a result, this would amount to a direct regulatory result. Of course, the extent to which transatlantic rule-making is viewed as normatively legitimate remains to be seen given that ICANN has recently attempted to increase or enhance participation and transparency in its rule-making practices.[90]

There are many regulatory benefits of the EU–US cooperation, not least the avoidance of trade conflict and interagency disputes. There is now an historically low number of trade conflicts pending before the EU and US at the WTO,[91] yet it remains a latent issue in all transatlantic rule-making. Moreover, a regulatory advantage of the WGCC would be to avoid ineffective agency-level bilateral models. For example, consider the recent Memorandum of Understanding between the Irish Data Protection Commissioner, as the data protection agency of the member state where most global social networking sites are headquartered,[92] and the US Federal Trade Commission on the operation of the EU-US Safe Harbour Agreement.[93] The recent NSA surveillance events demonstrate the obvious inadequacies of such a bilateral model and its failings to protect citizens' data, albeit in respect of a voluntary or hybrid regulatory regime.

The formulation of EU external cyber regulation with the US must be conducted so as not to create 'blind spots' of areas not within the framework. Its manifold components and externalities suggest that it may readily generate blind spots in the regulatory process. For example, the WGCC output could also be of much significance for cloud computing as a regulatory enterprise in so far as it could impact broadly upon understandings of territory, legality and cyber markets.[94] An EU–US expert working group on cloud computing was established by the Transatlantic Economic Council in 2011 which met in early 2012 and has to report to the EU–US Information Society Dialogue. However, the NSA surveillance has been mooted by a European Commissioner as a reason for Europeans not to trust US clouds and instead to build their own.[95]

90 See, for example, significant emphasis on the ICANN website on transparency and accountability-related activities. See www.icann.org/, accessed 23 December 2015.

91 For a recent survey of the European Parliament, see Library of the European Parliament, 'Principal EU–US disputes' (22 April 2013): www.europarl.europa.eu/RegData/bibliotheque/briefing/2013/130518/LDM_BRI(2013)130518_REV1_EN.pdf, accessed 23 December 2015.

92 For example, Facebook, Google, Twitter.

93 See www.ftc.gov/os/2013/06/130627usirelandmouprivacyprotection.pdf, accessed 23 December 2015.

94 Cf. media reports that the US Foreign Intelligence Surveillance Amendment Act (FISAAA) granted powers to grab EU data in US clouds: Nikolaj Nielsen, 'US free to grab EU data on American clouds' *EUobserver* (28 January 2013): http://euobserver.com/justice/118857, accessed 23 December 2015.

95 'Europe pushes own digital 'cloud' in wake of US spying scandal' *Euractiv* (29 August 2013): www.euractiv.com/infosociety/prism-cloud-european-silver-lini-news-530004, accessed 23 December 2015.

One may observe that EU–US rule-making is generally very sectoral or discrete and has a heavy dependence upon contemporary political affairs for its momentum. An EU agreement on data protection for transfers of personal data for law enforcement purposes was still actively under negotiation in early 2013. The WGCC began its work significantly prior to the outbreak of the NSA surveillance saga. This has since then called into question a broad range of EU–US data transfer agreements as well as the EU Data Protection Regulation negotiations. The European Parliament has voted to suspect all EU–US data transfer agreements on the foot of its enquiry on mass surveillance by the US. By contrast, the EU–US Justice and Home Affairs ministerial meeting in late 2013 stressed the importance of developing the EU–US negotiations on a data protection agreement, referencing the work of the EU–US ad hoc working group on the NSA surveillance saga.[96] Moreover, the regulatory impact of the EU–US WGCC is possibly of significance for, and in turn is related to, the on-going negotiations on an EU–US Data Protection Framework Regulation and an EU Data Protection Regulation. For example, the NSA surveillance affair has enhanced the controversy surrounding a draft provision of Article 42 of the draft regulation which would give an EU court authority over surveillance of EU citizen data pursuant to a foreign court order or other body.[97] The EU and US have recently reached an agreement on a data protection 'umbrella agreement' in the wake of the legal demise of the Safe Harbour Agreement before the CJEU.[98] Such developments have the capacity to significantly alter the dynamic of the EU–US rule-making.

The limited range of the WGCC mandate in the area of fundamental rights and data protection may thus need to be fundamentally revisited so as to acquire credibility and legitimacy. Moreover, its output seems increasingly eclipsed by EU and US internal rule-making developments. The European Parliament vote on the NSA surveillance and a European Parliament enquiry might have suggested a reduced impetus for the evolution of the regulation of cyberspace bilaterally, at least in the absence of a much stronger 'citizen-centric' component thereof. On the contrary, however, it has operated to spur the development of EU–US negotiations on a truly transnational instrument.

96 Joint Press Statement following EU–US Justice and Home Affairs Ministerial Meeting of 18 November 2013, Council 16418/13 (Brussels 18 November, 2013). See Council of the European Union, 'Report on the Findings by the EU Co-chairs of the Ad Hoc EU–US Working Group on Data Protection', Council doc. 16987/13 and European Commission, 'Rebuilding Trust in EU–US Data Flows' COM(2013) 846 final. The latter references the role of the US within the Council of Europe Convention on Cybercrime as evidence of promotion of privacy standards internationally, 9.

97 See Regulation (EU) 2016/679 of the European Parliament and of the Council of 27 April 2016 on the protection of natural persons with regard to the processing of personal data and on the free movement of such data (General Data Protection Regulation), entering into force in May 2016.

98 Case C-362/14 *Schrems* v. *Data Protection Commissioner* ECLI:EU:C:2014:317; see http://europa.eu/rapid/press-release_STATEMENT-15-5610_en.htm.

Conclusions

The case study of the rule-making of the EU in cyber policies is an instructive one, concerning the contours of internal and external security, as well as providing an insight into their specific relationship. The complexity of a regulatory process with many internal and external components raises the question as to its conceptual transparency, its functionality and systematic character. It has been argued here that the norm primacy accorded to the Council of Europe Convention has not yielded regulatory benefits. The account depicted here has demonstrated the primacy of external norms by the EU in its external and internal security making, as much as the overlapping and interlocking relationship between the internal and external dimensions thereof. While similarly prioritising the primacy of external norms, the external rule-making of the EU with the US envisages a bolder vision of security rule-making on a global level. The process and content of the case study outlined here provides evidence of the openness of the EU to external norms. This account has demonstrated how the internal/external dichotomy in EU security is very real and apparent. Its evolution reveals particular relationships between the two, dependencies and trade-offs. It also reveals contrasting but closely dependent approaches to the internal and external components of EU security. The traditionally asserted 'fluidity' of external and internal security is arguably inadequate when seen from the perspective of this account. Instead, external security reveals many significant dependencies upon internal security.

7 The EU's participation in the global legal order

Manifestations of sovereignty

Introduction

How the EU impacts, effects, participates and interacts in and with the global legal order presents many challenges for orthodoxy. One of the greatest challenges that it presents as a leading postnational democracy is argued here to be for our understanding of sovereignty. Accounts which depict or describe the EU as a postnational actor do not tend to invoke sovereignty, neither as a construct nor as a method or process thereof. Instead, such accounts are more concerned with the place within breakdowns of orthodoxy conceived broadly, the shortcomings of postnational democracy and its institutional components and rule-making practices. And there are many accounts in legal scholarship as to how the EU has evolved as an international actor, particularly after its last treaty revision process.[1] Such accounts suggest that the EU plays an 'active role in shaping the international order'[2] in terms of its objectives and practices and many policies, but it is similarly not a discourse mediated through sovereignty. The EU's participation in the global legal order is argued to show manifestations of 'late sovereignty', or at least to be atypical of postnational sovereignty.[3] It has spatial, action and transboundary dimensions that require unpacking. Sovereignty is arguably neither popular nor conventional, nor does it transpose itself into discourses of rule-making beyond the nation state. For some, to speak of sovereignty in the context of global governance leads to bewildering identification of a 'global sovereign'. International relations 'constructivists' emphasise that sovereignty in its internal and external facets is a socially constructed trait.[4] They

1 See Steven Blockmans, Bart van Vooren, and Jan Wouters (eds), *The Legal Dimension of Global Governance: What Role for the EU?* (Oxford University Press, 2012).

2 See Dimitry Kochenov and Fabian Amtenbrink (eds), *The EU's Shaping of the International Legal Order* (Cambridge University Press, 2014).

3 Manifestations: 'An event, action, or object that clearly shows or embodies something abstract or theoretical': www.oxforddictionaries.com/definition/english/manifestation, accessed 23 December 2015.

4 See John Searle, *The Construction of Social Reality* (Free Press, 1995); John Gerard Ruggie, 'Continuity and Transformation in the World Polity: Toward a Neorealist Synthesis' in Robert Keohane (ed.), *Neorealism and Its Critics* (Columbia University Press, 1986); see David Lake, 'The New Sovereignty in International Relations' (2003), 5(3), *ISR* 303.

are social facts that are usually produced and reproduced through the practices of states. Sovereignty comes from 'some place' and is heavily influenced by other social norms and practices. One of the most appealing and useful features of sovereignty for understanding the EU's actions in the world is that the EU, similar to sovereignty itself, has both an internal and external dimension.

As Keohane states, a means to interpret the essence of sovereignty is to view it as a thesis about norms of sovereignty being possibly violated.[5] Social norms are conventionally depicted as shared expectations on the part of a group about appropriate behaviour.[6] In the nation state context, when norms are espoused they may not make a difference but they are important sources of behaviour in world politics. Norms do not per se determine behaviour but they exercise an impact. However, for norms to be relevant they must be advocated. At supranational level – i.e. as to a regional organisation – these terms carry a different force, as considered here in. Norm agency is usually intended to imply where states act as advocates, non-state organisations act as advocates and international organisations act as norm agents.[7] The EU may be said to be a rising but complex norm agent because of its porous openness to *inter alia* external and internal norms and their interaction onwards into EU rules. The active and developing component of this process has the appearance of a manifestation, as a tendency, an incremental process or development. Norms act as a focal point for decentralised networks of organisations and individuals and, as a result, international organisations are major promoters of norms in world politics. This chapter focuses upon one aspect of the theorisation of sovereignty which is the manner in which norms are promoted by the EU through its participation in the global legal order.

This chapter argues that this participation may usefully be captured by sovereignty as an overarching framework beyond an analysis for power, influence and interactions between legal orders. It is argued that sovereignty comprises dynamic internal and external interfaces, and that it captures the flexible, fluid but also pragmatic way in which the EU gradually asserts itself in the global legal order. Accordingly, the account unpicks and unravels manifestations of the EU's emerging postnational sovereignty achieved through a consideration of social practice, active conduct, and the space of and for EU rules and their boundaries.

5 Robert Keohane, 'Stephen Krasner: Subversive Realist' (2010), APSA 2010, Annual Meeting Paper. Available at SSRN: http://ssrn.com/abstract=1643351, accessed 23 December 2015; Robert Keohane, 'Ironies of Sovereignty: The European Union and the United States' (2002), 42 *JCMS* 743; see Stephen D. Krasner, *Sovereignty: Organized Hypocrisy* (Princeton University Press, 1999).

6 For example, Martha Finnemore, *National Interests in International Society* (Cornell University Press, 1996), 22. Contrast Katerina Linos in her recent book who argues that there is a body of evidence indicating that international norms are spreading within regions across the globe and causing radical policy shifts: *The Democratic Foundations of Policy Diffusion: How Health, Family, and Employment Laws Spread Across Countries* (Oxford University Press, 2013).

7 See M. Finnemore and K. Sikkink, 'International Norm Dynamics and Political Change' (1998), 52 *IO* 887.

This chapter explores first, the lexicon of the 'postnational' as applied to the EU. It then assesses the understandings and many paradoxes of sovereignty. The next section considers the exceptionalism of EU sovereignty, including EU sovereignty. Finally, it considers what the EU participates towards the global legal orders and how it does this, in four subsections, as to its goals, social practices, the 'space' of and for EU rules, and the construction of (trans)boundaries under EU law.

By way of a preliminary overview, this chapter outlines what is understood by the term 'postnational' as applied to the EU and its legal order in this account.

The lexicon of the postnational

The demise of the nation state as a solitary actor and its increasing propensity to operate within transnational constructs is a fact of contemporary life. Nonetheless, it still remains the ultimate actor.[8] Terms such as 'postnational law' or 'postnational democracy' have been deployed to depict 'the state of the State' as much as the decline of the boundaries of societal orthodoxy.[9] Less so, the terms are used more incidentally in respect of the rule-making or legal instruments resulting therefrom, in the postnational 'space'.[10] Ostensibly, postnationalism implies that the performance of constitutionalism and politics is no longer configured around or constructed within the territorial strictures of the nation state. Postnationalism signifies the importance of the proliferation of new forms of law and politics, interactions between legal orders and political disordering.[11] Postnationalism is arguably less a study of single or specific instruments or policies and instead is probably more accurately a broader methodology to study shifts in norms, actors and processes.

However, postnationalism has not resulted in any accepted normative idea of postnational 'law' as a phenomenon, especially not in legal scholarship. Nor has it evolved with any express relationship to sovereignty as a construct, method or process of legal orders or ordering. At its height, the deployment of postnationalism in legal scholarship has even been critiqued as 'EU-centric'

8 See, most famously, Saskia Sassen, *Losing Control? Sovereignty in the Age of Globalization* (Columbia University Press, 1996); also Saskia Sassen, *Territory, Authority, Rights: From Medieval to Global Assemblages* (2nd edn, Princeton University Press, 2008).

9 See Colin Crouch, *Post-democracy* (Polity Press, 2004); Jürgen Habermas, *The Postnational Constellation: Political Essays* 1st edn (MIT Press, 2001); Jürgen Habermas, *The Crisis of the European Union: A Response* (Polity Press, 2012); Deirdre Curtin, *The European Union: A Postnational Democracy in Search of a Political Philosophy* (Kluwer Law, 1997).

10 See Damian Chalmers, 'Post-nationalism and the quest for constitutional substitutes' (2000), 27 (1) *JLS* 178; Karl-Heinz Ladeur, 'The Theory of Autopoiesis as an Approach to a Better Understanding of Postmodern Law From the Hierarchy of Norms to the Heterarchy of Changing Patterns of Legal Inter-relationships', EUI Working Paper Law No 99/3; Erik Eriksen, Christian Joerges and Florian Rödl (eds), 'Law and Democracy in the Post-National Union', ARENA Report No. 1/2006; Neil Walker, 'Postnational Constitutionalism and Postnational Public Law: A Tale of Two Neologisms' (2012), 3 *TLT* 61.

11 See Chalmers, n. 10.

and 'court-centric', thereby lacking relevance to any legal order or field outside the context of the EU, constructed largely through judicialised understandings of conduct.[12] Postnational conceptualisations of the EU are not perceived to have a broad reach precisely because, as some wryly, there is no postnational world.[13] Moreover, its inherent direction may become problematic. For example, can postnational legal orders such as the EU become post-postnational in the event of intense institutionalisation taking place between it and the US (for example, in the Transatlantic Trade and Investment Partnership (TTIP))?[14] Postnationalism may be said to capture most accurately the aspirations of the last treaty revision process of the EU. It was sought there to create an autonomous democratic life of the EU, legal personality, dispersed external executive power and a regularisation of its most sensitive field for nation state sovereignty, its Area of Freedom, Security and Justice (AFSJ). In this regard, to speak of the EU as a postnational democracy is more commonplace in scholarship.[15] Postnational democracy has a heavy descriptive component in the EU treaties, expressly developed in the autonomous section on the democratic life of the EU. Its 'promise' is of significance to many.[16] However, this is not to reify the significance of the use of the postnational. The lexicon of the postnational is not necessarily a term of art and rather a broader one to understand the development of the EU. Yet it is not one which offers an account of the dynamics of power or the superstructure of hierarchy and authority. What this account attempts to develop, then, is the usefulness of sovereignty for the depiction of the postnational as it applies to the EU.

The 'useful uselessness' of sovereignty

Overview

Sovereignty is conducted within a rhetoric that is usually conducted either in terms of *negativity*, loss, breakdown and reference to the past,[17] or in terms

12 Gregory Shaffer, 'A Transnational Take on Krisch's Pluralist Postnational Law' (2012), 23(2) *EJIL* 565; Nico Krisch, *Beyond Constitutionalism: The Pluralist Structure of Postnational Law* (Oxford University Press, 2011).

13 Ibid.

14 Established after the EU–US Summit in 2011, followed by an Interim Report on 19 June, 2012. See Final Report High Level Working Group on Jobs and Growth: http://trade.ec.europa.eu/doclib/docs/2013/february/tradoc_150519.pdf, accessed 23 December 2015. See Marija Bartl and Elaine Fahey, 'A Postnational Marketplace: Negotiating the Transatlantic Trade and Investment Partnership (TTIP)' in Elaine Fahey and Deirdre Curtin (eds), *A Transatlantic Community of Law: Legal Perspectives on the Relationship between the EU and US Legal Orders* (Cambridge University Press, 2014).

15 See Chalmers, n. 10.

16 Armin Van Bogdandy, 'The European Lesson for International Democracy: The Significance of Articles 9–12 EU Treaty for International Organizations' (2012), 23 *EJIL* 315.

17 See Joschka Fischer, 'Europe's Sovereignty Crisis': www.project-syndicate.org/commentary/europe-s-sovereignty-crisis, accessed 23 December 2015.

of *positivity*, which is constructive – e.g. as to sovereignty in conflict,[18] competitive sovereignty, mixed sovereignty or pooled sovereignty. In this way, it offers a parallel to postnational rule-making in its emphasis upon disorder but also upon the space of postnational rule-making. The essential incoherence and even uselessness of sovereignty in contemporary legal scholarship is an omnipresent feature, be it in UK constitutional law, supranational discourse or emerging polities.[19] Its ability to confuse and cloud debate is one frequently observed, especially across subject disciplines.[20] Similarly, its tendency to raise the rule of recognition 'finders trail' garners it little support. The contestable and *acriticerial* nature of sovereignty is asserted as both a normative and descriptive standard, yet few accounts of sovereignty may be said to be truly preoccupied with the latter.[21] As a result, sovereignty remains a strikingly malleable 'construct', with broader appeal than its detractors suggest,[22] despite assertions of its demise and futility. It is argued that the meaning of sovereignty is open to change across time and space, more so than ever before.[23] Others depict sovereignty as a common ground where the concerns of lawyers and political scientists can meet.[24] The need for a conceptual framework for sovereignty to settle immediately a series of paradoxes often involving legitimacy and authority makes it no small task. The discursive nature of sovereignty can render it attractive to emergent polities, less so for 'deeper' integration mechanisms.

The classical 'orthodoxy', if one may term it that, is well put by Loughlin, reminding us that it is a relational interface between law and politics that separates

18 Samantha Besson, 'Sovereignty in Conflict' (2004), 8(15) European Integration Online Papers 1. Available at SSRN: http://ssrn.com/abstract=594942, accessed 23 December 2015.

19 See Hans Lindahl and Bert van Roermund, 'Law Without a State? On Representing the Common Market' in Zenon Bankowski and Andrew Scott (eds), *The European Union and its Order: The Legal Theory of European Integration* (Blackwell/Wiley, 2000), 1; Bert Van Roermund, 'Sovereignty: Unpopular and Popular,' in Neil Walker (eds), *Sovereignty in Transition: Essays in European Law* (Hart, 2003), 33. But see Alison Young, 'Sovereignty: Demise, Afterlife or Partial Resurrection?' (2011), 9(1), I.CON 163, arguing that it requires a shift in focus from a definition of sovereignty in terms of law-making power to an analysis of sovereignty in terms of power over constitutive rules. See Jean Cohen, *Globalization and Sovereignty Rethinking Legality, Legitimacy, and Constitutionalism* (Cambridge University Press, 2012).

20 See Beth Simmons, 'Review Essay: Is Sovereignty still Relevant' (2000), 94(1), *AJIL* 226, emphasising the distance between disciplines on the place of law in the global context. Similarly Cohen, ibid., adopts no specific definition of law in this account, despite the place of law and legality within her account. See also Nick Barber, 'The Afterlife of Parliamentary Sovereignty' (2011), 9(1) *I.CON* 144.

21 See Samantha Besson, 'Sovereignty in Conflict' (2004), 8(15), *European Integration Online Papers* 1. Available at SSRN: http://ssrn.com/abstract=594942, accessed 23 December 2015.

22 On its evolution, see Jens Bartelson, *A Genealogy of Sovereignty* (Cambridge University Press, 1995), 88; Quentin Skinner, 'The Sovereign State: a Genealogy' in Hent Kalmo and Quentin Skinner (eds), *Sovereignty in Fragments: The Past, Present and Future of a Contested Concept* (Cambridge University Press, 2010).

23 See Jens Bartelson, 'The Concept of Sovereignty Revisited' (2006), 17 *EJIL* 463.

24 Ibid.

and binds both domains together.[25] Nonetheless, his assertion that the proliferation of new international institutions does not in any way necessitate a *new* form of sovereignty, whereby it remains undisturbed by international integration, is argued here to be far from compelling.[26] It does not engage with the enabling characteristics of postnational actors/organisations and their participation in the global legal orders. It appears to this author more compelling to argue, as Keating does, that although sovereignty may be ebbing away, new sovereignty claims are being made all the time.[27] For example, in the context of the EU, while there may be no single European demos, he proposes instead 'plurinational democracy', to locate democracy *inter alia* in communities of will.[28] The openness of such a construction and its realist acceptance of the complex dual role of the EU alongside its member states is worth reflecting on. The sovereign state is self-evidently unlikely to remain the only locus of political authority and community in the future, but at the same time it remains a very potent, even tricky, source of authority and community.[29] Nonetheless, there is one particularly valuable feature of sovereignty and that is its ability to form a lexicon for the transition of the world of sovereign states to a world where sovereignty has been relocated in many different levels, above and beyond the nation state.[30]

Bellamy's assertion of sovereignty and post-sovereignty as two sides of the one coin are argued to be particularly problematic in so far as he states that post-sovereignty views other forms of sovereignty as a threat to rights. As he states, the EU certainly reflects the positive and negative aspects of the passage from sovereign to post-sovereign (promotion of liberal democracy versus the race to the bottom and/or legitimacy challenges), as much as an awkward space between them – for example, the limited integration of the EU's AFSJ. However, others contend with some force that the difficulty with post-sovereignty is its blindness to the epistemic as much as the normative role of sovereignty, irrespective of what it is attached to.[31] Rather, Besson has claimed, post-sovereignty fails to engage with the countless later claims to *finalité* that will arise. Yet there is something rather unpalatable about an assertion, as Besson makes, as to the 'correct' use of sovereignty, given the highly constructivist nature of sovereignty and its acknowledged contestability. It is constantly the subject and object of

25 Martin Loughlin, 'Ten Tenets of Sovereignty' in Neil Walker (eds), *Sovereignty in Transition* (Hart, 2003), 55. See Hans Lindahl, to the effect that it elaborates the *contingent* unity of a political community: 'Why Sovereignty?' in Richard Rawlings, Peter Leyland and Alison Young (eds), *Sovereignty and Law: Domestic, Regional & Global Perspectives* (Oxford University Press, 2013).

26 Because it is a foundational concept of the discipline of public law, see Loughlin, ibid., 56.

27 Michael Keating, 'Sovereignty and Plurinational Democracy. Problems in Political Science' in Neil Walker (eds), in *Sovereignty in Transition*, (Hart, 2003), 191.

28 Keating, ibid., 208.

29 See Stephen D. Krasner, *Sovereignty: Organized Hypocrisy* (Princeton University Press, 1999); Wouter Werner and Jaap H. de Wilde, 'The Endurance of Sovereignty' (2001), 7 *EJIR* 283.A.

30 Neil Walker, 'The Cosmopolitan Local: Neil MacCormick's Post Sovereign World' in John Eric Fossum and Agustin Jose Menendez (eds), *The Post-Sovereign Constellation* (Springer, 2011).

31 See Samantha Besson, 'Sovereignty in Conflict' (2004), 8(15), EIO Papers 1. Available at SSRN: http://ssrn.com/abstract=594942, accessed 23 December 2015, 18.

aggressive reinterpretation arising from globalisation, new claims to territoriality and the EU itself. Contrariwise, theorisations of its essential features by Besson by means of 'cooperative sovereignty' suggest that its dynamism and reflexiveness undermine her efforts to dichotomise the correct and even 'incorrect' use of sovereignty. Yet it is equally unsatisfactory or inadequate to settle on flexibility or malleability alone as the gold standard. These latter developments suggest distinct new challenges for sovereignty – for understanding, for example, new layers of autonomous action.

The compartmentalised debates on the force of the nation state or new manifestations of sovereignty remain an enduring feature of this analysis. This leads to a more specific discussion on the place of the EU therein and its starting points and premises.

Sovereignty and EU exceptionalism

EU scholarship on sovereignty begins from the premise of its exceptionalism as a construct. In the worlds of the greatest critics of claims of EU exceptionalism in discussions of sovereignty, the EU is inconsistent and contradictory as an entity – and not necessarily a straightforward model for an organisational representation of sovereignty.[32] There is a dominance of *tripartite* formulations of sovereignty in EU law scholarship itself.[33] For example, Chalmers suggests that sovereignty has been cast in three ways in the EU legal order. The first sees sovereignty as a series of activities which go to make up a domestic human order which transcends and constrains government, protected from EU law as it is a governmental order.[34] The second views sovereignty as something that ordains EU law and grants it authority and retains the prerogative to patrol the democratic quality of EU law.[35] The third argues that if EU government involves these bodies as most capable of expressing the will of this sovereign human order in its decision-making, it can enjoy sovereignty.[36] However, overall, he argues that the 'genius and folly of EU debates on sovereignty lie in their fluidity'. Yet there is a tremendous gap concerning how cultural, geographic and geopolitical considerations come into play more broadly in non-European analyses of

32 See the transcript of the interview with Krasner 'Sovereignty: An Interview', available at: http://globetrotter.berkeley.edu/people3/Krasner/krasner-con3.html, accessed 23 December 2015.

33 See Jean Cohen, *Sovereignty and Globalization: Rethinking Legality, Legitimacy and Constitutionalism* (Cambridge University Press, 2012), emphasising dualistic sovereignty as an optimum descriptor of contemporary global governance – that is, the importance of the nation state, without developing the relevance of law therein.

34 Damian Chalmers, European Restatements of Sovereignty in Rawlings, Leyland and Young (n. 25), Chapter 11.

35 Ibid., 3, citing Jens Bartelson, *A Genealogy of Sovereignty* (Cambridge University Press, 1995) 88 and Benno Teschke, 'Geopolitical Relations in the European Middle Ages: History and Theory' (1998), 52 *IO* 325, 350–355.

36 Ibid.

sovereignty.[37] In a similar methodology, Besson outlines the three main camps within EU sovereigntists to be the national intergovernmentalists, the European supranationalists, both advocating unitary accounts of sovereignty, and then the post-sovereigntists.[38] Such tripartite models used to explain and understand sovereignty to demonstrate its flexible lexicon, its multifaceted dimension and its constructability. Sovereignty theorisations remain awkwardly wedded to taxonomies of their content, usually tripartite ones, as if to reinforce its inherent intractability. Such tripartite analytical lens engage little with its exceptionalism despite operating from the assumptions thereof, and instead treat it as *sui generis.*

Much scholarship on sovereignty and the EU has been developed prior to more recent invocations in the EU treaties to evolve as a postnational democracy. For example, for Krasner, the EU remains solely a product of sovereign states and as a *sui generis* organisation, he argues that it is not capable of replication or imitation. He appears fixed to the idea that the EU Member States have effective democratic sovereignty but not Westphalian sovereignty. For him, withdrawal of member states from the EU is a not viable option nor is a truly federalised United States of Europe, but this analysis begs the question as to its application to contemporary developments in the EU legal order.[39] These innovations include withdrawal from the Union, a (postnational) democratic life of the Union, the development of formal legal coherence of EU action in the world by creating specific external representation in the form of the ('actively' named) European External Action Service, separate legal personality,[40] and the 'conventionalisation' of the most sensitive field traditionally guarded jealously by the member states, the EU's AFSJ. It also precedes a vast range of legislative efforts to manipulate legal constructs so as to save the Eurozone through international agreements by the member states, *outside* the EU treaties and *outside* EU accountability and legitimation structures.[41] These developments demonstrate

37 See Antony Anghie, 'Rethinking Sovereignty in International Law' (2009), 5 *ARLS* 291; Michael Byes and Adriana Sinclair, 'When US scholars speak of sovereignty, what do they mean?', TransState Working Papers 597, No. 44, 1. See the historical account of Brendan Simms, *Europe: The Struggle for Supremacy, from 1453 to the Present* (Lane, 2013).

38 See Samantha Besson, 'Sovereignty in Conflict' (2004), 8(15) EIO Papers 1.

39 Stephen Krasner, *Sovereignty: Organized Hypocrisy* (Stanford University Press, 1999).

40 See, of many, Ramses Wessel, 'Revisiting the International Legal Status of the EU' (2000), 5 *EFAR* 507; Rafael Leal-Arcas, 'EU Legal Personality in Foreign Policy?' (2006), 24 (2), *BUILJ* 65; Matthias Ruffert, 'Personality under EU Law: A Conceptual Answer towards the Pluralisation of the EU' (2014), 20 *ELJ* 346.

41 See Bruno De Witte, 'Using International Law in the Euro Crisis Causes and Consequences', ARENA Working Paper No. 4, June 2013; Allan Rosas, 'The Status in EU Law of International Agreements Concluded by EU Member States' (2011), 34(5) *Fordham International Law Journal* 1304; Bruno De Witte and Thomas Beukers, 'Case C-370/12, Thomas Pringle v Government of Ireland, Ireland, The Attorney General, Judgment of the Court of Justice (Full Court) of 27 November 2012', (2013), 50(3) *CMLR* 805; see Elaine Fahey and Samo Bardutzky, 'Judicial Review of Eurozone Law: The Adjudication of postnational norms in the EU courts, plural: A Casestudy of the European Stability Mechanism' (2013), 34, *Michigan Journal of International Law Online*, http://mjilonline.org/?p=694, accessed 23 December 2015.

the weakness of postnational democracy as an ideal and its incompleteness, especially in the face of crisis.

The EU's late sovereignty: the development of post-sovereignty

Walker's formula of *late sovereignty* as a development of postnational sovereignty merits further attention here. As Walker states, late sovereignty is still sovereignty. 'Late sovereignty', in his own words, was 'by way of a retreat' from the assumptions of 'post-sovereignty', which he explains as taking effect 'without returning to the oxymorons of disaggregation or the myopia of the *unitary* approach'.[42] It conceives of sovereignty in terms of a plurality of unities and in terms of the emergent possibilities of the relationships among this plurality of unity. For Walker, 'late sovereignty' is characterised with an atypical typology, which includes fundamental continuity over discontinuity, a distinctive phase in the career of the term, irreversibility, no way back to early sovereignty and transformative potential. He maintains that it is distinctive in that the claim to authority flowing from it is no longer combined with the notion that it need be monopolistic, within the territorial boundaries of the polity. The advantage of 'late sovereignty' is that it explicitly captures new and supplementary tiers of transnationally connected legal and political authority. More significant is his acceptance of the possibility to conceive of autonomy without territorial exclusivity. Arguably the most problematic criterion is the 'no way back' element, now defunct after the possibility of withdrawal from the Union being provided for in the treaties.[43] Walker's defence of the precariousness of late sovereignty encompasses conflict and boundary maintenance, diffusion of sovereign power and reflexivity, and suggests a high degree of conceptual elasticity.[44] For Walker, however, late sovereignty ultimately permits an organisation to flourish in a broad range of contexts. It offers a wide variety of mechanisms to understand participation in the global legal order.

The present account would readily subscribe to later accounts of MacCormick, particularly on the nature of a kind of compendious legal external sovereignty exercised towards the rest of the world, written before innovations in the EU treaties on legal personality. Nonetheless, they appear to have featured significantly (implicitly) in his work in terms of their possible legal and political

42 Neil Walker, 'Late Sovereignty in the European Union' in Neil Walker (ed.), *Sovereignty in Transition* (Hart, 2003), 1; see also Neil Walker, 'Sovereignty Frames and Sovereignty Claims' in Richard Rawlings, Peter Leyland and Alison Young (eds), *Sovereignty in Question* (Oxford, 2013), Chapter 2.

43 Article 50, which was in force at the time of Walker's piece.

44 Neil Walker, 'Late Sovereignty in the European Union' in Neil Walker (ed.), *Sovereignty in Transition* (Hart, 2003), 1, 23; see Neil Walker, 'Surface and Depth: The EU's Resilient Sovereignty Question', in Jurgen Neyer and Antje Wiener (eds), *Political Theory of the European Union* (Oxford University Press, 2010).

impact.[45] The essence of the attractiveness of the formulation of MacCormick was that sovereignty had never been lost in the process of European integration. Politically, it had enhanced the action of its members collectively and perhaps even individually, in his assessment. Rather, the process of division and combination had taken us beyond the sovereign state, albeit well beyond it.

It is argued here that those who contend that new and evolving international institutions do not necessitate a new conceptualisation of sovereignty, such as Loughlin, are unduly myopic to the challenge of postnational rule-making.[46] Such a premise has been developed on the basis that sovereignty is the representation of autonomy of the political and provides the foundational concept for public law. Yet this same premise seems to fail to explicitly acknowledge changes in the nature of international organisations and the empirical rise of postnational rule-making.[47] It is worth noting that for all of the provocation of critics of the EU specifically such as Krasner, they must be remarked to have a particularly limited perspective on the EU and not a particularly contemporary one. The nature of EU regulatory powers and their use, increasingly beyond their boundaries in law, practice and competence shows its limits. Nonetheless, its use thereof for the betterment of its subjects is significant in the context of its place as an aspirant postnational democracy. Similarly, the efforts of the EU to gain specific new statuses in international organisations is of significance. It is vivid evidence of active and participatory practice in the global legal order, even if esoteric.[48]

The EU's participation in the global legal order

Postnational rule-making with a goal of the 'good life'

The diffusion of higher standards, practices and the offer of the 'good life'[49] and well-being for its peoples may be said to represent the broadest premise of the EU as a new international organisation and postnational democracy, although it is not

45 Neil MacCormick, *Questioning Sovereignty: Law, State and Nation in the European Commonwealth* (Oxford University Press, 1999), 133.

46 Martin Loughlin, 'Ten Tenets of Sovereignty' in Neil Walker (eds), *Sovereignty in Transition* (Hart, 2003), 55.

47 Michael Zürn, 'The politicization of world politics and its effects: Eight propositions' (2012), 6 (1) *EPSR* 47; Gary Marks and Liesbet Hooghe, 'Delegation and Pooling in International Organizations' (2015), 10, *Review of International Organizations*, 305.

48 Jan Wouters, Jed Odermatt and Thomas Ramopoulos, 'The EU in the World of International Organizations: Diplomatic Aspirations, Legal Hurdles and Political Realities', KU Leuven Working Paper No. 121 – September 2013, https://ghum.kuleuven.be/ggs/publications/working_papers/new_series/wp121-130/wp121-ramopoulos-odermatt-wouters-1.pdf, accessed 23 December 2015.

49 On what is the good life, this account does not purport to advocate the classical political theory interpretation thereof, and instead implies the benefits of EU integration as conceived in the EU treaties – for example, in the preambles to the TFEU and TEU in particular, beyond the goal of the 'ever closer union'.

the only premise of a postnational democracy.[50] The same can be said for many places, countries and bodies or regimes predicated upon similar ideals, yet which might be said to fall short of a liberal democracy.[51] More specifically, a central difficulty associated with the development of the EU's AFSJ, its most sensitive and evolving field but also the most closely associated with the nation state in terms of offering justice, peace, security and overall well-being, is that it has evolved with considerably less coherence than desirable in its efforts to deepen cooperation, substantively and procedurally – e.g. procedural before the substantive, variable geometry, human rights instruments with specific or limited effects. It has occurred in a manner which does not offer its citizens the benefits of a 'good life' overall. For example, the status of the AFSJ as a policy field or mode of governance remains contentious.[52] There are also many who protest as to its justice deficit, but it is never stated to the effect that the 'good life' is jeopardised.[53]

The development of the AFSJ is a vivid reminder of the limitations of aspirations beyond the nation state. Also, constructions of the good life are too easily premised on the malleable boundaries of EU law. The rule-making toolkit of the EU to act as an innovative organisation is incredibly limited. Moreover, the construction of competence where it straddles classical internal market law and the AFSJ demonstrates how the EU has yet to carve out a sophisticated rule-making toolkit.

Participation within the global legal order as a social practice

Sovereignty is an inherently *social* concept in that it entails the recognition by other similar entities that an entity is also 'one of them'.[54] It thus implies a social relationship of formal equality.[55] Participation in the global legal order is argued

50 See Colin Crouch, *Post-democracy* (Polity Press, 2004); Jürgen Habermas, *The Postnational Constellation: Political Essays* (1st edn, MIT Press, 2001); Jürgen Habermas, *The Crisis of the European Union: A Response* (Polity Press, 2012) who both focus upon citizen participation and the attainability of some form of meaningful representative democracy over the good life at post-national level.

51 On Singapore, see 'Singapore is taking the first steps to true democracy', *The Guardian* (10 May, 2011): www.theguardian.com/commentisfree/2011/may/10/singapore-election-democracy-new-media accessed, 23 December 2015; 'Is Culture Destiny? The Myth of Asia's Anti-Democratic Values' *Foreign Affairs* (November/ December 1994): www.foreignaffairs.com/articles/50557/kim-dae-jung/is-culture-destiny-the-myth-of-asias-anti-democratic-values, accessed 23 December 2015.

52 Helena Carrapiço and Florian Trauner (eds), 'The External Dimension of EU Justice and Home Affairs: Post-Lisbon Governance Dynamics' (2012), 17(2) *EFAR* 1.

53 See Dimitry Kochenov, Grainne de Búrca and Andrew Williams, *Europe's Justice Deficit?* (Hart, 2014).

54 David Lake, 'The New Sovereignty in International Relations' (2003), 5 (3), *International Studies Review*, 303.

55 See Hedley Bull, *The Anarchical Society: A Study of Order in World Politics* (Macmillan, 1977/ Columbia University Press, 2002).

to be a broad construct. It involves understanding the EU as an actor – i.e. what it is and what it does. Some, such as Cohen, have sought to refine the global legal order as an evolving political construct in terms of political participation, within a highly specific formulation of political rights as part of a constitutionalised version of the international system.[56] As such, a thesis of constitutionality presupposes a particular view and definition of 'law' in that context. There is a hypothetical yet highly 'active' content to the measurement of sovereignty with regard to the EU. Some measure the loss of sovereignty in 'real' versus 'formal' terms of active participation in the global arena, and this account draws from this as a point of reflection.[57]

One such arena for analysis is Union participation in international organisations as a social practice, generating recognition, perception and acceptance. *Internal* legal order issues mostly dominate the question of Union participation in, for example, international organisations. The EU treaties provide permissively for participation in Article 218 TFEU, for UN participation in Article 220 TFEU, and permissive third country and international organisation representation in Article 221 TFEU. The EU treaties are considerably more detailed with regard to treaty negotiation and conclusion than with regard to actual participation in international organisations. The EU treaties may be argued to have provided for an incomplete or open-ended legal construction of *active* participation in international organisations.[58] It is worth reflecting on the value that scholarship places on the EU treaties construction thereof. Legal scholarship appears to place a high premium on the ability of the EU to participate externally. It varies from being 'imperfect' or having 'persistent shortcomings' to being open, flexible and permissive.[59] In fact, the EU treaties maintain a silence concerning the active social practices and conventions such as the right to participate or even to become a member of international organisations, not concerning itself with social activities such as discussion, cooperation or negotiation. Representation in international organisations between the institutions is often a source of conflict and may be governed by pragmatism, something which international relations scholars focus upon in the greatest detail.[60] While, for example, the Commission's role as

56 Jean Cohen, *Sovereignty and Globalization: Rethinking Legality, Legitimacy and Constitutionalism* (Cambridge University Press, 2012). See Gráinne De Búrca, Review, *Global Law Books*: www.globallawbooks.org/reviews/detail.asp?id=776, accessed 23 December 2015; Friedrich Kratochwil, Review of 'Sovereignty and Globalization: Rethinking Legality, Legitimacy and Constitutionalism' (2014), 27 *LJIL* 297.

57 Alan Hervé, 'The Participation of the European Union in Global Economic Governance Fora' (2012), 18 *ELJ* 143.

58 Ibid., 161.

59 See Piet Eeckhout, *EU External Relations Law* (2nd edn, Oxford University Press, 2011), 220.

60 Hervé, n. 57; compare Sophie Meunier and Eugenia da Conceicao-Heldt, 'Speaking with a Single Voice: Internal Cohesiveness and External Effectiveness of the EU in Global Governance'(2014), 21 *JEPP* 961; Edith Drieskens and Louise G. van Schaik (eds), *The EU and Effective Multilateralism: Internal and External Reform Practices* (Routledge, 2011).

negotiator has been endorsed in the treaties in Article 17 (1) TEU, there are clear exceptions for common foreign and security policy. Instead, what is referred to as a 'bicephal arrangement',[61] including the presence of member states, the presidency of the EU and Commission, has prevailed in the OECD, the United Nations Conference on Trade and Development and the Socio-Economic Council of the United Nations. This can create external and internal problems – external, for third parties, and internal, as between the rotating presidency and the member states who (i.e. the latter) are compelled by this arrangement to listen and defer (i.e. remain silent).[62] Here, the principle of sincere cooperation does not suffice and case law alone may be insufficient to govern institutional inertia or turf battles. Yet ambiguity in social and active practices is long tolerated as part of EU external relations law.

A balanced and effective external representation may afford broad benefits to the EU, but it may be at the expense of circumscribing the actions of the institutions in external relations, often the Commission. As a result, some consider the distinction between a formal loss of sovereignty (for the member states) and a gain in terms of real sovereignty (for the EU member states) as a dichotomy.[63] Yet it is a complex dichotomy to accept. Some posit a gain for the EU in the context of understanding how the EU can reform global governance.[64] There are manifold assumptions, explicit and implicit, in such a thesis concerning the nature of actual and potential global influence through sovereignty. And examples from one context – e.g. the specificity of international economic law – may not be so easily transposed to another. Nevertheless, the enabling character of sovereignty at the postnational level arguably remains insufficiently studied. States can clearly enter, for example, international agreements or can set up new organisations or institutions, so long as it is without force. This 'characteristic' and practice is more commonplace outside a domestic order with a single hierarchy of authority. Nonetheless, the 'enabling' component appears key to understanding the formal loss and/or gain of sovereignty. This question of enablement is an active one which requires considerable room for manoeuvre, and the chapter thus returns to consider this in further detail. It reflects next on the formulation of the space for and of EU rules, and the impact of EU rules externally.

The 'space' of EU rules and the 'global approach'

There are specific assumptions made in contemporary scholarship worth reflecting upon on the physical or territorial space of EU 'external' rule-making,

61 Derived from the Greek, meaning 'two-headedness'.

62 Mary Farrell, 'EU Representation and Coordination at the United Nations' in Katie Verlin Laatijainen and Karen E Smith (eds), *The European Union at the United Nations* (Palgrave, 2006).

63 Hervé, n. 57, 161.

64 Ibid.

outside the EU, *vis à vis* international law. It raises the question as to how it should impact on our understanding of EU rule-making and the EU's participation in the international legal order. Some offer reasons to explain the success of and reasons for the use of EU law *instead of* international law, including path dependence, geography, ease of decision-making and the effectiveness of the EU.[65] In this analysis, there is a normative assumption as to a physical gap between EU and international law as a regulatory choice. It presupposes that they are distinct rule-making processes and distinct forums capable of such a comparison, which is not necessarily methodologically accurate.

The external impact of the EU's rules – i.e. in the context of the metaphysical space for EU rules – is both a normative and descriptive challenge, but it is a different question from EU law in place of international law as a regulatory choice. Yet it is a question which also flows from considering the space of EU rules. Some, such as Young, have contended that the depiction of the EU as a global shaper of rules has been an exaggerated one of influence, especially in literature on the EU's regional capacity, drawing extensively on literature on what the EU *says* and *does* rather than what it *achieves*.[66] Young challenges the explicit assumption that the EU always seeks to export or upload EU regulatory solutions globally and instead pursues a more relative regulatory solution overall. However, as a proposition it requires more nuancing, not least from a legal perspective.

It is increasingly common for the EU to harbour 'global governance' goals with its third country partners – for example, the aims of the EU–US Transatlantic Trade and Investment Partnership (TTIP), aiming for global standards, similar to the EU–US cybercrime and security negotiations, also aiming for global standards as an outcome but arguably differing somewhat from the 'global approach' to AFSJ data transfer, as depicted here. Also, it may be both over-inclusive and inaccurate to depict the EU's rule-making which has implications, effects and force outside its territory as 'global' rule-making per se, thereby formulating the rule-making in territorial terms.[67] Descriptions of the (regulatory) impact of the EU often do appear to overstate its influences, possess different understandings of what is regulatory impact. It also is easy to neglect outlining instances where the EU did *not* exercise regulatory

65 Anne Thies and Bruno de Witte, 'Why Choose Europe? The Place of the European Union in the Architecture of International Cooperation', in Steven Blockmans, Bart van Vooren, and Jan Wouters (eds), *The Legal Dimension of Global Governance: What Role for the EU?* (Oxford University Press, 2012), 23.

66 Alasdair Young, 'Perspectives on the Changing Global Distribution of Power: Concepts and Context' (2010), 30 (1), *Politics* 2; see Alasdair Young and John Peterson, *Parochial Global Europe: 21st Century Trade Politics* (Oxford University Press, 2014).

67 See Joanne Scott, 'Extraterritoriality and Territorial Extension in EU Law' (2014), 62 *AJCL* 87; Joanne Scott, 'The New EU Extra-territoriality' (2014), 51 *CMLR* 1343. See Geert De Baere and Cedric Ryngaert, 'The ECJ's Judgment in Air Transport Association of America and the International Legal Context of the EU's Climate Change Policy' (2013), 18 *EFAR* 389.

influence.[68] However, as a broader proposition, the space of EU rules is argued here to require more nuancing, method and study as to its components, especially in the context of the AFSJ. In short, there are as many methodological as substantive challenges to such a thesis, which this text has sought to address as part of a research agenda. This leads to the question of the construction of boundaries and transboundaries, which is now considered in further detail.

Transboundary control and EU law

While there has been a charted empirical explosion in the late 20th century in the number of so-called 'transnational' cases arising, where national laws are applied extraterritorially, to attempt to typologise categories of control as it manifests itself in 'transboundary' action – descriptively or normatively – is a steep challenge.[69] It reflects the enduring relevance of boundaries as interests for political ends. Extraterritorial laws have been argued to be a necessary impetus to spur negotiations and provide incentives to cooperate internationally.[70] In this regard, territoriality and extraterritoriality are and seem likely to remain legal constructs defined traditionally by claims to and resistance from authority. As Buxbaum states, the essence of such claims to authority is that particular actors usually wish to promote specific substantive interests.[71] As a result, practical but mainly political questions inevitably dominate these constructs. As Lindahl has argued persuasively, through the guise of alegality, no legal order is in reality thinkable absent boundaries in space, time, subjectivity and content.[72] This is because legal boundaries join and separate within the unity of a legal order.[73] This does not necessarily meet the challenge of the postnational level where one witnesses a specific reconfiguration of directions of authority.

68 See R. Daniel Kelemen, *Eurolegalism: The Transformation of Law and Regulation in the European Union* (Harvard University Press, 2011; on the judicialisation of governance); R. Daniel Kelemen, 'Globalizing EU Environmental Regulation' (2010), 17(3), *JEPP* 335; Anu Bradford, 'The Brussels Effect' (2012–2013) 107 *NULR* 1; Scott (n. 67).

69 Rodney Falvey and Peter J Lloyd, 'An Economic Analysis of Extraterritoriality', Working Papers Series 675 (1999), Department of Economics, The University of Melbourne.

70 See Austen L. Parrish, 'Reclaiming International Law from Extraterritoriality' (2009), 93 Minnesota LR 815; see Jennifer Zerk, 'Extraterritorial Jurisdiction: Lessons for the Business and Human Rights Sphere from Six Regulatory Areas' (2010) Harvard Corporate Social Responsibility Initiative Working Paper No. 59 available at www.hks.harvard.edu/mrcbg/CSRI/publications/workingpaper_59_zerk.pdf, accessed 23 December 2015.

71 Hannah Buxbaum, 'Territory, Territoriality and the Resolution of Jurisdictional Conflict' (2009), 57 *AJCL* 631.

72 Hans Lindahl, *Fault Lines of Globalization: Legal Order and the Politics of A-Legality* (Oxford University Press, 2013).

73 Nonetheless, the specific argument of 'alegality' remains a particularly obscure and difficult one to apply or even to transpose or apply to the EU context.

The phenomenon of the EU leveraging its rule-making outside its territory has been depicted variously as 'territory extension' or 'counter-territoriality'.[74] Yet the traditional 'triumvirate' of sovereignty, territory and jurisdiction conventionally used to theorise borders of laws is arguably of little use in the conceptualisation of much contemporary conduct of the EU.[75] Instead, the globalised world of transboundary conduct and overlapping jurisdiction suggests that these three elements merge more frequently.[76] That EU law should similarly reflect this is not surprising. Moreover, the conduct of the EU externally as a legal actor is not necessarily unitary and instead its actors remain non-unitary. Thus, to assert that the EU acts unilaterally so as to expand its territory has been argued here not to grasp the structural indirectness of the EU's rule-transfer. This point is neatly demonstrated by recalling Scott's argument as to 'territorial extension' of EU law,[77] who proposes 'territory extension' as a (positive) phenomenon of EU rule-making beyond its territory, without necessarily addressing the authority or legitimacy of this endeavour of postnational rule-making. One may note how few legal theorisations of the EU develop extraterritoriality or territorial extension from the premise of broader theorisations of conduct and necessity – for example, cosmopolitanism – so as to justify moral, ethnic or other legal duties outside its territory.[78] From the perspective of sovereignty, there is something unsatisfactory about constructing territorial extension alone as a (quasi-)normative standard, if it is that at all, because of the failure to engage with the blurring of sovereignty, authority and territory therein.

Conclusions

This book has sought to place sovereignty in the context of postnational rule-making and to consider the exceptionalism of EU sovereignty. Postnationalism is more accurately a broader methodology to study shifts in norms, actors and processes, and fits well with the task of unpacking the global reach and effects of EU law. It has been argued here that those who argue that new and evolving international institutions do not necessitate a new conceptualisation of sovereignty are unduly myopic to the challenge of postnational rule-making. EU scholarship on sovereignty begins from the premise of its exceptionalism. However, much scholarship on sovereignty and the EU has been developed prior to more recent invocations in the EU treaties to evolve as a postnational democracy.

74 See Joanne Scott, 'Extraterritoriality and Territorial Extension in EU Law' (2014), 62 *AJCL* 87; Joanne Scott, 'The New EU Extra-territoriality' (2014), 51 *CMLR* 1343.

75 Paul Schiff Berman, 'The New Legal Pluralism' (2009), 5 *ARLSS* 225; Buxbaum (n. 71).

76 Antony Anghie, 'Rethinking sovereignty in international law' (2009), 5 *ARLSS* 291.

77 See n. 74.

78 Compare Noah Feldman, 'Cosmopolitan Law' (2007), 116 *YLJ* 1022 on the normative form of cosmopolitanism in extraterritoriality.

Sovereignty as an inherently social concept entails the recognition by other similar entities that an entity is also 'one of them'. This implies social recognition as a standard or practice. Participation by the EU in the global legal order is argued here to be grounded in understanding the EU as an actor. Legal scholarship appears to place a high premium on the *ability* of the EU to participate externally as an actor, seamlessly, coherently and with consistency. Accordingly, as has been argued here, the *enabling* character of sovereignty at the postnational level appears insufficiently studied.

This book has focused upon one aspect of Krasner's theorisation of sovereignty and norms that is said to be unexplored, which is the manner in which norms are promoted. It is this particular angle that the present account has drawn from, examining how the EU develops and practises its autonomous constructed sovereignty in its AFSJ, both internally and externally. The case studies of norm promotion in the AFSJ, cybercrime and transatlantic rule-transfer demonstrate a variety of haphazard practices, as much as a commitment to external norms. Norm promotion as considered here performs a useful function if it can pinpoint the internal and external facets of EU action through law. Similarly, if it can assist identifying practices of 'enablement', it then has a useful methodological purpose. Moreover, the identification of norm promotion can also pinpoint the relationship between its rule-making and participation in the global legal order.

Three specific elements of the global reach and effects of EU law have been canvassed here throughout through examination of three components – first, internal/external coherence, second, the construction of competence and action, and third, territorial and boundary questions. The three case studies of norm promotion, cybercrime and rule-transfer all demonstrate internal and external incoherence between the aims and means of EU rule-making. All three case studies also raise issues as to the boundaries of competence construction and the reach of the 'internal'. The case studies demonstrate the fluidity of directions of authority and the construction of the external and fluid (cybercrime), with a dominant external component (norm promotion) and with reverse territory claims (rule-transfer).

As has been demonstrated here, legal texts providing for active participation in the global legal order can be almost imperfect even in integrated spheres of action. What is more pressing to consider is the merger of sovereignty, territoriality and jurisdiction in a global world as an emerging matter for EU law, one that requires more attention to methodologies of rule-making.

8 Conclusion

The global reach of EU law has been argued here to be a multidirectional phenomenon which offers insights into the flourishing and failings of EU integration processes. This book has sought to look beyond 'headline' approaches to the global reach of EU law in understanding EU rule-making. Through a closer attention to methodology (e.g. examining form, process and content), the text has sought to develop a richer perspective on rule-making. It has focused upon the dynamic between the internal and external elements of EU law and policy in various ways. As such, it has sought to bring order to them. The AFSJ provides a rich array of case studies demonstrating global reach, often multidirectional, whose unpacking is rewarding and insightful.

The study of rule-transfer has been argued to offer a practical insight into the EU's role in the world and its global impact. Such a study is, of course, more usually 'internally' focused rather than externally so – i.e. upon the EU and its subjects rather than the world. Rule-transfer is argued to represent a useful future research agenda for legal scholars on account of its accommodation of the external functioning of EU law, the centrality of movement and dynamic processes therein, and the behavioural direction of EU law analysis.

As Chapter 2 has argued, the global reach of EU law is not necessarily a wholly positive narrative. It has been shown here that there are reasons to harbour concerns about the global reach and effects of EU law, why it can occur but also how we understand its evolution. An aggrandisement of EU influence, competence, scope and even territory may increasingly score lowly in terms of social legitimacy, both inside and outside the EU. The divergences of methodology and meaning to the global reach of EU law are reflective of the flexibility of its means. The malleability of the 'internal' and the 'external' appear as causative of the global reach and effects of EU law, but there are more pressing concerns for reflection. The de facto and de jure ambiguity of the internal and external intersection in EU law raises many possible issues of social legitimacy.

This book has argued that how we understand EU action – globally, its reach, its actions specifically through law and its effects – is heavily dependent upon our theorisation of actors engaging in rule-making beyond the nation state. Chapter 3 has considered how our contemporary understanding of actors is dominated by doctrinalism and formalism and sits ill with contemporary practices of rule-making beyond the nation state. Leading theorisations of EU action in the world paradoxically dominant upon legal theory do not account well for contemporary rule-making practices in EU law, either internally or with external effects or in the global legal order. There are many paradoxes and limitations as to the EU as a legal actor in the world. The 'bicepheral' stance of the EU in theory and in practice operates to be excusatory and indulgent of the overreach of EU powers. This is particularly the case in the global context. The EU appears exceptionalist as a *sui generis* entity but is also a useful case study of evolution and change. There are also compelling reasons to recalibrate our understanding of actors by way of a future research agenda, focusing specifically upon the EU. It forms an important dimension of the global reach of EU law that requires considerable unpacking, methodology and multidisciplinary engagement.

This book has generally made the claim for the benefits of tracing textual methodologies for the study of EU rule-making so as to assist in understanding the relationship between internal and external EU action through law. As the specific case study of the AFSJ in Chapter 4 has demonstrated, the use of external norms in EU rule-making is in effect an internalisation of those norms. Yet their use and place in rule-making operates also as an expression of external norms. The internalisation of external norms is less haphazard than the external expression of norms. Rather, the EU almost always practises some form of external norm primacy in directives, but more generally that the EU mainly practises haphazard norm promotion in its rule-making, more as to form than substance. Rule-making practice gives no indicator of international political processes but rather instead, demonstrates EU willingness to set, lead or follow international best practice.

Chapter 5 explored a more esoteric but also active case study of the global reach of EU law. EU 'internal' security has been shown there to readily embrace 'external' transatlantic security but similarly EU security rules under development may be said to demonstrate the migratory effects of EU–US legal rules by way of some form of rule transposition or 'rule-transfer,' as defined and developed in this account. The transposition of transatlantic justice and home affairs measures, such as EU–US PNR and EU–US TFTP into EU law, raises questions about appropriate legal standards and safeguards. This case study in particular demonstrates how rule-transfer in this field is fraught with challenges. The exercise of tracing transatlantic rule-transfer provides an insight with which to view the global reach and effects of EU law and the precariousness of the internal and external which the EU readily manipulates. This particular case study demonstrates that it is not a fully complete architecture within which to view EU rule-making. Nonetheless, as a methodology to break down evolutions in rule-making, it is clear and insightful and a means to put 'daylight' upon even highly controversial forms of EU rule-making.

The case study on cybercrime and cybersecurity rule-making outlined in Chapter 6 showed how although the EU gives primacy to external norms – i.e. a Council of Europe Convention in both its contemporary internal and external rule-making in security – it still produces very different regulatory results despite the commonality of the norms used. It has not produced particularly comprehensive, systematic or conceptually transparent processes in either forum. Rather, external security reveals many dependencies upon internal security and the multidirectional porousness of the global reach of EU law. The dynamism of the global reach of EU law may nevertheless be captured through methodology, and specifically through tracing internal and external norms within rule-transfer.

Several of the case studies (e.g. Chapters 4 and 5) conducted have been shown to demonstrate the primacy of external norms by the EU in its external and internal security making, as much as the overlapping and interlocking relationship between the internal and external dimensions thereof. It is an important thesis to be considered. While similarly prioritising the primacy of external norms, the rule-making of the EU with the US in particular envisages a bolder vision of security rule-making on a global level. The process and content of the case study outlined here provides evidence of the openness of the EU to external norms. However, as the case study on this question conducted in Chapter 4 indicates, practice is not necessarily a firm indicator of contemporary international political processes involving the EU.

Finally, this book then took a different turn in Chapter 7 to further advance its thesis. The global reach of EU law is indicative of broader developments in how we understand the 'postnational'. Postnational rule-making as conducted by the EU is argued to be usefully captured by sovereignty as an inherently *social* concept, in that it entails the recognition by other similar entities that an entity is also 'one of them'. Participation in the global legal order requires an understanding of the nature of the EU as an actor – i.e. what it is and what it does. One such arena for analysis is Union participation in international organisations as a social practice, generating recognition, perception and acceptance, which this book has examined in detail. It has thus been argued here that the 'enabling' character of sovereignty at the postnational level has been insufficiently studied. As a broader proposition, the space of EU rules is argued here to require more nuancing, method and case studies as to its components. Rather, the merger of sovereignty, territoriality and jurisdiction in a global world requires more attention to methodologies of rule-making, not least in the context of the EU.

Index

For Product Safety Concerns and Information please contact our EU representative GPSR@taylorandfrancis.com
Taylor & Francis Verlag GmbH, Kaufingerstraße 24, 80331 München, Germany

www.ingramcontent.com/pod-product-compliance
Ingram Content Group UK Ltd.
Pitfield, Milton Keynes, MK11 3LW, UK
UKHW011018180926
475701UK00004B/811

* 9 7 8 1 1 3 8 6 0 6 6 6 1 *